MW01039675

RECONSTRUCTING CARE IN TEACHER EDUCATION AFTER COVID-19

This collection explores the changing meaning and enactments of care in teacher education in light of the COVID-19 pandemic, from preservice teachers and teacher candidates to in-service teachers and education faculty.

Over 50 international teacher educators explore the complicated concept of care in different content areas, learning contexts, and communities of learners, using different conceptual frameworks and methodological orientations. Throughout, this book situates research and reflection at the nexus of teacher education, care, and COVID-19 in order to reconstruct care in post-pandemic teacher education.

Timely and incisive, this collection raises important questions and offers relevant examinations to consider how post-pandemic teacher education as a field will move forward in preparing and caring for those who will, in turn, care for their future students. The book is essential reading for teacher educators, scholars, and anyone interested in the notion of care in education.

Melanie Shoffner is Professor of English Education in the College of Education at James Madison University, USA.

Angela W. Webb is Associate Professor of Science Education in the College of Education at James Madison University, USA.

RECONSTRUCTING CARE IN TEACHER EDUCATION AFTER COVID-19

Caring Enough to Change

Edited by Melanie Shoffner and
Angela W. Webb

Routledge
Taylor & Francis Group

NEW YORK AND LONDON

Cover image: © Getty images

First published 2023
by Routledge
605 Third Avenue, New York, NY 10158

and by Routledge
4 Park Square, Milton Park, Abingdon, Oxon OX14 4RN

Routledge is an imprint of the Taylor & Francis Group, an informa business

© 2023 selection and editorial matter, Melanie Shoffner and Angela W. Webb; individual chapters, the contributors

The right of Melanie Shoffner and Angela W. Webb to be identified as the authors of the editorial material, and of the authors for their individual chapters, has been asserted in accordance with sections 77 and 78 of the Copyright, Designs and Patents Act 1988.

All rights reserved. No part of this book may be reprinted or reproduced or utilised in any form or by any electronic, mechanical, or other means, now known or hereafter invented, including photocopying and recording, or in any information storage or retrieval system, without permission in writing from the publishers.

Trademark notice: Product or corporate names may be trademarks or registered trademarks, and are used only for identification and explanation without intent to infringe.

Library of Congress Cataloging-in-Publication Data
Names: Shoffner, Melanie, editor.
Title: Reconstructing care in teacher education after COVID-19 : caring enough to change / edited by Melanie Shoffner and Angela W. Webb.
Description: First Edition. | New York : Routledge, 2022. | Includes bibliographical references and index.
Identifiers: LCCN 2021061443 |
Subjects: LCSH: Teaching--Moral and ethical aspects. | Teachers--Training of--Evaluation. | COVID-19 Pandemic, 2020-
Classification: LCC LB1027.5 .R4197 2022 | DDC 370.71/1--dc23/eng/20220322
LC record available at https://lccn.loc.gov/2021061443

ISBN: 978-1-032-15599-9 (hbk)
ISBN: 978-1-032-15598-2 (pbk)
ISBN: 978-1-003-24487-5 (ebk)

DOI: 10.4324/9781003244875

Typeset in Bembo
by Taylor & Francis Books

This book is dedicated to those who choose to enter the classroom—who are not deterred by the world around them—who allow us to join them on their journey.

Angela: It is hard to think about the immense role of care in education without wondering who takes care of the carer. For me, that person is my husband, Brian Webb. Thank you for all the big and small ways that you care for me and encourage me—in my work as in our life.

Melanie: I have the good fortune to know many teacher educators who give the best of themselves to bring out the best in our preservice teachers. Only one of them is Kristina Doubet. Thank you for caring enough to do the hard work—and laughing enough to get us through it.

CONTENTS

ILLUSTRATIONS

Figures

Tables

CONTRIBUTORS

Melanie Shoffner, PhD, is a professor of education at James Madison University (Virginia, USA), where she teaches classes in English language arts methods, curriculum theory, and young adult literature. Her research addresses issues of English language arts teacher preparation, preservice teacher development, and reflective practice. She is the current editor of *English Education*. In 2016–17, she was a Fulbright Scholar at Babeş-Bolyai University (Romania). Her previous edited books with Routledge include *Exploring Teachers in Fiction and Film: Saviors, Scapegoats and Schoolmarms* (2016) and *Teacher Representations in Dramatic Text and Performance: Portraying the Teacher on Stage* (2019).

Angela W. Webb, PhD, is an associate professor of science education in the College of Education at James Madison University (Virginia, USA), where she teaches courses in general methods, science methods, and curriculum theory. Her scholarship centers primarily on the preparation and early career development of science teachers, with specific attention to science teacher identity. Her work on teacher education and induction has been published in *Theory Into Practice, Journal of Educational Research and Practice, Teacher Education and Practice*, as well as the edited book *Newly Hired Teachers of Science: A Better Beginning* (Luft & Dubois, Eds.), among others.

Melony Allen, PhD, is an instructional coach in the Alamance-Burlington school system (North Carolina, USA). She researches the intersection of teachers' visions and instructional adaptations.

Louise Ammentorp, PhD, is a professor in the Department of Elementary and Early Childhood Education at The College of New Jersey (USA). Her research interests include best practices in teacher preparation and P-6 classrooms, focusing on the integration of nature and the arts in the curriculum, outdoor education, and social-emotional learning.

Ingrid Anderson, EdD, is faculty in the Infant Toddler Mental Health Graduate Certificate and Master of Early Childhood: Inclusive Education degree at Portland State University (Oregon, USA). Her research interests address early childhood educator emotional wellbeing.

Jennifer Baumgartner, PhD, is an associate professor of early childhood education at Louisiana State University (USA), where she teaches undergraduate courses in the PK-3 teacher certification program and graduate courses in child development and theory. Her research interests include teacher stress and teacher education.

Crystal L. Beach, PhD, is an academic specialist, student-teacher mentor, and teacher educator in Northeast Georgia (USA). Her research interests include literacies, identity, multimodality, and technologies in the English language arts classroom.

Melissa Riley Bradford, PhD, is a professional lecturer in Ikeda/Soka Studies and Educational Leadership at the DePaul University College of Education (Illinois, USA), where she also serves as the director of the principal preparation and superintendent internship program.

Samantha Elliott Briggs has a doctoral degree in instructional leadership from The University of Alabama (USA). Dr. Briggs has nearly 30 years of experience in education as an urban school teacher, adjunct professor, curriculum writer, consultant, and director of non-profit education program. She is the director of the GEAR UP Alabama grant.

Stuart Carroll, Ph.D., is an associate professor of elementary and early childhood education at The College of New Jersey (USA). His work focuses on humane, holistic practices in teacher education.

Ann D. David, PhD, is an associate professor at the University of the Incarnate Word in San Antonio, Texas (USA) and a former high school English teacher. Her research focuses on the teaching of writing, how preservice teachers learn to teach writing, and youth writers.

James de Winter leads the secondary physics postgraduate Initial Teacher Education course (PGCE) at the Faculty of Education, University of Cambridge (UK). He is a member of the Physics Education Research Group at the University of Uppsala, Sweden, where he researches preservice and early career physics teachers.

Kara DeCoursey is a doctoral student and graduate assistant in the School of Teacher Education and Leadership at Utah State University (USA). She is an instructor for a reading assessment and intervention course in the elementary education department at USU. Kara earned a master's degree in curriculum and instruction and is a former elementary grades teacher.

Elisabeth Etopio, PhD, is a clinical associate professor and assistant dean for teacher education at the University at Buffalo (New York, USA). Her research focuses on factors influencing preservice teachers' professional development, including the social contexts of teaching and learning and its intersection with aspects of cognition, affect, and behavior.

Martez Files is currently working on his PhD in educational studies in diverse populations in the School of Education at The University of Alabama at Birmingham.

Jessica Gallo, PhD, is an assistant professor of English education at the University of Nevada, Reno (USA). Her research focuses on English teacher preparation, middle and secondary writing pedagogy, and rural education.

Christian Z. Goering, PhD, is professor and co-coordinator of English education at the University of Arkansas (USA), where he leads the Northwest Arkansas Writing Project. His current scholarship explores how English teachers take up music in their teaching, especially student songwriting.

Julie Gorlewski, PhD, is professor and chair of the Department of Learning and Instruction at the University at Buffalo (New York, USA). Her research examines implementing district-centered transformative teacher education, collaborating to create professional development for culturally diverse schools, and cultivating professional dispositions with preservice and practicing teachers.

Kathryn Hackett-Hill is a doctoral student in Curriculum and Instruction at the University of Arkansas (USA). She is a National Writing Project Teacher-Consultant and ARTeacher Fellow. Her research interests include writing instruction and arts integration in the secondary English language arts classroom.

Rosalyn Hyde, PhD, is a Principal Teaching Fellow in mathematics education at the University of Southampton (UK). She leads the secondary mathematics postgraduate Initial Teacher Education course and supervises MSc and PhD courses. Her research centers on mathematics teaching and initial teacher education, particularly for secondary mathematics teachers.

Nozomi Inukai, PhD, is a Translation, Research and Translation Fellow at DePaul University's Institute for Daisaku Ikeda Studies in Education in the College of Education (Illinois, USA).

Hannah Jurkiewicz graduated with a BA in English from the University of Alabama at Birmingham and is now pursuing a Master's in secondary education. She is passionate about advocating and improving adolescent mental health. While at UAB, she volunteered as an SEL educator and worked with the Red Mountain Writing Project.

Meghan A. Kessler, PhD, is currently an assistant professor of teacher education at the University of Illinois Springfield (USA). Her research investigates teacher education policy and practice, particularly teachers' lives and the enactment of policy and reform.

Deepti Kharod, PhD, is an assistant professor at the University of the Incarnate Word in San Antonio, Texas (USA) and a former kindergarten teacher. Her research focuses on care and play-based learning and teaching.

MinSoo Kim-Bossard, PhD, is an associate professor in the Department of Elementary and Early Childhood Education at The College of New Jersey (USA). Her research and teaching focus on Asian American teacher voices, immigrant mothering, arts integration, and inclusive education in early childhood education.

Ekaterina Koubek, PhD, is an associate professor and TESOL coordinator at James Madison University (Virginia, USA), where she teaches both undergraduate and graduate courses in TESOL programs. Her research examines preservice teacher attitudes and beliefs, action research in teacher preparation programs, and high-impact practices on student engagement.

Devon Lejman is a high school English teacher in central Indiana (USA). She graduated from Ball State University with a degree in English education and a minor in autism spectrum disorders. Devon is also the lead writing instructor for the Indiana Writer's Center summer youth program.

Narelle Lemon, EdD, is an interdisciplinary researcher in the fields of education, positive psychology, and arts, holding the position of Associate Professor in Education at Swinburne University of Technology in Melbourne, Australia.

Lauren Madden, PhD, is a professor of elementary science education in the Department of Elementary and Early Childhood Education at The College of New Jersey (USA). She coordinates the environmental sustainability education minor and graduate certificate programs.

Sharon McDonough, PhD, is an academic researcher in the fields of wellbeing, resilience, and teacher educator work at Federation University Australia, Ballarat.

Her research investigates mindfulness in education, self-care and wellbeing to empower educators, and communitiy members.

Abigail Navarro Muñoz is a senior at the University of Nevada, Reno (USA), majoring in secondary education, English, Spanish and minoring in geography. Her research analyzes the ways in which students navigate transitions and changes within their education through a geographic lens.

Tiffany Karalis Noel, PhD, is a clinical assistant professor and director of doctoral studies in the Department of Learning and Instruction at the University at Buffalo (New York, USA). Her research addresses teachers' professional identity development and the role of equity and inclusion in cultivating supportive and sustainable educational environments.

Ceridwen Owen finished her PhD at Monash University (Melbourne, Australia) in 2020 on the everyday work and becoming of early-career English teachers in Victoria, Australia. She is currently a teacher of English at a high school. Her research interests are in teacher development and becoming, and the transition of preservice teachers to the teaching profession.

Kathryn Parthun earned her bachelor's in behavioral neuroscience and Master's in education from Purdue University (Indiana, USA). She is currently the Director of Social and Emotional Learning for Lafayette School Corporation, focusing on brain-aligned strategies for staff and students for a healthier, more regulated community.

Tonya B. Perry is a professor of secondary English education at the University of Alabama at Birmingham (USA). Her research focuses on literacy instruction in secondary schools, primarily in the areas of writing, rural and urban education, and teacher preparation. She is the PI for the GEAR UP Alabama grant.

Ashton Ray holds a master's degree in English from The University of Alabama at Birmingham (USA). She is a graduate coach for the GEAR UP Alabama grant.

Holly Sheppard Riesco is a doctoral student at the University of Arkansas (USA) in the curriculum and instruction program in English education. Her research focuses on the valuation of students' lived literacies through rhetorical practices in English language arts.

Catherine Scott, PhD, is an associate professor of education at Coastal Carolina University (South Carolina, USA). She researches normative practices in science, technology, engineering, and mathematics (STEM) education and Montessori pedagogical practices.

Melanie Shoffner, PhD, is a professor of education at James Madison University (Virginia, USA). Her scholarship examines issues of English language arts teacher preparation, preservice teacher development, and reflective practice.

Rebecca Smith, EdD, is an assistant professor in the School of Education at the University of Portland (Oregon, USA). She teaches methods and research courses to undergraduate and graduate students. Her research areas include teacher learning and professional development, culturally responsive practices, and innovative technologies.

Jeff Spanke, PhD, is an assistant professor of English at Ball State University (Indiana, USA), where he teaches courses in young adult literature, rhetoric and composition, and English education. His research interests include preservice teacher identity, mental health, and the role of citizenship education in English language arts.

Paul Sutton, PhD, is an assistant professor of education at Pacific Lutheran University (Washington, USA). He teaches secondary methods, multicultural education, sociocultural foundations of education, and introductory writing. His publications and presentations examine the collaborative practices of teachers as they develop problem-based learning curriculum.

Tamara Tallman, PhD, is an assistant professor in the Department of Elementary and Early Childhood Education at The College of New Jersey (USA). She teaches literacy and social studies methodologies courses as well as middle level education courses.

Gavin Tierney, PhD, is an assistant professor in the Department of Secondary Education at California State University, Fullerton (USA). His research focuses on youth participatory design within research-practice partnerships, classroom assessment, and youth identity development and engagement, all with an emphasis on educational equity.

Jacob Warren is a graduate student and graduate assistant at the University of Arkansas (USA). He earned an MA in curriculum and instruction from the University of Mississippi as well as a Bachelors of Arts in English and communications from Millsaps College.

Angela W. Webb, PhD, is an associate professor of science education in the College of Education at James Madison University (Virginia, USA). Her scholarship centers primarily on the preparation and early career development of science teachers, with specific attention to science teacher identity.

Anne Elrod Whitney, PhD, is a professor of education at the Pennsylvania State University (USA), where she works with prospective and experienced teachers, as well as doctoral students, in writing, literacy, and professional development. Her research focuses on writing as a tool for living and learning, in classrooms and beyond.

Larrell Wilkinson, PhD, is an Associate Professor of community health & human services at the University of Alabama at Birmingham (UAB). Dr. Wilkinson has a Master of Science in public health, specialized in health promotion, education, and behavior. He also holds a PhD in health services policy and management

Amanda Winkelsas, PhD, is a clinical assistant professor and director of the Teacher Residency Program in the Department of Learning and Instruction at the University at Buffalo (New York, USA). Her research focuses on teacher diversity, cultivating community knowledge for education, and innovative, community-centered models for teacher education.

Jennifer A. Wolfe, PhD, is an associate professor of mathematics education at The University of Arizona (USA). She was recently awarded a university Teaching Excellence Award for her efforts to effectively implement research-based equitable teaching practices for engaging students through collaborative group work.

Camie Wood is a graduate student at the University of Arkansas (USA) who previously worked as a teacher at the secondary level in Spanish and social studies. Her research interests include education systems, the effects of trauma on student success, and learning outcomes for students with exceptionalities.

Lin Wu, a first-generation immigrant from China, is an assistant professor of teacher education at Western Oregon University (USA). His research interests include culturally responsive pedagogy, multicultural teacher education, and critical race theory.

Elizabeth Laura Yomantas, PhD, is an assistant professor in the Department of Humanities and Teacher Education at Pepperdine University (California, USA). Her research interests include critical allyship and culturally responsive experiential education.

FOREWORD

I've written in the last few years (2018, 2020) about a school district in Gaines-ville, Georgia, that has earned my admiration. Writing about schools for me has often centered on their emphasis on "accountability," with data, data, and more data serving as the means of informing teachers and students about their achievements. It's a discouraging, demoralizing, dehumanizing environment in general. The COVID-19 pandemic has exacerbated the problems originating in emotional trauma in many ways. School officials often care more about "learning loss" according to those accountability measures than about the health and well-being, including the mental health, of the people who occupy school commu-nities. It does not help when citizens occupy school board meetings demanding that those weak-kneed teachers get back to work and stop whining about masks and vaccinations. And this Critical Race Theory business has got to stop imme-diately, because my kid feels bad about learning about racism. Who cares about how your kids feel when their lives are never included in the curriculum?

And then, to the rescue of my sensibilities, came Hall County, Georgia. Their district motto is "The Most Caring Place on Earth." The shocking thing is that it's not just a slogan. They really work at caring.

I learned of this unusual place through a former student of mine who is parti-cipating in longitudinal research covering nine years. She entered the study in her third year of college, when her teacher education coursework began. She then worked in two school districts that she found unsatisfying, with the second so oriented to corporate policies that she quit after one year and spent a year in the hospitality business. She finally ended up in Hall County, where she felt that her own primary orientation to students was matched by the district's philosophy and practices. When I wrote about it for the *Atlanta Journal-Constitution*, I heard from people asking, how do I apply for a job there?! That essay continued to circulate online for at least a year, occasionally getting new life and, for me, new inquiries about how to contact their administration. It's a place that teachers wish they could work, instead of the heartless, data-driven schools that employ them.

The question remains, then, what does it mean to care, beyond the slogans and pieties? Is hanging a poster of different-colored kittens snuggling together, accompanied by a "Celebrate diversity" slogan, sufficient? Or is caring more like hard work, undertaken in school contexts where the value is on outcomes, making care a quality that requires concerted attention and continual monitoring?

When my former student went to her first school orientation in Hall County, the district superintendent spoke about the importance of human relationships, above all else. Do not focus on test scores or real estate values tied to test scores, he urged the faculty. Focus instead, he said, on how everything educational follows from developing and fostering productive relationships within the district.

Kids in the district require care. It's not affluent or privileged. The city is home to many chicken processing plants, where immigrant workers pluck and slice poultry along with a native workforce. Both populations often have children who do not graduate high school. Many of the immigrant families are harassed by immigrant officials looking for someone to deport, and many families have been split up in the name of law enforcement. Poultry plant conditions have become especially dangerous during the pandemic, forcing employees to work at close quarters to maximize productivity. Some kids are homeless, some work multiple jobs before and after school, some have started families of their own. The district's test scores, as might be predicted, do not top the state's charts. But the superintendent, at the point of orientation, entreated the teachers to tune out the noise about test scores and focus on making the school feel positive to kids, teachers, counselors, principals. It sounds like a good place for the cafeteria staff, grounds crew, and custodians as well.

But that is not enough. The district isn't satisfied with verbal pleas. It works at the whole-school level to assess their students' emotional needs and do something to provide a nurturing environment to support them. Here's how one such initiative was described by a local reporter (Podo, 2019). The program was designed to make sure that the students' mental health needs are understood and addressed:

> Step one started with listening to students. "A kid who's in their seventh house in the last three months and has a step dad that's beating them and a mother who's addicted, just doesn't care much about advanced algebra," Hall Superintendent Will Schofield said during a board meeting on Nov. 18. "It's not that they don't want to learn advanced algebra, it's not even on their radar screen." . . . "There are kids having issues with depression, different types of abuse, anxiety, divorce, sexuality issues, relationship drama — so many issues," Joy Schofield said. "It's just overwhelming to see the sheer number of issues our kids are facing everyday and see it all in one place."

When schools like this one enroll a large population of students of color whose heritages get little representation in the curriculum, the students often feel alienated and estranged, and often drop out more for emotional and material reasons than academic shortcomings. Throw in the sorts of traumas described in the news report, and the feelings multiply. The Hall County mental health initiative begins with asking students what they think, what they have experienced, and what they need. It begins with their subjective experiences and not "objective" tests designed to determine their academic achievement.

Among the activities in the program was a sentence-completion task in which students were asked to complete the following sentence: "If my teacher really knew me, they would know…" Answers included: "If my teacher really knew me, they would know how much potential I have if someone just gave me the chance. I could help guide others in the right direction and also myself, but it's hard when you lack hope." Another wrote, "If my teachers really knew me, they'd know that I've been verbally abused all my life and treating me unfairly makes me feel like I can't do anything."

It takes a courageous administrator to ask kids what is wrong with the school. The students' insights into the school's operation might be embarrassing to leaders who often prefer to act as though their institution is run so well that complainers reveal their own character flaws, rather than problems in the institution. It then takes a visionary leader to figure out what to do with the information in sensitive, empathic ways.

Caring is complicated. Much of what is written in the name of care concerns nurturing of the sort I've reviewed, and I'm all for it. But there is also a need for some level of performance to be expected. In our research we have identified a common tension between *rigor and relationships*. We borrow "rigor" from our interviews, where teachers use it to describe high academic standards. These can come in conflict with the need to foster relationships, in that making demands on people often produces obstacles and frustrations for them as they push themselves into new levels of performance. This sense of academic standards can also be harsh and unempathic. It's a difficult line to walk with sensitivity and appropriate attention to both rigor and relationships.

I'll confess that my responses to my graduate students' writing is, they tell me, quite severe. One noted that in her dissertation, my first nurturing comment came well after page 100. My follow-up question was simple: How many of your dissertation articles got published? The answer: All of them. I hope that the care I took in providing a demanding review outweighed any feel-good moment they might have experienced with lush praise of the sort that does little to advance the quality of the work.

And that complication, that tension between rigor and relationships, brings us to *Reconstructing Care in Teacher Education after COVID-19: Caring Enough to Change*. I have mostly talked about schools, the destination for candidates in teacher education. Teacher candidates who spend many hours in practica in corporate-style schools are being socialized to those values, no matter what they hear in college classrooms. Often that dissonance between university ideals and school realities is the hardest part of their transition to full-time teaching.

Teacher education itself, then, must work hard to develop notions of care that both fit university ideals and are practicable in schools, or at least provide a way to try to reconcile the two. Promoting care in universities may be as challenging as it is in schools, given that universities are responsive to the same economic constraints, ideological battles, and growing neoliberal management as schools are. If anything, university traditions make "knowledge" the most important commodity available in college, one that allows for mammoth, alienating lecture halls, lectures in small classrooms, and a "no-excuses" perspective on students accompanied by a "no responsibility" view of faculty when it comes to nurturing the emotional life and mental health well-being of students. Many faculty regard students as impediments to their research, what with their neediness and growing pains. The broader culture of universities has little interest in or patience for students beyond their academic productivity. When neither the university nor the schools provide positive settings for promoting healthy emotional growth, it makes the task of encouraging care among prospective teachers a major challenge, one that cannot be achieved through slogans and posters.

Care comes in many forms, often within uncaring institutions. The editors and contributors have provided readers with a compelling set of chapters to consider in undertaking a care-driven education for teacher education students. The timing is ideal, given how COVID has amplified so many tensions and conflicts and brought mental health crises into focus for educators. This volume provides a variety of perspectives on care that the thoughtful teacher educator may consider in supporting students in such challenging times. I hope that it gets wide distribution and attention, and that the issues it raises become part of the discourse of education as the notion of care gets refined and applied in ways that benefit teachers, students, and anyone else involved in the educational system.

Peter Smagorinsky, Distinguished Research Professor of English Education, Emeritus, The University of Georgia, USA

References

Podo, K. (2019, November 23). Why Hall County is tackling student mental health issues. *Gainesville Times.* www.gainesvilletimes.com/news/education/why-hall-county-made-stand-tackle-student-mental-health-issues.

Smagorinsky, P. (2018, January 1). What if schools focused on improving relationships rather than test scores? *Atlanta Journal-Constitution.* www.petersmagorinsky.net/About/PDF/Op-Ed/Relationships.html.

Smagorinsky, P. (2020). The essential role of relationships and emotional life in schooling. *School Administrator,* October, 36–39.

ACKNOWLEDGMENTS

This book was fueled by equal amounts rage, caffeine, alcohol, chocolate, and pasta, without which we could not have managed during this two-year (and counting) pandemic while teaching, meeting, writing, emailing, and grading.

*

Our thanks to Simon Jacobs and AnnaMary Goodall at Routledge for their interest in the book and guidance toward its completion. We also thank the anonymous reviewers for their time with and pertinent feedback on our initial proposal.

*

Many thanks to the people in our professional lives who motivated us to create this book; without our BFFs leading the way, we might have decided to spend more time in the hammock.

*

Many thanks, as well, to our colleagues who demonstrate on a daily basis that care can look and sound like many things but it always comes from the heart.

INTRODUCTION

Care after COVID—Moving Forward as Caring Teacher Educators

Melanie Shoffner and Angela W. Webb

> She cares about each and every one of her students and understands the importance of mental health, especially during these trying times.
>
> She was extremely stoic and did not care about us as people.
> Angela's course evaluations (Fall 2020)

> Some days it felt like you did not have a clue that we were struggling so much or just didn't care.
>
> She showed immense caring for us by reaching out when she noticed changes in engagement or attitude.
> Melanie's course evaluations (Fall 2020)

How interesting it is to learn that your preservice teachers consider you a caring and uncaring teacher educator in the same set of course evaluations—in the midst of a pandemic, while teaching classes and managing meetings, while supporting our students and helping our families, while working from home and living on Zoom. These comments are only one example of many that we could offer; the two of us have had any number of emails, conversations, and interactions over these past COVID-infused years that prove our preservice teachers believe we gave them exactly what they needed and, yet, nothing that they needed. We suspect most teacher educators found themselves in similar situations as higher education (and the world with it) turned upside down: trying to give our students what they needed and somehow failing and succeeding in doing just that.

We know that care is a tricky concept, in definition and enactment—although the pandemic was not the cause of this revelation. We both have considered issues of care in the classroom for years, first as secondary teachers in science

DOI: 10.4324/9781003244875-1

(Angela) and English (Melanie) and now as teacher educators who understand the importance of relational teaching (Cochran-Smith, 2003; Noddings, 2012). We are increasingly frustrated with the commodified versions of care in higher education that treat the social processes of learning as objective, quantifiable outcomes (Ball, 2004). We are often dispirited by the celebrated and often unrealistic views of care expected by students and colleagues alike: that care is unidirectional, that care is maternal, that care is sacrifice. And then COVID hit.

As this is our first pandemic, we optimistically believed we would be past this global nightmare by the time this book was published. Yet, here we are: still struggling with an ever-mutating virological disease, still mired in the ever-increasing inanity of political and personal debate. When COVID brought everything to a halt in the spring of 2020, we did not know how to prepare ourselves—much less, our students—for the unfolding fallout in higher education, generally, and teacher education, specifically, but we did our best to manage the unprecedented pivots (two words we hope never to hear again). Part of that management was finding our footing as caring teacher educators who were supportive of and responsive to our preservice teachers. Because the kids were not alright.

Multiple studies have documented that rates of stress, anxiety, and depression increased for university students over the course of the pandemic (e.g., August & Dapkewicz, 2020; Camacho-Zuñiga et al., 2021; Son et al., 2020) in response to issues of isolation, uncertainty, financial support, illness, and death. After a brief respite, and despite utter uncertainty about what came next, higher education moved online in the spring of 2020, which brought its own issues. As Carrillo and Flores (2020) report in their review of online teaching and learning in teacher education, COVID lockdowns and remote learning only exacerbated existing issues of internet access and digital literacy and revealed the importance of social support networks.

Clearly, the pandemic wreaked havoc with teachers and students in K-12 schools; at the same time our university-level students were struggling, so, too, were the populations that our preservice teachers work with and hope to teach. Moving into schools—through university field experiences, during student teaching practica, and as novice teachers—now means "meeting the social-emotional needs of children and implementing trauma- and healing-informed practice, all while making up for learning loss and preparing for the coming unpredictable combinations of distance learning, blended learning, and in-classroom learning" (Darling-Hammond & Hyler, 2020, p. 457). Teacher educators have always understood that there are important aspects of teaching that must be learned on the job (Feiman-Nemser, 2003) but we, too, are struggling with how to prepare our preservice teachers to enter this brave new world that has such issues in it, one that already includes severe teacher shortages: "Nearly one in four teachers surveyed in early 2021 said they were likely to quit their jobs and be out of the classroom" by the end of the calendar year (Rodriguez-Delgado et al., 2021, para. 4).

The pandemic has revealed the complexity of care in teacher education by emphasizing the complexity inherent of teaching. Nothing requires us to return to our previous understandings and enactments of care, however. In fact, we argue the opposite here: that our navigation of COVID requires us to reconceptualize what we know and reconsider what we do post-pandemic as caring teacher educators.

The Complexity of Care

Care is a complex endeavor in education, with no one standard definition and no one recognized enactment:

> Caring is one of those things that most educators agree is important in working effectively with students, but they are hard pressed to characterize it in actual practice, or to put a functional face on it that goes beyond feelings of empathy and emotional attachment. (Gay, 2018, pp. 57–58)

Still, within such ambiguity lies an understanding that care is dependent on interactions with and receptiveness to others. There might be no concrete way to define those interactions and receptions; what one person interprets as overstepped boundaries and unwanted attention could be understood as welcomed connection and thoughtful interest by another. However, the central element of care remains that of relationships.

Nel Noddings (2005) offers what has become a foundational understanding of care in teacher education: the relational interaction of carer and cared-for that centers responsiveness. In Noddings' (2005) construction of care, the carer's role is "to listen attentively and to respond as positively as possible" (p. xiv) in order to meet the expressed and inferred needs of the cared-for. This explanation of care appears deceptively simple if understood as the cared-for saying what they want and the carer providing it. As Noddings (2005) explains,

> Both carer and cared-for contribute to this relation. If, for whatever reason, the cared-for denies that she or he is cared for, there is no caring relation. When that happens, it is not necessarily the fault of the carer; it may be that the cared-for is stubborn, insensitive, or just plain difficult…[or]…the situation in which carer and cared-for meet may make it difficult to establish caring relations. (p. xv)

To create and sustain the relational interactions fundamental to care requires a level of trust on both sides (Noddings, 2012). However, care is also dependent on contextual factors that are often outside the control of either the cared-for or the carer (e.g., culture, identity, emotion). Noddings' construction of care does not come without issue nor does it stand alone.

Other constructions of care often take up these contexts and, in doing so, add additional complexity to our understanding of it. Many educators argue that care must be cognizant of students' ethnic, racial, and cultural identities (e.g., Delpit, 1995, 2002; Ladson-Billings, 1994, 1995; Love, 2019; Valenzuela, 1999). Gay's (2018) presentation of culturally responsive teaching, for example, takes up the concept of culturally responsive care. In addressing caring for versus caring about, Gay's language is similar to Noddings': "While *caring about* conveys feelings of concern for one's state of being, *caring for* is an active engagement in doing something to positively affect it. Thus, it encompasses a combination of concern, compassion, commitment, responsibility, and action" (Gay, 2018, p. 58). Where Gay's conception diverges, however, is in its recognition that educators must respond to ethnically and racially diverse students in purposeful ways. Culturally responsive care requires actions and emotions that support students' "improved competence, agency, autonomy, efficacy, and empowerment" (p. 58) as both learners and as individuals. To do so, educators must recognize and respect the ethnic, racial, and cultural diversity of those they care for.

The emotions associated with care add another layer of complexity to understanding and enacting care in educational contexts (e.g., O'Connor, 2008; Zembylas, 2005). Isenbarger and Zembylas (2006) point to the emotional work involved in caring for others. The resulting intentions, actions, and understandings are "often invisible, unacknowledged, or devalued…[despite being seen as]…natural or effortless" (p. 123). Often, this emotional work can only be enacted and expressed in socially expected and accepted ways in education (and in doing so, becomes emotional labor). Even though the work can be a "rewarding, fun and exciting part" (p. 124) of teaching, this commodification of care and concomitant expression of regulated emotions can also lead to burnout.

The educational setting is another contextual factor shaping understandings and enactments of care. At the university level, which encompasses teacher education, care is "a function of personal belief and institutional philosophy" (Zembylas, 2017, p. 4), elements that might be at odds with one another. Faculty can express care in many different ways (e.g., holding high expectations, listening to students' concerns, offering authentic praise) but that care is still bound by the university context. Developing caring relationships, then, is often an act of resistance (Walker & Gleaves, 2016), since faculty might need to be "resistors of discourses, institutional policies, [and] damaging emotional labour" (p. 74) in order to enact relational care.

However care is conceptualized (and there are certainly more constructs than we have offered here), caring engages varied personal and professional perspectives in response to different contexts. If we are willing to recognize that the students we teach are not a standardized product, we must also be willing to see that the care we enact is not, either—especially so with the seismic shift of COVID-19.

Navigating the Ecosystem

Disruptions in life are not the exception; we need only look to nature to prove the rule. As the COVID-19 pandemic sparked in 2019, what would become one of the most destructive wildfire seasons in recorded history began around the world (e.g., National Centers for Environment Information, 2020; Sullivan, 2021; Wheeling, 2020). When any ecosystem endures major disruption and destruction—such as that from wildfires and pandemics—it is changed significantly but not rendered lifeless: Over time, the ecosystem is repopulated and rebuilt and communities are renewed, albeit different from what they once were.

Similarly, COVID-19 has disrupted the ecosystem of education and care is one of many areas to suffer. The pandemic's destruction of community—the daily interactions, the casual conversations, the developed connections—changed the relational landscape for both teachers and students; COVID's upheaval in learning was magnified by the upheaval in relationships between teachers and students. Yet, in ecological succession, wide-spreading, fast-growing, tolerant pioneer species arrive after the disruption, stabilizing the environment before slowly giving way to the reestablishment of communities. Similarly, our understandings and enactments of care can be the necessary pioneer species in the landscape of teacher education as we recover and rebuild post-pandemic. By reimaging ideas and enactments of care in the (hopefully) waning days of COVID-19 and all its variants, we can reconstruct teacher education to respond to the pandemic's disruption of our environment and better support those who prepare to teach after that disruption.

Expanding our understandings and enactments of care in teacher education post-COVID recognizes and respects the disruption to what has always been a complicated endeavor. Every day, we navigate the disparate needs and wants of students and colleagues, the theoretical groundings and contextual beliefs of the profession, and the expectations and demands of institutions, while attempting to codify complex concepts like diversity, equity, reflection, dispositions—and care. Preparing preservice teachers for their future students, classrooms, and communities is complex and layered (Darling-Hammond & Bransford, 2005). They must learn to analyze beliefs and create new ideas while developing subject matter knowledge and understandings of learning and learners as they cultivate practices for teaching (Darling-Hammond & Bransford, 2005; Feiman-Nemser, 2003; Zeichner & Liston, 2013). Enacting care through all of this adds yet another component to this complicated ecosystem of teacher education, as the pandemic revealed to all of us.

Perhaps not surprisingly, the two of us hold similar views of care. Asked to define it in our own words, we would offer that care is manifested in our relationships with, acceptances of, and responses to preservice teachers as individuals with specific needs. And yet, we are very different people who enacted care quite differently in our COVID-colored classrooms. During the height of the pandemic, Angela incorporated informal weekly check-ins in her classes that used memes and light-hearted questions while hosting virtual coffee hours for her preservice teachers; Melanie instituted a slower start to virtual classes, with time for general conversation and greetings, and consistently negotiated due dates for assignments. Now, in what we resignedly call a "normal" semester, we continue to reshape enactments of care in our teaching and they continue to be different versions of our shared belief. Angela has instituted flexibly scheduled online meetings, in addition to regularly scheduled in-person office hours, to offer support to students during a hectic semester of coursework and practicum. Melanie has integrated more assignments that allow students to present ideas and understandings in spoken, rather than written, form. From informal feedback, students seem to agree with the impetus behind this change: Recording a video is less stressful than writing a paper (and usually more entertaining for the professor). And still, we know that the care we work to show our preservice teachers may not be perceived as such because of the complex and relational nature of caring.

Why We Need This in Teacher Education

We hope that, by the time this book is published, the world will have moved forward into some reconstitution of normal that recognizes our collective trauma from this pandemic. Teacher education is standing at this same junction: We can dismiss the last two years as an anomaly and return to our usual practices or we can acknowledge that this pandemic opens up new directions and different practices.

We stand at the precipice of a new, uncharted situation, armed with the opportunity to disrupt the status quo of care (since the status quo is no longer quo). We do not dare attempt to put a positive spin on the COVID-19 pandemic yet we realize the power in questioning whether how we cared for preservice teachers and teacher educators in the past must be our path moving forward. The disruption of COVID-19 requires different, if not new, considerations and enactments of care within the current paradigm of teacher education. We are still riding the waves of the pandemic, unfortunately, and thus still making sense of its impact but this should not stop us from asking whether we return to pre-pandemic normal, shelve the issue for future generations of teacher educators to handle, or take the opportunity for a paradigm shift in our field (Kuhn, 1996).

As Kuhn (1996) explains, "During revolutions, scientists see new and different things when looking with familiar instruments in places they have looked before" (p. 111). This pandemic has many hallmarks of physical revolutions that have come before, with its destruction, difficulty, and death, but it also carries the inspiration of intellectual revolution by "loosening the rules" (p. 84) of how we think about care in teacher education. If we move through our current ecological destruction, might we not reach a new paradigm of teacher education that offers a changed view of "the field, its methods, and its goals" (p. 85)?

We know the adage of putting on our own masks before helping others with theirs, even if we have not flown in two years. We are also well aware of the gendered views of care in teaching and learning: While "good teachers care, and good teaching is inextricably linked to specific acts of caring" (Rogers & Webb, 1991, p. 174), good takes on a different meaning when women are involved in that care. Care for the self must be present in our minds and in our practice so that we are as mentally and emotionally healthy as possible in order to care in authentic ways for the preservice teachers with whom we work. Even as we write this, however, we are looking surreptitiously at each other and shaking our heads: Neither of us is particularly good at this, perhaps because we are so often left to determine and meet these needs for ourselves (and there is just so damn much to do).

A shift in teacher education, whether paradigmatic, ecological, animal, or mineral, will not be easy but it will be necessary if we are to address the disrupted systems, structures, and practices that exacerbate the need for care now. In doing so, we must resist westernized, commercialized, white centering perspectives of caring and accept that care, grounded in the relational, means that our understandings of care must also be grounded in the awareness of relational complexity.

Today, that includes the myriad ways in which complex and sometimes fragile relationships can be rocked by current events and injustices. Care must acknowledge the context and lived experiences of all parties, which requires us to see the whole rather than the part put forward in the moment. Moving through a pandemic has involved the whole person, not a separate piece, and that requires us to rethink our understandings and enactments of care now and going forward. Through this book, we hope to provoke these necessary conversations and actions: ones that recognize the intersectionalities of identities that define, determine, and inform teacher educators' caring as well as preservice teachers' perceptions and interpretations of that care.

What's to Come

The COVID-19 pandemic forced us to reconsider and reconceptualize what it means to care and how that care can be enacted for all those involved in teacher education, from preservice teachers and teacher candidates to novice teachers and education faculty. Our response is reflected in the chapters of this book, looking through the lenses of different content areas and contexts, different constituents, and different conceptual frameworks and methodological orientations.

Part One: Programmatic Approaches to Care includes six chapters that explore varied experiences with and perspectives on care at the program level. Four chapters show how programs contended with reconceptualizing and reprioritizing care during the pandemic. In the opening chapter, Ann D. David and Deepti Kharod consider the ways in which their Catholic university's teacher education program reconciled sacred care with secular expectations of accreditation, since the wheels of program accreditation continued to turn even in the midst of the pandemic. In Chapter 2, Rebecca Smith, Paul Sutton, and Gavin Tierney re-envision care in teacher education through a renewed focus on students' expressed needs against the backdrop of key sociopolitical contexts (i.e., the pandemic, racial injustice, social upheaval). Similarly, Amanda Winkelsas, Tiffany Karalis Noel, Julie Gorlewski, and Elisabeth Etopio's co-constructed narrative in Chapter 5 highlights the ways in which a teacher education program grappled with care and empathy for students and faculty during the pandemic. In Chapter 3, Cami Wood, Jacob Warren, Holly Sheppard Riesco, Kathryn Hackett-Hill, and Christian Goering reflect on concrete actions for institutionalizing critical care pedagogy, balancing critical consciousness and compassion, to best meet the needs of all students in teacher education programs.

The two remaining chapters in Part One offer insights into how we can support our students' resilience and wellbeing. In Chapter 6, Jeff Spanke, Devon Lejam, and Kathryn Parthun consider the responsibility of teacher educators to treat (and teach) preservice teachers as we are educating them to treat their future students: as whole humans with a variety of lived experiences, emotions, and needs. Jennifer Baumgartner and Ingrid Anderson provide a specific way to offer that support to preservice teachers in Chapter 4: the Self-Care Problem Solving Pathway. Using specific questions and targeted reflection, teacher educators can help preservice teachers navigate the complex emotions that will inevitably arise during their teaching experiences post-COVID.

Part Two: Care in the Content Areas narrows the breadth of programmatic care to examine care in specific contexts. Two chapters focus on early childhood and elementary student teaching seminar courses. MinSoo Kim-Bossard, Lauren Madden, Stuart Carroll, Louise Ammentorp, and Tamara Tallman reflect in Chapter 10 on their responses to preservice teachers' emerging needs during the 2020–21 academic year by implementing curricular changes and mental health check-ins while modeling self-care and advocacy efforts. In Chapter 7, Catherine Scott and Melony Allen examine the shifts that occurred in their preservice teachers' understandings and enactments of care while student teaching during the pandemic.

The other chapters in Part Two are situated within the context of subject-specific methods courses. Chapter 8 presents Ekaterina Koubek's efforts to enact care in Teaching English to Speakers of Other Languages courses before and during the COVID-19 pandemic to consider how her personal pedagogy will enact care post-COVID. In Chapter 9, Jennifer A. Wolfe describes the different practices used in her mathematics methods course during the pandemic to develop positive mathematics identities, build authentic caring relationships, and cultivate a collaborative learning environment with her preservice teachers.

Part Three: Care and Teacher Educators includes three chapters that highlight the perspectives of the teacher educators themselves. The chapters in this section delve into the pandemic experiences of teacher educators as they worked to make sense of the extensive upheaval in K-12 and post-secondary education and offer implications for their work with and care for preservice and novice teachers. In Chapter 12, Jennifer Baumgartner and Angela W. Webb reflect on their evolving understandings of care during the pandemic, connecting their experiences to the importance, complexity, and cost of caring as teacher educators. In addition to reflection, teacher educators engaged in self-study to learn more about their practice during the pandemic and to inform their care for preservice teachers post-pandemic. Nozomi Inukai and Melissa Riley Bradford use self-study in Chapter 11 to examine how Buddhist compassion offers new understandings of and efforts to create care in their teacher education courses during and post-pandemic. Rosalyn Hyde and James de Winter also use self-study in Chapter 13 to examine their understanding of preservice teachers' needs in England and make sense of their current and future responses to those personal and professional needs.

Clearly, the implications of COVID-19's disruption extend beyond teacher education programs and educators to novice and inservice teachers. The chapters in *Part Four: Care in the Classroom* explore the experiences of inservice teachers during the pandemic to inform the ways in which we can better care for preservice teachers in our teacher education programs post-pandemic. In Chapter 15, Kara DeCoursey takes a longitudinal look at the experiences of novice teachers during the pandemic—from their student teaching into their first year in the classroom—to depict the ways listening, connecting, and coming together in intentional spaces can support preservice teachers in their teacher education programs and beyond. Complementing the experiences of the student-teachers-turned-novice-teachers in DeCoursey's chapter, Crystal Beach writes from her unique perspective as a teacher educator, student-teacher mentor, and high school teacher in Chapter 14 to redefine what care can mean when working with student teachers in the field. Sharon McDonough and Narelle Lemon's Chapter 16 closes out this section by building from their research with Australian inservice teachers during the pandemic to propose principles for teacher education that support care and wellbeing for preservice teachers.

Part Five: (Re)Framing Care includes six chapters that offer frameworks that extend or problematize constructs of care. In Chapter 20, Jessica Gallo and Abigail Navarro Muñoz use the lens of cultural geography to draw on place, space, and identity in order to examine students' and teachers' pandemic experiences; through this lens, they discuss the value of the culture teachers and students create through relationships with one another in their learning environments. Two chapters in this section draw our attention to groups disproportionately impacted by the pandemic and its political wrappings. Lin Wu details the ways in which he supported the wellbeing of his Asian American preservice teachers in Chapter 17 by embodying culturally responsive caring via careful contextualization of COVID-19 and its related anti-Asian rhetoric. Tonya B. Perry, Martez Files, Samantha Elliott Briggs, Hannah Jurkiewicz, Ashton Ray, and Larrell Wilkinson locate their consideration of care in Black rural areas during the pandemic; in Chapter 18, they discuss ways in which critical caring pedagogy can be applied in teacher education to better meet the needs of and care for students in Black rural spaces in responsive, equitable ways.

Elizabeth Laura Yomantas uses found poetry in Chapter 19 to introduce the concept of "harboring" that offers a framework centered on reclaiming humanity and connecting with one another in new ways. Pushing back against mainstream conceptions of self-care, in Chapter 21, Ceridwen Owen and Anne Elrod Whitney present teacher learning communities as powerful sites for collective and liberatory self-care that afford space for processing and reflecting on the social and political conditions surrounding the work of teaching, drawing connections to how this sort of care can support preservice and inservice teachers as well as teacher educators beyond the pandemic. Meghan A. Kessler brings the book's consideration of care to a close. In Chapter 22, she focuses on the structural, cultural, and political contexts teachers work in and against, offering the Identify-Interrogate-Advocate framework as a way to enable preservice teachers' contextualization of their teacher-selves and their work to build emotional resilience and support their abilities to critique and advocate within their contexts.

References

August, R., & Dapkewicz, A. (2020). Benefit finding in the COVID-19 pandemic: College students' positive coping strategies. *Journal of Positive School Psychology, 5*(2), 73–86.

Ball, S. J. (2004). "Education for sale! The commodification of everything?". King's Annual Education Lecture, University of London. https://nepc.colorado.edu/sites/default/files/CERU-0410-253-OWI.pdf.

Bellas, M. L. (1999). Emotional labor in academia: The case of professors. *The Annals of the American Academy of Political and Social Science, 561*(1), 96–110.

Camacho-Zuñiga, C., Pego, L., Escamilla, J., & Hosseini, S. (2021). The impact of the COVID-19 pandemic on students' feelings at high school, undergraduate, and postgraduate levels. *Heliyon, 7*(3), e06465.

Carrillo, C., & Flores, M. A. (2020) COVID-19 and teacher education: A literature review of online teaching and learning practices. *European Journal of Teacher Education, 43*(4), 466–487.

Cochran-Smith, M. (2003). Sometimes it's not about the money: Teaching and heart. *Journal of Teacher Education, 54*(5), 371–375.

Darling-Hammond, L., & Bransford, J. (Eds.). (2005). *Preparing teachers for a changing world: What teachers should learn and be able to do.* Jossey-Bass.

Darling-Hammond, L., & Hyler, M. (2020). Preparing educators for the time of COVID…and beyond. *European Journal of Education, 43*(4), 457–465.

Delpit, L. (1995). *Other people's children: Cultural conflict in the classroom.* Norton.

Delpit, L., & Dowdy, J. K. (Eds.). (2002). *The skin that we speak: Thoughts on language and culture in the classroom.* The New Press.

Feiman-Nemser, S. (2003). What new teachers need to learn. *Educational Leadership, 60*(8), 25–29.

Gay, G. (2010). *Culturally responsive teaching: Theory, research, and practice* (2nd ed.). Teachers College Press.

Isenbarger, L., & Zembylas, M. (2006). The emotional labour of caring in teaching. *Teaching and Teacher Education, 22*(1), 120–134.

Kuhn, T. (1996). *The structure of scientific revolutions* (3rd ed.). University of Chicago Press.

Ladson-Billings, G. (1994). *The dreamkeepers: Successful teachers of African American children.* Jossey-Bass.

Ladson-Billings, G. (1995). Toward a theory of culturally relevant pedagogy. *American Educational Research Journal, 32*(3), 465–491.

Love, B. L. (2019). *We want to do more than survive: Abolitionist teaching and the pursuit of educational freedom.* Beacon Press.

National Centers for Environment Information. (2020). Wildfires – December 2020. National Oceanic and Atmospheric Administration. www.ncdc.noaa.gov/sotc/fire/202012.

Noddings, N. (2005). *The challenge to care in schools: An alternative approach to education.* Teachers College Press.

Noddings, N. (2012). The caring relation in teaching. *Oxford Review of Education, 38*(6), 771–781.

O'Connor, K. E. (2008). "You choose to care": Teachers, emotions and professional identity. *Teaching and Teacher Education, 24*(1), 117–126.

Rogers, D., & Webb, J. (1991). The ethics of caring in teacher education. *Journal of Teacher Education, 42,* 173–181.

Rodriguez-Delgado, C., Wang, F. K-H., Hays, G., & Chavez, R. (2021, November 23). Schools across the country are struggling to find staff. Here's why. PBS News Hour www.pbs.org/newshour/education/schools-across-the-country-are-struggling-to-find-staff-heres-why?

Son, C., Hegde, S., Smith, A., Wang, X., & Sasangohar, F. (2020). Effects of COVID-19 on college students' mental health in the United States: Interview survey study. *Journal of Medical Internet Research, 22*(9), e21279.

Sullivan, H. (2021, August 12). Summer of fire: Blazes burn across Mediterranean with more extreme weather forecast. *The Guardian.* www.theguardian.com/environment/2021/aug/13/summer-of-fire-blazes-mediterranean-more-extreme-weather-forecast.

Valenzuela, A. (1999). *Subtractive schooling: U.S.-Mexican youth and the politics of caring.* State University of New York.

Walker, C., & Gleaves, A. (2016). Constructing the caring education teacher: A theoretical framework. *Teaching and Teacher Education, 54,* 65–76.

Wheeling, K. (2020, November 30). Australia's most extreme bushfire season, statistically speaking. EOS Buzz. https://eos.org/research-spotlights/australias-most-extreme-bushfire-season-statistically-speaking.

Zembylas, M. (2005). *Teaching with emotion: A postmodern enactment.* Information Age Publishing.

Zembylas, M. (2017). Practicing an ethic of discomfort as an ethic of care in higher education teaching. *Critical Studies in Teaching & Learning, 5*(1), 1–17.

Zeichner, K. M., & Liston, D. P. (2013). *Reflective teaching: An introduction* (2nd ed.). Routledge.

PART I

Programmatic Approaches to Care

1

CARE, ACCREDITATION, AND COVID

The Intersection of Sacred and Secular in Teacher Education

Ann D. David and Deepti Kharod

In Spring 2018, the Teacher Education Department at the University of the Incarnate Word (UIW) in San Antonio, Texas, embarked on the journey of program improvement with an eye toward national accreditation. An initial program review by an external reviewer was not as positive as the department might have wished yet unsurprising in its critiques. While it offered observations and suggestions toward improvement, the department decided to follow its own path.

This chapter offers the authors' perspectives on moments that required departmental decisions to follow one path and not another, as well as the larger contexts within which those decisions took place. Those moments and perspectives—both before and during the COVID-19 pandemic—show how the department shifted its priorities for decision making from compliance with standards and accreditation toward departmental and university identities grounded in care and the sacred. Further, as discussions and decisions came to be guided by the university mission's focus on human dignity, the department transitioned to a knowledge community centered around care for students and for one another. While the requirements of compliance and accreditation did not change, the department's approach did, and decisions made using that new approach centered on dignity and caring in ways that they had not prior to the pandemic. The story of our department offers teacher education programs a map for responding to the continuing impacts of COVID-19 on preservice teachers (PSTs), teacher education programs, and K-12 classrooms in the midst of continued compliance and accreditation pressures.

We organize our chapter by considering three questions:

- How does the institution's Catholic mission center or challenge the program's approaches to care?

DOI: 10.4324/9781003244875-3

- In what ways do sacred understandings of care intersect with the secular accreditation standards that drive the work of teacher education?
- How has the development of a faculty community helped us to navigate inherent tensions between the sacred and secular?

Care and the Catholic Identity

Inspired by Judeo-Christian values, the Catholic Intellectual Tradition, and Catholic Social Teaching, UIW aims to educate students who will become concerned and enlightened citizens within the global community. The university is committed to educational excellence in a context of faith in Jesus Christ, the Incarnate Word of God. Thus, through a liberal education, the university cultivates the development of the whole person and the values of life-long learning. To that end, faculty and students support each other in the search for and communication of truth, thoughtful innovation, care of the environment, community service, and social justice (University of the Incarnate Word, Mission Statement, n.d.).

At UIW, the mission is not a statement that administrators merely gesture toward but a standard to which the institution and individuals within it hold themselves. The university's mission infuses conversations, decisions, and interactions, which means that serving one another, human dignity, the search for truth, and social justice are constant companions. While central to UIW's identity, the mission is not a statement of religious indoctrination: UIW hires for commitment to the mission but not to Catholicism. There is an expectation that all employees value human dignity and a reflective approach to faith, often expressed through interfaith dialogues. Similarly, Noddings' (2005) notions of care are built around relationships of care and trust with students, dialogue, and self-improvement.

That said, understanding the Catholic underpinnings of the mission and how those concepts guide work is important. There is an underlying belief that the mission flows from the Holy Spirit. The work of living the mission and values, while never perfect, is aimed at fulfilling the will of God to serve others and work for justice. UIW's mission is grounded in incarnational spirituality—a belief that Jesus is present in each human—and the Catholic Intellectual Tradition. Growing out of this belief and tradition is the mission's focus on social justice, which in Catholic framing is called Catholic Social Teaching (CST).

The principles of CST address the practicalities of how UIW expresses its mission and values in the world. The Teacher Education Department grounds its programmatic identity on supporting a diverse student body to become successful teachers (Ardley et al., 2020; Dallavis, 2014; Sleeter et al., 2014). A third of our department's students are first-generation college students, and 78% are PSTs of color, predominantly Latinx. In a Catholic context, the vocation of teaching is more than a job; it is a calling from God that an individual discerns, often over a lifetime. Discernment is discovering the work that uses one's talents to bring joy, defined not as personal happiness but as the "interior conviction that what one is doing is good even if it does not make one happy or content" (Himes et al., 1995, p. 49). The call to teaching often begins with a desire to serve and care for children, to help them fulfill their potential, all while developing one's own identity as an educator (Heller, 2020).

Within this vocation is also the knowledge that the educational structures within which one labors as a teacher are unjust for a vast majority of the children served. CST addresses this by acknowledging that "structures have to be accepted but at the same time criticized always" (Himes et al., 1995, p. 50). Teaching, then, involves "work[ing] to change structures that are unjust" (p. 50) so that all children can participate in school. These same ideas apply to the department's work of preparing PSTs: There are unjust structures that teacher educators have to both accept and work to change. While our work as a department prior to the pandemic always focused on supporting individual PSTs, it was not equally focused on changing unjust structures.

In a book about care and the COVID-19 pandemic, it is worth noting that UIW was founded by nuns whose community was started to care for victims of a yellow fever epidemic ravaging San Antonio in the mid-1800s. The Sisters of Charity of the Incarnate Word after serving as nurses, opened an orphanage and school to serve San Antonio's children and founded UIW to prepare nurses and teachers. The department's path, then, has always been closely aligned with the notion of vocation and the university's mission, both grounded in caring for others.

Navigating Sacred Identity and Secular Accreditation

Moving away from compliance toward a stance that centers the dignity of PSTs and their future students requires finding connections between the two, then highlighting human dignity while ensuring that the compliance requirements are fulfilled. As one example, the Texas Education Agency (TEA) requires a 2.5 GPA for all programs in the state, while the UIW Teacher Education Program requires a 2.75 GPA. The 2018 external program review praised the diversity of the program's students yet simultaneously recommended raising the GPA requirement to 3.0. However, a 3.0 GPA requirement is known to inhibit diversity in preservice teacher cohorts and has mixed results as a predictor of teacher success (Van Overschelde & López, 2018). This guidance to raise GPA requirements conflicted with our program's identity in serving diverse undergraduates, as well as the need to prepare more teachers of color (Texas Education Agency, 2019a). Our discussions on which path to choose were left unresolved: The department did not want to raise the GPA requirement but previous accreditation decisions had often focused on compliance.

Across the next several semesters, the conversations changed, specifically to focus on care (Noddings, 2005, 2018), as Deepti offered her knowledge and expertise of care theory during meetings and Ann connected these ideas to the

UIW mission and CST. The pandemic's upheaval further clarified the need to support PSTs as people experiencing disruption and trauma, a stance grounded in the university's mission and its focus on human dignity. Lastly, the calls for racial justice sparked by George Floyd's murder in May 2020 focused the need to support the racially diverse students in the program. Over time, the department's approach became one guided by *both* meeting accreditation standards *and* caring. In this case, that meant acknowledging the tension around GPA requirements, while maintaining the 2.75 requirement for admission.

Beyond this example are the requirements that pervade the work of teacher education and the need to comply with those requirements for continued programmatic existence. Documents and standards from both the TEA and the Association for Advancing Quality in Educator Preparation (AAQEP) include language addressing teachers' need to engage in practices that support diverse students. In the Texas Pedagogical and Professional Responsibility Competencies (Texas Education Agency, 2019b), "diverse learners" is the oft-repeated phrase with few mentions of culture or context. Without ever defining diverse learners, the competencies make it easy to ignore culture, race, language, or a host of other student characteristics. The AAQEP Standards address diverse learners with somewhat more specific language, framing the work of teacher candidates as grounded in "culturally responsive practice" and "intersectionality" (Association for Advancing Quality in Educator Preparation, 2021).

The university mission's focus on the search for truth reminded faculty to engage in hard conversations about how programs can become more culturally sustaining and draw on students' extensive and diverse funds of knowledge (Moll et al., 1992). The department found spaces between the sacred and the secular, particularly because the AAQEP Standards articulated a focus on culture and context in a way that previous Texas-based competencies' language did not. As we thought about making a rubric based on AAQEP standards, we also needed to use the language of the university's mission as a guide in the ongoing work of operationalizing the accreditation standards (Twale & Ridenour, 2003).

Developing Community in the Sacred-Secular Tension

The unfolding of these events, and the work to resolve these tensions, were inseparably connected to our relationships as colleagues and people and our emergent knowledge community (Craig, 1995). Our department grew into a knowledge community because the experiences of the pandemic moved us toward meetings as places to construct knowledge in the moment—individually and collectively—through lived experiences, rather than external rules or expectations, because there were no rules for educating PSTs in a pandemic. Additionally, our care for one another moved from the standard "How are you?" toward relational caring, which attends to whether or not individuals feel "cared for" (Noddings, 2005, p. 1). The stress of the pandemic pushed the department further down the path toward a caring knowledge community than we might have gone otherwise.

We come to the work of teacher education from different professional and spiritual identities. Ann taught high school English and her graduate work was in curriculum and instruction, specifically literacy. Deepti taught in elementary self-contained classrooms and her graduate work was in early childhood education. Ann is Catholic and Deepti is Hindu. Ann is tenured and Deepti is on the tenure-track. What we share, though, is greater. We both ground our scholarship in socio-constructivist understandings of learning alongside care and inter-connectedness. Our professional foundations are grounded in our spiritual foundations, faiths with long intellectual traditions and a belief that human dignity is at the center of our work as teachers, teacher educators, and people. Being guided by our professional and spiritual identities offers unique perspectives on an unprecedented time in teacher education while impacting the ways in which we engaged in the communal work of accreditation.

We, obviously, did not create this community alone, and we acknowledge that ours are only two perspectives on this process. Yet our individual attention to care and mission were factors that supported the department in moving past a compliance mindset that puts checklists above people and leaves care out of the equation entirely. What follows is a discussion of how different events, and responses to the pandemic, created opportunities for this shift to a caring community.

During a departmental work session in mid-January 2020, talk turned to how little we knew about what happens in one another's courses and classrooms. In a small program where most classes have one section, there is little need to collaborate on teaching, although we often shared how a class went or brainstormed ideas for instruction. That day, we enthusiastically took a step toward getting to know one another as teachers by creating a pineapple chart (Gonzalez, 2016) to welcome each other into our classrooms to observe and learn (one faculty member added a note to the chart to say, "You are welcome anytime!"). Each member of the department committed to visiting at least one colleague's class over the next few weeks.

The visits happened over late January and February across all classes. During department meetings, a school meeting, and hallway conversations, faculty shared their experiences of observing one another's classes, and they became "stories to live by" (Craig, 2013) as faculty members. These stories, crafted from sharing classrooms with one another, revealed ways that we narrated ourselves and our values into our department and university. As excited as we were to share and learn together, these stories grounded us when the pandemic shutdown hit.

Opening classroom doors to each other and seeing one another as teachers proved to be invaluable in navigating the paradox of isolation and invasiveness of online learning and teaching. Noddings (2018) describes the central role of interpersonal reasoning which manifests in a caring relationship through the question, "Explicitly or implicitly, what are you going through?" (p. 236). As virtual learning took hold at the start of the pandemic, faculty conversations focused almost exclusively on students' struggles, particularly changing responsibilities of family and home, as well as the lack of access to basic resources for survival and learning. Faculty meetings had time dedicated to discussing strategies for supporting students, with emails and texts following up on those discussions. Conversations about students' welfare, though, opened the doors to conversations about one another's welfare.

As an emergent knowledge community, we were pulled toward caring for one another. The communal experience of visiting classrooms just prior to the pandemic—as colleagues, not evaluators—pointed toward other possibilities for community in this virtual space. Ann hosted several Zoom morning coffee talks for the department, and people dropped in as their schedules allowed. Those were important moments of collegiality, and they began to be about our own experiences with the pandemic, not just our students' experiences. For example, in addition to managing the transition to online teaching, Ann was transitioning her own children to online learning. Meanwhile, in Deepti's household, many responsibilities changed hands as her once self-reliant parents minimized outdoor activities and errands. Sharing the challenges we faced began to foster a more caring stance toward one another, reminding us again of the centrality of interpersonal reasoning for ensuring dignity.

Even in a pandemic, though, accreditation never stops. The work, interrupted in March, resumed in May, when Black Lives Matter (BLM) protests were erupting, and the larger political climate contributed to stress, anxiety, and worry. Fortunately, departmental meetings and work sessions had begun to include check-ins where we asked each other about our families and personal wellness and needs. One colleague facilitated a scavenger hunt, and Deepti engaged us in a guided contemplation to reflect and laugh together during work sessions. From being faculty colleagues, we were becoming a faculty community. Relationships, which are considered "ontologically basic" (Noddings, 2012, p. 771) in care ethics, became integral to the community—and all of this happened via Zoom as we had not seen one another in person for months.

By appreciating one another as humans first, even differences of opinion could be discussed with more listening and compassion, which points to an idea Noddings (2005) calls motivational displacement: We "must take into account the feelings and desires that are actually there and respond as positively as [our] values and capacities allow" (p. 2). From this stronger, care-focused position, we could pivot back to the accreditation work without falling back into prioritizing compliance. The new place of caring allowed for a continued turn in accreditation conversation to centering the needs of our PSTs in ways that compliance had previously made more challenging.

Social inequities, now highlighted by BLM protests and compounded by the pandemic, were a persistent drag on students' success, yet changing the program and policies to acknowledge that reality had not previously been successful. One of the ways that the department had designed support for its diverse PSTs was staking a claim to preparation in culturally responsive teaching (Gay, 2010; Nieto, 2013) through a course of that same title. Ann, who has been teaching Culturally Responsive Teaching since 2015, was particularly focused on how that class—and by extension, the program—could meet the moment to better prepare students to become culturally responsive and sustaining educators. She admitted early on that she was not sure she was fully up to the task and sought support from colleagues. As a faculty community, our emerging expressions of vulnerability allowed for important and uncomfortable conversations that had once been masked by the empty language of standards, such as "students with diverse backgrounds and needs" (Texas Education Agency, 2019b), but now demanded explicit attention.

As the pandemic, protests, and politics continued, this greater comfort with the sacred continued to influence the department's work. In designing a new course, Social Emotional Learning and Classroom Management, and revising Culturally Responsive Teaching, the department incorporated unambiguous words, such as *compassion, equity,* and *social justice* into the course description, overview, and outcomes. These words reflect values embodied in the department's mission statement. This highlighting of values-based language occurred in spite of the fact that national accreditation (Association for Advancing Quality in Educator Preparation, 2021) and state teacher competencies (Texas Education Agency, 2019b) lacked these terms. The design process for these courses served as one of the most robust instances of a collaborative and values-based approach to decision-making. In centering care and the sacred inherent in the university's mission, our emergent knowledge community is better prepared to face the continued and uncertain impacts of the pandemic as we return to face-to-face classes and PSTs graduate and go into classrooms of their own.

Changing Language: Acknowledge the Tension, Center the Sacred

The inherent points of tension between the sacred and the secular became apparent as we, the authors, reflected on program improvement experiences over the past two years. During this departmental work, conversations were more frequent, yet still only occasional, as department faculty interrogated how well program goals, processes, and artifacts embodied the university's stated mission and role as a Hispanic-Serving and Minority-Serving Institution. We, the authors, often engaged in dialogue outside of departmental meetings that led us to interrogate the specific points of tension between the sacred and the secular, as well as to look for bridges between the two. For example, we noted that TEA (2019a) plans to highlight teacher education programs that prepare PSTs of color (p. 33–34). This secular concept aligns well with ideas about social justice in the UIW Mission.

So why do we feel a tension between compliance and mission? Is it because secular demands for compliance-based education are uncomfortable with the idea of human dignity? Is it possible for a sacred orientation, one centered on care, to lead to successful, secular accreditation? We answer these questions in the affirmative. Our evidence for the answers grows out of the experience of crafting policy language in meetings, and how it shifted and changed over the two years of accreditation work. Initially, there was discomfort with the language of care and dignity because it had not been a part of the discourse of the department, despite the Catholic context. But discourse patterns can change in ways that acknowledge the tension while reorienting to the sacred. We offer three examples of this language shift, each building on the previous.

First, from 2018 to 2019, the department articulated and operationalized the program's professional dispositions standards and processes including assessing, facilitating reflection about, and holding students to professional standards. While eventually coming to a developmental stance toward dispositions, there was a tendency to consider how to ensure that the program had a way to support decisions to remove students from placements or the program. The final dispositions document included headings like "Cultural and Social Responsiveness" and "Health and Wellness" but language closely aligned to the mission statement, like *compassion, care*, and *human dignity*, was left out. It proved too difficult to operationalize these terms, to turn them into checklists of observable and measurable behaviors, so the group was uncomfortable committing to that language.

Second, after COVID-19 interrupted the accreditation work between March and May 2020, work restarted with a focus on developing rubrics to assess how program benchmarks met AAQEP Standards 1 and 2 (Association for Advancing Quality in Educator Preparation, 2021). During these work sessions, we experienced another fork in the path, with accreditation and mission pulling conversations and understandings in different directions. As discussed before, the department supported culturally responsive teaching but the integration of culturally responsive and sustaining practices had not expanded beyond a specific course in the ensuing decade. Initial reads of the AAQEP Standards began with a standard focus on what our PSTs learn about lesson planning and teaching. Early on in the conversation, though, the references to culturally responsive practice and intersectionality in the standards facilitated a deeper, richer discussion about how these practices weave their way into the program, not just in the single course with the right name. Ann opened up this rubric discussion to consider how the university's mission and Catholic identity, as well as culturally responsive and sustaining practices, could be operationalized in assessment systems. CST, after all, points not just to individual human dignity, but also to the systems that create or reinforce inequity. In this case, as with GPA, the department chose the path that was guided by care, dignity, and the university's mission by integrating the language of dignity and mission into the rubrics.

Third, in the spring of 2021, the department rewrote the mission statement for the teacher education program. In an earlier draft from May 2020, the language centered on standards of excellence (e.g., exemplary education, student-centered, theory and practice) with a nod to mission focus (e.g., value-based, socially just). Its general language of "affecting mankind in positive ways" lacked the force of what the department was willing to stand behind by May 2021. In sharp contrast, the final version stated that the department's values reflect CST through relationships, social justice, human dignity, and a culturally sustaining approach. As one of the team observed, the first draft was about the program ideals, not about the students. In the final version, words and phrases that had seemed nebulous in early discussions, such as "human dignity," became solid in a world suffering through a pandemic and uprisings for racial justice:

Teacher Education Mission Statement

The Dreeben School of Education Teacher Education Program's mission is to prepare educators who are guided by compassion, social justice, human dignity, and innovation. We are committed to ensuring a high-quality teacher preparation experience that combines theory with practical application. Reflective of Catholic Social Teaching, we value a culturally sustaining approach to teaching, contributing to a diverse teaching profession, and nurturing strong relationships with students and the community.

Conclusion

Does our experience hold meaning for a secular education program? Again, we answer yes. The tension, we propose, lies in the fact that accreditation is observable and measurable and, therefore, commodified. Human dignity, and the care necessary to acknowledge and value it, cannot be commodified in the same kinds of ways, though they are observable. We have found that our path to resolving the sacred-secular tension is embracing and more intentionally living the mission of the university. We have also committed to telling the story of our department as one that supports PSTs of color by focusing on developmental practices (Ardley et al., 2020). These commitments mean living in the tension, making choices that support PSTs in finding joy in their future work, and changing systems that replicate injustice. This stance will be essential going forward as we move out of the pandemic and strive to recover as individuals, institutions, and nations. By prioritizing human dignity and educating for the common good, which Wells (2015) describes as "where individual and community goods overlap" (p. 49), our teacher education program can continue to make choices that align with our mission and address long-term inequities that the pandemic has made more visible, all while meeting accreditation standards.

References

Ardley, J., Goodloe, A., & Kerns, K. (2020). Building capacity in the successful preparation of teachers of color: Effective retention strategies. *Kappa Delta Pi Record, 56*(4), 160–163.

Association for Advancing Quality in Educator Preparation. (2021). *Guide to AAQEP accreditation*. https://aaqep.org/files/2020-Guide-to-AAQEP-Accreditation.pdf.

Craig, C. (1995). Safe places on the professional knowledge landscape: Knowledge communities. In J. D. Clandinin and M. F. Connelly (Eds.), *Teachers' professional knowledge landscapes* (pp. 137–141). Teachers College Press.

Craig, C. J. (2013). Coming to know in the 'eye of the storm': A beginning teacher's introduction to different versions of teacher community. *Teaching and Teacher Education, 29,* 25–38.

Dallavis, C. (2014). Culturally responsive caring and expectations for academic achievement in a Catholic school. *Journal of Catholic Education, 17*(2), 154–171.

Heller, R. (2020, April 27). Why we teach: A conversation with Sonia Nieto. *Phi Delta Kappan.* https://kappanonline.org/why-we-teach-sonia-nieto-interview-teaching-heller.

Himes, M. J., Pilarski, J., & McNeill, D. P. (1995). *Doing the truth in love: Conversations about God, relationships, and service.* Paulist Press.

Gay, G. (2010). *Culturally responsive teaching: Theory, research, and practice* (2nd ed.). Teachers College Press.

Gonzalez, J. (2016). How pineapple charts revolutionize professional development. *Cult of Pedagogy.* www.cultofpedagogy.com/pineapple-charts.

Moll, L., Amanti, C., Neff, D., & Gonzalez, N. (1992). Funds of knowledge for teaching: Using a qualitative approach to connect homes and classrooms. *Theory Into Practice, 31*(2), 132–141.

Nieto, S. (2013). *Finding joy in teaching students of diverse backgrounds: Culturally responsive and socially just practices in U.S. classrooms.* Heinemann.

Noddings, N. (2005). 'Caring in education', *The encyclopedia of pedagogy and informal education.* https://infed.org/mobi/caring-in-education.

Noddings, N. (2012). The caring relation in teaching. *Oxford Review of Education, 38*(6), 771–781.

Noddings, N. (2018). *Philosophy of education* (4th ed.). Routledge.

Sleeter, C. E., Neal, L. I., & Kumashiro, K. K. (2014). *Diversifying the teacher workforce: Preparing and retaining highly effective teachers* [eBook edition]. Routledge.

Texas Education Agency. (2019a). *Texas accountability system for educator preparation (ASEP) manual 2019–2020.* https://texreg.sos.state.tx.us/fids/202005274-1.pdf.

Texas Education Agency. (2019b). *Preparation Manual Pedagogy and Professional Responsibilities EC–12 (160).* www.tx.nesinc.com/content/docs/TX160_Pedagogy_PrepManual.pdf.

Twale, D. J., & Ridenour, C. S. (2003). The sacred and the secular: Aligning a Marianist mission with professional standards of practice in an educational leadership doctoral program. *Journal of Catholic Education, 7*(2), 181–196.

University of the Incarnate Word. (n.d.). *UIW Mission.* www.uiw.edu/mission.

University of the Incarnate Word. (n.d.). *Catholic intellectual tradition.* www.uiw.edu/mission/missionsupport.html#catholicsocialteaching.

Van Overschelde, J. P., & López, M. M. (2018). Raising the bar or locking the door? The effects of increasing GPA admission requirements on teacher preparation. *Equity & Excellence in Education, 51*(3–4),223–241.

Wells, C. A. (2015). Finding the center as things fly apart: Vocation and the common good. In D. S. Cunningham (Ed.). *At this time and in this place: Vocation and higher education* (pp. 47–71). Oxford University Press.

2

REDEFINING CARE IN TEACHER EDUCATION

Responding to Teacher Candidate Needs after COVID

Rebecca Smith, Paul Sutton, and Gavin Tierney

Teaching has long been viewed as a caring profession but COVID-19 brought unprecedented challenges to the field of education as the care needed for students and teachers alike grew tremendously. These challenges also impacted the mental health of those in the learning community. Self-reported incidents of depressive and anxious behavior were heightened in the general public during the pandemic (Wang et al., 2020), and the impact on college students appears to be severe. In one study of 791 US college students, ages 18–30 (Conrad et al., 2021), one third of students reported having to physically relocate, leading to grief, loneliness, and anxiety. Additional fears related to illness, loss of jobs, and infecting family members also contributed to the stress college students experienced throughout the pandemic (Zhai & Du, 2020). The comprehensive strain of the pandemic, particularly on college students, leads to a call for teacher educators to re-envision how we care for our teacher candidates.

Purpose of This Study

In this chapter, we explore how teacher educators in a post-pandemic world are called to refigure understandings and enactments of care and carry those revised understandings and enactments forward into their in-person, online, or hybrid practice with teacher candidates. While research on care in education exists, there is limited research on the pedagogy of care in higher education (Walker & Gleaves, 2016). This chapter contributes to the literature on how to care for teacher candidates during a time of crisis, such as the COVID-19 pandemic, but also informs methods for enacting care at all times so students are more authentically heard and supported in their learning.

This chapter was borne out of a larger collaboration of seven teacher educators and two doctoral students from universities across the United States who came

DOI: 10.4324/9781003244875-4

together virtually in Fall 2020 to support each other in our own competencies in online teaching during COVID-19. The three authors of this chapter were particularly drawn to understanding how to care for teacher candidates during this unique and challenging time in education, and thus we utilized data from the larger research project to inform this chapter. We argue for an extension of Noddings' (1988) care framework to adequately and authentically support teacher candidates needs related to pre-existing inequities spotlighted by the pandemic and virtual learning. The following research questions guided this study: How can teacher educators demonstrate care for teacher candidates? How does the context of the COVID-19 pandemic impact how we consider and define the elements of care?

Framing Care in Education

Noddings (1988) frames the aims of care in education around modeling, dialogue, practice, and confirmation. Modeling requires that "teachers treat students with respect and consideration and encourage [students] to treat each other in a similar fashion" (p. 223). Dialogue, defined as ongoing conversation where "conclusions are not held by one or more of the parties at the outset" (p. 223), calls for teachers to model respect and consideration by co-constructing solutions with students. Noddings explains that "in a classroom dedicated to caring, students are encouraged to support each other; opportunities for peer interaction are provided, and the quality of the interaction is as important as the academic outcomes" (p. 223). The practice Noddings refers to describes ways that teacher educators can provide teacher candidates with opportunities to practice care toward each other and their future students. This might include strategies such as intentional small group work to solve problems of practice in the classroom as well as explicit, ongoing discussions with teacher candidates about how they can become teachers who not just understand the ethical dimensions of their instructional decision-making but can operationalize that thinking into concrete practices in their K-12 classrooms. By confirmation, Noddings describes a dynamic whereby teachers empower students to identify and clarify their purpose in life and work to support them in that effort. We argue these frames are relevant in teacher education today, yet, the need to contextualize care is also a critical, missing component.

Noddings' (1988) care framework has provided meaningful guidance for educators seeking to care for their students, and we seek to apply lessons from prior research to teacher education. Walker and Gleaves (2016) explored faculty perceptions of care in teaching, finding that caring teachers (1) have relationships at the center (i.e., quickly learning students' names, responding to emails in a timely manner, initiating contact with students when challenges arise); (2) are compelled to care (i.e., spending multiple hours supporting students, facilitating learning in various ways, explicitly supporting student diversity); and (3) view caring as resistance (i.e., defending students when needed, questioning institutional policies). These findings support both the relational and action-oriented nature of care for students. Another study (Anderson et al., 2020), which focused on student perceptions of good teaching at a New Zealand university, found that "they described good teachers as people who care about their discipline, care about teaching and care about students, powerfully influencing students' engagement with subject matter, enthusiasm for learning and aspirations for the future" (p. 1). While perceptions of care from both the teacher and student perspective have variations, they focus on relationships.

Noddings' care has also been used as a framework in teacher education programs. For instance, Rabin (2020) found that an ethics of care framework can help teacher candidates and mentor teachers effectively traverse the power dynamics within this relationship. In addition, Benson (2008) explored the efficacy of Noddings' (1988) care theory in supporting teacher candidates identifying as queer. Findings indicated that queer students did welcome care from their professors and their sense of wellbeing benefited from the enactment of care; however, the lack of explicit care for the needs of queer students is a limitation of the framework's responsive to students' needs. These studies support the use of care in navigating various relationships within teacher education; however, there also appears to be gaps in utilizing care as a framework for explicitly addressing issues of equity and justice within the curriculum and instruction. We argue that Noddings' framework needs to include an integration of the sociopolitical context that impacts our teacher candidates and teacher educators today.

Methodology and Data Sources

This study reports targeted findings that emerged from a larger research study involving seven teacher educators from four institutions who met regularly during Fall 2020. The original study focused on how we could effectively teach and facilitate discussions in online learning spaces. The three authors of this chapter found that care for our teacher candidates was an emergent theme in the data collected for the larger study. Thus, we have utilized transcripts from seven focus group interviews with teacher candidates from four institutions to address our research questions.

The 18 participants for the study were enrolled in an undergraduate or graduate teacher licensure program in the fall of 2020 and had completed a language arts methods course online due to the COVID-19 pandemic. The 45-minute interviews were conducted and recorded via Zoom and then transcribed by graduate research assistants. The authors did not interview their own teacher candidates for this research project, and all participant identities are protected with pseudonyms. Interviews consisted of six questions related to the teacher candidates' experiences in their online methods course: (1) Tell me, generally, about your experience in your methods course. What was challenging; what was beneficial? (2) Did your class focus on discussion? (3) What is a discussion? How did your understanding change, if at all, during your course? (4) What in the course helped you prepare to enact discussions in your own classroom and during student teaching? (5) Do you feel prepared to teach text-based discussions in your own classroom/during student teaching? (6) If your instructor were to teach this course again, what feedback would you give them?

The data analysis entailed a multi-step, collaborative process (Saldaña, 2016). First, the research team collaborated in real time via Zoom to review focus group transcripts, which had been uploaded to Dedoose. The research team utilized a priori coding, in which we identified a set of pre-established codes based on the literature review and our own experiences as participant researchers in this study. Examples of a priori codes included *context: online learning, context: COVID, modeling,* and *assumed needs.*

This coding process was useful due to the application of Noddings' (1988) preexisting care framework from which we were framing our exploration. In addition to the a priori codes, the team also conducted open coding of the data, where parts of the qualitative data were broken down into meaningful codes for comparison across the data set (Saldaña, 2016). Examples of open codes included *instructional flexibility and adaptability, context: Black Lives Matter, vulnerability, adjusting in response to teacher candidate needs,* and *community.*

After this first cycle of collaborative coding, the research team individually coded the remaining transcript data, utilizing the existing codes. After all data were analyzed by each researcher, the codes were transformed into broader themes that assigned meaning to our initial codes. This process included looking at individual and overlapping codes in and across data and creating initial memos and then themes. Major themes emerged from (1) codes that identified how teacher candidates saw care in the setting and relationship with the university instructor (e.g., *listening to teacher candidate concerns, vulnerability*); (2) codes that identified the larger sociopolitical context in which care existed (e.g., *context: Black Lives Matter, context: COVID*); and (3) codes that identified how teacher educators enacted care in their classrooms (e.g., *adjusting in response to teacher candidate needs, modeling*). These themes are discussed further in our findings. Other themes less focused on care were also identified but excluded from this chapter.

Findings

Several key findings emerged from the qualitative data analysis. Teacher candidates appreciated the accommodations made and flexibility demonstrated by teacher educators to respond to their needs. These spaces of care helped candidates feel a strong connection to their instructors and to each other as they struggled to complete coursework. In addition, teacher candidates appreciated the vulnerability teacher educators showed as they, too, struggled to deal with the near-constant disruptions of teaching during a pandemic. Candidates perceived this vulnerability as a form of modeling that helped them learn how to deal with unanticipated crises, how to care for themselves and those around them, and how to deal with unprecedented external, sociopolitical events while teaching.

Creating a Setting for Care

The first theme that emerged from the data was creating a setting for care through individual and community relationships. The first quality of creating a setting for care was how relationships were built between the teacher educator and the teacher candidates. This was evidenced by related codes occurring in and across the data, such as *listening to teacher candidate concerns* (17 instances across four institutions) and *vulnerability* (20 instances across four institutions). While the specific qualities of individual relationships shifted, it appeared that the teacher educators tried to build relationships with the teacher candidates in their classes, as one candidate explained in talking about communication with their professor:

> I think the fact that he's always willing to answer our questions via text, via email, via whatever we're most comfortable with definitely had a lot to do with my engagement and how much I wanted to share myself and discuss in the classroom.

This teacher candidate later discussed the importance of the professor knowing them on a personal level: "Two out of the three classes he was my professor and he knew about my situation." It appeared that a trusting relationship between the teacher candidate and the teacher educator was established and maintained over time, so that care could be enacted.

Another teacher candidate discussed the relational way the professor led class activities, demonstrating how she, too, was engaging in the work, particularly in trying to facilitate online discussions: "It felt nice knowing she was in the same— our professor was in the trenches with us in some sense, and I think that was really admirable to kind of watch her go through." This quotation demonstrates a way that caring relationships were built into the teacher educator's practice.

The relational practices extended beyond individual relationships that teacher educators built with specific candidates into the classroom community they created. Data analysis indicated that there was a community of care established in these virtual classrooms, creating settings in which care could exist. One teacher candidate discussed the classroom community:

> I also think it's very important when it comes to building a classroom environment. [The professor] allowed a lot of relevancy and distractions in online learning so that we could release things. So that we were able to learn because our well-being came first.

In this quotation, the candidate identified how the professor built a classroom environment where their humanity and "well-being" came first. One interesting aspect of this quotation is the fact that the student linked relevancy and distractions as important qualities of the classroom environment, highlighting the need for classrooms to be authentic and inclusive learning spaces. Further, this comment hints at a classroom community that was co-constructed with the teacher candidates, where all members of the community dictated what was meaningful and relevant. This community was built online when the professor provided multiple entry points into class activities, such as allowing teacher candidates to engage in the chat feature on Zoom and utilizing breakout rooms. The chat was mentioned as more of a student-led space that could be a different or parallel conversation to what was being discussed verbally. While the candidate discussed how the chat helped them stay engaged, it also represents a caring learning environment where teacher candidates' voices are valued.

Considering Sociopolitical Contexts of Learning and Being

The second theme was the teacher educators' awareness of the social and political contexts in which their teacher candidates existed. The unique nature of the sociopolitical context during the COVID-19 pandemic highlighted a need to recognize and explore the impact on candidates' lives and learning and the ways in which they existed in the world at that time. This was evidenced by related codes occurring in and across the interview data, such as *Context: COVID* (56 instances across four institutions) and *Context: Black Lives Matter* concerns (five instances across two institutions). While there were fewer instances of codes around Black Lives Matter, we included it as part of this theme to identify the complex experiences of teacher candidates as they navigated a multitude of sociopolitical contexts.

Some of the ways that teacher educators demonstrated consideration of their teacher candidates' sociopolitical contexts of learning and being included supporting candidates as they navigated the dual contexts of a global pandemic and the Black Lives Matter movement following the murder of George Floyd. One teacher candidate reflected on their professor's support:

> I just started crying about how hard my teaching and classroom placement has been going because of my situation. I was homeless... My mom kicked me out of my house because I'm dating a Black woman. And then my dog almost died because...the vets wouldn't take my dog in because my fiancé was Black. And it was all in the midst of the Black Lives Matter protest and it was just really fucked up and, in the midst of all of this, I was...trying to figure out how to do school work.

In this quotation, the teacher candidate does not necessarily highlight what responses the teacher educator had, but the candidate felt open to reaching out and discussing the contexts in which they were struggling. The multiple external stressors impacting this student beyond the classroom were also impacting their own learning.

The sociopolitical contexts impacting teacher candidates emerged when discussing their personal struggles but also when thinking about teaching as a practice. Another teacher candidate from a different institution talked about how their practice as a student teacher existed in the context of historical racism and racial injustice:

> I just speak a lot of truth when it comes to racism and making sure that people are seen, especially if it's the Indigenous people or Black people and making sure that white fragility isn't just taking over the conversations ... I'm sick and tired of white fragility taking over the conversation.

In this quotation, the teacher candidate speaks to how teaching practice cannot exist outside of the sociopolitical contexts in which students and teachers exist. Ignoring the lived realities of our students perpetuates white fragility and racism. As this teacher candidate recognizes, teaching is an act of participation with the world.

Modeling Care for Students and Self

A third key theme that arose in the data was modeling care for students and self, specifically the teacher educator modeling care for teacher candidates. The value and expression of care surfaced in an affective manner when candidates discussed social and emotional health, of themselves, their K-12 students, or of the teacher educator. This was evidenced by related codes occurring in and across the interview data, such as *modeling* (28 instances across four institutions) and *adjusting in response to teacher candidate needs* (15 instances across three institutions). Across these codes, we noted a theme of creating a safe and inclusive learning environment mentioned as foundational for effective learning, as highlighted by one teacher candidate:

> If your students don't feel safe or comfortable in your classroom, then they're not really going to participate or have valuable discussions because they don't feel comfortable, but if you've created an atmosphere of security and safety, then it's going to lead to more in depth discussion.

Another teacher candidate felt their teacher educator advocated for them in the midst of the challenges of the pandemic, claiming the professor said, "Let me advocate for you. Let me see what I can do. And then let's figure out a plan for what we can do for your assignments and that's what we did. And then I felt very relaxed and less overwhelmed and less anxious." This teacher educator modeled listening to the needs of their student and adapted their care to meet these needs.

The impact of teacher educators' modeling care, particularly around issues of candidate mental health, appeared to have positive impacts on the teacher candidates. One candidate said of their professor, "He really energized me and gave me hope and [I] realized, this is worth it because this is not the end all, be all of what teaching is." The teacher educator modeled an attitude of hope during this time of crisis and was able to help the candidate envision an educational landscape in the future beyond the pandemic.

Another teacher educator modeled a classroom community where questions were welcome:

> Our class was very open with each other and we were all into the discussions we had in class and we were all asking questions. Our class community was pretty close. We felt like we could be honest with [the professor].

It appeared that modeling care for teacher candidates by providing safe spaces to ask, answer, and discuss questions helped to strengthen the class community, allowed candidates to be vulnerable themselves, and helped them feel like valued members of the learning community.

Discussion and Implications

In reflecting on the themes identified above, the data suggest that these teacher candidates desired caring classroom spaces in which two key criteria were present: (1) room for deeper relationships through which teacher educators can respond to the impacts of the sociopolitical context teacher candidates face, and (2) community involving the teacher educator modeling what care looks like in the moment and over time. These findings suggest how teacher educators can demonstrate care for teacher candidates and how the COVID-19 pandemic impacts how we consider the elements of care moving forward.

First, it is clear that relationships remain at the core of a caring classroom, as has been highlighted in numerous studies on care in education, both in the teacher-student relationship (e.g., Walker & Cleaves, 2016) and in the student teacher and mentor teacher relationship (e.g., Rabin, 2020). Furthermore, it appears that empathy and trust are critical for developing these relationships, particularly when the teacher educator is open to ongoing dialogue with teacher candidates that leads to a less hierarchical power dynamic in the learning environment. The COVID-19 pandemic brought teacher educators into the homes and lives of our candidates in unprecedented ways. Yet, this insight into the humanity of our teacher candidates—their window into our own private lives when teaching remotely—has the potential to redefine authentic relationships in teacher education.

Second, Noddings' (1988) framework of care must retain a focus on teacher educators' explicit modeling of care for teacher candidates. In this study, teacher candidates recognized the value of collaborative, caring, and honest relationships with their professors, and they transferred this knowledge into their own K-12 classrooms in the way they showed care for their students. Additionally, we advocate for modeling to include a focus on vulnerability, which is largely missing from current research around care. When teacher educators publicly accept their own failure, share ways they struggle, or acknowledge ways they need to improve, they provide teacher candidates with a roadmap they can use to do the same with their future students.

Third, the data suggest that teacher candidates crave support related to the sociopolitical context to be integrated within a broader philosophy of care in the teacher education classroom. However, our data also suggest that such a setting for care is only possible if enough trust is built between teacher educators and teacher candidates so that candidates feel comfortable sharing their anxieties, exhaustion, and overall mental health struggles with teacher educators. Perhaps honoring these "distractions" can enable deeper learning to occur.

Care Beyond COVID

The pandemic has highlighted numerous equity issues that directly impacted K-20 education and yet, the lessons we are learning from COVID-19 can be applied beyond the pandemic, particularly to how we care for teacher candidates. The call to consider context in education is not new; Ladson-Billings (1995) recognized the importance of context in her theory of culturally relevant pedagogy, including understanding the institutional, cultural, and social contexts experienced by students. Furthermore, Gay (2013) argued that "instructional practices should be shaped by the sociocultural characteristics of the settings in which they occur" (p. 63). This study occurred during the unique context of a pandemic, and yet, no matter the context, a deliberate integration of a contextualized care framework in teacher education can benefit teacher candidates and their students. This pedagogy of care could include the teacher educator designing specific learning experiences that address the social context surrounding teacher candidates' preparation but it might also include indirect ways teacher educators provide candidates with opportunities to discuss the challenges of balancing the demands of their coursework with non-academic demands and co-constructing solutions. Similar to K-12 students' need to feel a sense of belonging in order to fully engage academically in classroom spaces (Cobb & Krownapple, 2020), so too do teacher candidates who sometimes struggle to balance their professional and personal lives need caring classrooms for deeper learning.

All three implications have consequences for how teacher educators approach their teaching practice. Teacher candidates expressed a desire to be listened to, to be cared for, and to have the larger sociopolitical context acknowledged and perhaps brought into the teacher education classroom space. Although these desires have taken on new urgency as a result of the pandemic, teacher educators would be wise to consider how they can reorient their classrooms around these principles. The work of becoming a teacher is intellectually and emotionally exhausting. Being mindful of the stress that teacher candidates bear, and taking both big and small steps to better care for them, will ensure they have the capacity to learn the complex work of teaching and will provide them with a powerful model for how they should work with their future students.

Conclusion

This study highlights the need for teacher educators to listen to the expressed needs (Noddings, 2012) of their teacher candidates, particularly as those needs relate to navigating sociopolitical contexts. As the COVID-19 pandemic ravaged communities, teacher candidates found themselves dealing with both the existential threat the pandemic posed to what they imagined teaching to be and the very real, physical threat the pandemic posed to their personal safety. In such traumatic times, demonstrating care for teacher candidates demanded teacher educators take a revised approach to what care looks like in the teacher education classroom, whether virtual or in-person. As we move beyond the pandemic, teacher educators must model care and vulnerability, must establish trust with teacher candidates, and must honor the lived experiences of their candidates beyond the classroom by bringing this context into their curriculum and instruction to better support candidates' needs.

References

Anderson, V., Rabello, R., Wass, R., Golding, C., Rangi, A., Eteuati, E., & Bristowe, Z. (2020). Good teaching as care in higher education. *Higher Education, 79*(1), 1–19.

Benson, F. J. (2008). *Teacher educators' practice of queer-care: A necessary expansion of Noddings' model of care.* ProQuest Dissertations Publishing.

Cobb, F., & Krownapple, J. (2020). *Belonging through a culture of dignity: The keys to successful equity implementation.* Mimi and Todd Press.

Conrad, R. C., Hahm, H. C., Koire, A., Pinder-Amaker, S., & Liu, C. H. (2021). College student mental health risks during the COVID-19 pandemic: Implications of campus relocation. *Journal of Psychiatric Research, 136,* 117–126.

Gay, G. (2013). Teaching to and through cultural diversity. *Curriculum Inquiry; 43*(1), 48–70.

Ladson-Billings, G. (1995). Toward a theory of culturally relevant pedagogy. *American Educational Research Journal, 32*(3), 465–491.

Noddings, N. (1988). An ethic of caring and its implications for instructional arrangements. *American Journal of Education, 96*(2), 215–230.

Noddings, N. (2012). The caring relation in teaching. *Oxford Review of Education, 38*(6), 771–781.

Rabin, C. (2020). Co-teaching: Collaborative and caring teacher preparation. *Journal of Teacher Education, 71*(1), 135–147.

Saldaña, J. (2016). *The coding manual for qualitative researchers* (3rd ed.). Sage Publications.

Walker, C., & Gleaves, A. (2016). Constructing the caring higher education teacher: A theoretical framework. *Teaching and Teacher Education, 54*, 65–76.

Wang, C., Pan, R., Wan, X., Tan, Y., Xu, L., Ho, C. S., & Ho, R. C. (2020). Immediate psychological responses and associated factors during the initial stage of the 2019 coronavirus disease (COVID-19) epidemic among the general population in China. *International Journal of Environmental Research and Public Health, 17*(5), 1729.

Zhai, Y., & Du, X. (2020). Addressing collegiate mental health amid COVID-19 pandemic. *Psychiatry Research, 288*, 113003.

3

ON A JOURNEY INTO THE UNKNOWN

Critical Care Pedagogy, COVID, and Teacher Education

Camie Wood, Jacob Warren, Holly Sheppard Riesco, Kathryn Hackett-Hill, and Christian Z. Goering

As teacher educators, the topic of *good* teaching comes up frequently (Au, 2009; Cochran-Smith at al., 2009; Ladson-Billings, 1995). In fact, when we consider *good* teaching in our education classes, we often picture classrooms that center rousing dialogue and constant interaction to challenge students' thinking. These practices are designed to ensure that all students are able to engage fully in the learning process, making discussions about dialogue and interactions critical in teacher education programs. Through education-focused critical dialogues, pre-service teachers are asked to reflect on trending practices in education and to determine ways to implement those practices into their future classrooms.

Unfortunately, when the COVID-19 pandemic hit, teachers at every level scrambled to find footing for good teaching as school buildings shut down. Sparking a drive toward innovation, many K-12 teachers rose to the challenge, learning how to (re)apply their practices, strategies, and tools through previously unused and unfamiliar platforms, whether creating physical copies of work and texts that students without internet could access at home or creating interactive web-based lessons. This brought changes in teacher education classrooms, as well. Not only were classes for preservice teachers switched to virtual platforms but teacher educators and preservice teachers now had to reimagine the classroom practices supporting student engagement. In facing the redevelopment of practice through these unfamiliar platforms, we, as teacher educators, became convinced that the redesign of coursework must also focus on caring classroom practices within colleges of education during and after the pandemic.

Here, we—the authorial team of Camie, Jacob, Holly, Katie, and Chris—consider the question of institutionalizing caring classroom practices and argue that centering care as an instructional practice can only benefit our preservice teachers. In reflecting on what caring classroom practices should look like in

DOI: 10.4324/9781003244875-5

colleges of education, an essential question emerged for us: *Why should we—and how can we—enact a critical care pedagogy within teacher education programs, now and in the future?* This chapter explores specific classroom practices centering on critical care pedagogy and questions how we, as teacher educators, might institutionalize these practices in colleges of education.

Positionality

We connected around these issues during a series of unstructured conversations in the spring semester of 2021 that, in turn, engendered a movement toward change in our educational practices. Camie, a former high school social studies and Spanish teacher, is in her third year as a doctoral student, focusing on education policy and teacher education. Jacob and Holly are second year PhD students focusing on English and literacy education. A first-year doctoral student, Katie joined the conversations while wrapping up a high school English teaching career and planning a move to focus on English and literacy teacher education. Alongside Chris, a professor of English education, each author brings K-12 humanities-focused teaching experiences, as well as their own graduate student experiences, to bear on the conversation surrounding the incorporation of caring classroom practices in colleges of education during and after the COVID-19 pandemic.

We met through Zoom to discuss questions of care in colleges of education. Our conversation revolved around our personal experiences with the unexpected issues—such as disconnection from colleagues, remote or hybrid learning, and balancing high expectations with compassion for our students—that we confronted during the pandemic as doctoral students, instructors of preservice teachers, a secondary teacher, and a professor. Our conversation also turned toward what we did personally to overcome the tensions of the pandemic and led us to determine what we, as graduate students and future teacher educators, would want from institutions that were concerned with enacting care after COVID. We continued this conversation through face-to-face meetings and the collaborative writing of this chapter, keeping in mind our common goal of creating a path for care within teacher education programs.

Reflecting on the Issues

Before the pandemic, educators and researchers explored the ideas that stress, anxiety, and trauma can lead to learning impairments. Newman et al. (2021) demonstrate that stress is one cause of memory problems, and Jones and Nangah (2021) show that traumatic emotional experiences contribute to engagement barriers in higher education. We see this not only in research but also in the effects of stress and traumatic experiences on our preservice teachers and ourselves as graduate students and teacher educators as the pandemic persists.

As the number of cases of COVID-19 increased in the spring of 2020, so did the number of universities that shut down their campuses and switched classes to virtual settings, raising in both student and faculty anxiety and tension about the shift needed to continue effective teaching and learning practices during COVID. Switching to a virtual platform meant that there were few opportunities for conversations and questions before or after class, no accidental meetings at a campus event or in the library. This type of informal communication was replaced by more formal meetings on virtual platforms, which meant an increase in the number of meetings needed in order to communicate well and build relationships. While the effort to build relationships and reduce feelings of isolation were appreciated, many were overwhelmed with the number of meetings they were attending and found it necessary to work longer hours to complete assignments on time or meet research deadlines. Setting boundaries between work and home life became increasingly difficult. While some flourished in this environment, many found it difficult to distinguish between working hours and personal hours while working from home.

In our conversations about the changes that COVID wrought on us as graduate students and teacher educators, we learned how we coped differently to manage the workload and stress of the moment. For example, while some excelled in the online environment, others preferred more direct instruction and collaboration in a face-to-face community. In addition, our systems of stress relief varied by individual means. Some used apps on their phones to block notifications during certain hours of the day (or night); others took pets for walks, visited family, or strolled around their neighborhoods. The differences explored during our conversations offered a hint of what is needed to support preservice teachers and their instructors in enacting caring classroom practices. In exploring our conversations through the lens of critical care pedagogy and critical consciousness, we came to acknowledge that caring classroom practices are necessary to meet the differentiated needs of individuals and must be institutionalized in colleges of education.

Critical Consciousness and Care

Paulo Freire (1970) notes that creating a critical consciousness of institutional systems develops students' ability to enact changes in their world. To develop critical consciousness, instructors can approach their content through the lens of critical pedagogy, which promotes "transformative ideals of democratic schooling" (Darder et al., 2017, p. 2) and asks students to consider the systems of power and inequity in the institutionalized disciplines. According to Freire (1970), critical consciousness is enacted when an individual reflects and then acts. Furthermore, in *Teaching to Transgress*, bell hooks (1994) suggests that the development of critical consciousness in college courses can exist in a caring and open environment that still challenges students. She notes, for example, how she approaches the criticality of her classes from a place of compassion because she acknowledges that there is "some degree of pain involved in giving up old ways of thinking and knowing and learning" (p. 43). With that acknowledgement, she has learned to "include recognition of [that pain]...and talk about the discomfort of it" (p. 43).

To us, critical care pedagogy is about a balance of critical consciousness that establishes quality learning outcomes for preservice teachers and compassion for the trauma that many preservice teachers have faced during the pandemic. Like hooks (1994), we believe that acknowledging preservice teachers' pain and anger toward the pandemic is key to building that compassionate relationship between those within teacher education spaces. The onus is on the teacher educator, who is a symbol of the institution and the profession, to design and implement a course and classroom environment that supports and challenges preservice teachers after COVID and models the care they should enact in their future classrooms.

We acknowledge that, in our position as teacher educators, we must challenge our preservice teachers to become critically conscious thinkers, both during and after the COVID-19 pandemic. However, we must also acknowledge our roles as compassionate instructors who consider the impact that COVID-19 and other societal ills have had on our preservice teachers. In recognizing the need for the development of critically conscious preservice teachers while supporting their emotional needs through our classroom practices, we have done what Freire (1970) suggests: We both reflected on our preservice teachers' social and emotional lives in relation to our classes and acted with compassion within our roles as teacher educators, ultimately modeling practices that could be carried on in their future classrooms. By combining the ideas of critical consciousness and care, we believe instructors of preservice teachers can establish an expectation of their critical awareness while offering clear communication and supporting a space that encourages positive relationships in a class setting.

As we considered how to best institutionalize caring classroom practices in colleges of education during our conversation, we determined that critical care pedagogy in teacher education means prioritizing student safety, emotional well-being, and strategic assistance alongside academic proficiency (Jeffrey et al., 2013) that challenges student thinking and extends ideologies. Critical care pedagogy means making a genuine effort to understand and respond to students' knowledge, experiences, and feelings for cultivating a robust and welcoming environment where students are empowered learners and instructors are advocates (Piorkowski & Scheurer, 2000). It means communicating a subtext of care beyond words and through actions, attitudes, and policies. Moreover, it also means that teacher educators take on institutionalized forms of oppression within teacher education and challenge preservice teachers to confront those oppressive systems in their future teaching careers.

In instituting caring classroom practices, we believe that actionable steps for creating a more compassionate and relational environment after COVID-19 will benefit teacher educators and preservice teachers alike. Care can be a verb, after all, and is manifested through "careful listening, intense dialogue, and emotional support [that] sustain[s] the cooperative construction of understanding" (Mahn & John-Steiner, 2002, p. 51). To this, we add the ideas of critical consciousness from Freire (1970) so that teacher educators can reflect on and enact care within their disciplines while extending preservice teachers' academic knowledge.

Toward A Plan of Action

If care is to be institutionalized and formalized within the system of teacher education, it should be built into the heart of that system: the classroom. Teacher education classrooms provide the opportunity to foster and model versions of critical care that can be carried out of teacher educators' classrooms and into preservice teachers' future classrooms. As an historical precedent for systems of care, John Dewey conceived of classrooms as central places in a modern democracy that "allowed for the fullest development of everybody…[and] embraced a range of ideas, such as tolerance, fair play, critical intelligence, and respect for others" (Rury, 2020, p. 128). For Dewey (1923), the knowledge that emerges from classrooms is "humanistic in quality, not because it is about human projects in the past, but because of what it does in liberating human intelligence and human sympathy" (p. 269). Dewey's vision, nearly a century after his articulation, still has a place in the academy, and it is incumbent on us to continue to bring it to fruition, especially in the midst of an ongoing pandemic. COVID-19 has pushed us to reimagine and reinvent the spaces in which we live and work, and now, more than ever, we must prioritize the "fullest development of everybody" (Rury, 2020, p. 128) by improving and expanding the ways we care through incorporating caring classroom practices based in critical care pedagogy that challenge and support preservice teachers to "rewrite" (Freire, 1985) these spaces with us as more inclusive, equitable, and joyful for all.

It would be easy to announce a perfunctory commitment to care amongst all members of an educational institution. Campus-wide emails from a provost or chancellor, for example, carry with them the implication of a top-down structure that, over time and through the day-to-day interactions of academic life, can become merely performative and certainly rudderless. If we are to institutionalize caring classroom practices in colleges of education, however, it is important to have top-down initiatives work in conjunction with grassroots efforts, and we must hold campus leaders responsible for these pronouncements and the commitment they imply. If an email announces support and care for campus communities, who carries out that care? Often, it is the people—the students and faculty—who work together to deliver action that turns the performative into the proactive. We must also hold our leaders to their stated commitment to support these actions by working to institutionalize caring practices as policy. Thus, we center our shift towards a new community of care for those in teacher education by intentionally focusing on caring classroom practices that embrace diversity, engender positive relationships, and enable critical consciousness as a foundation to begin our quest toward institutionalizing caring classroom practices that are also sustainable.

Self-Awareness in Teacher Education Classrooms

Becoming aware of and articulating beliefs, thoughts, and emotions is essential for understanding the behaviors, identities, and biases we enact (DeMink-Carthew et al., 2020). In an educational setting, for example, teacher educators' and preservice teachers' heightened self-awareness can potentially elucidate values, expectations, and interests in the classroom community, empowering all to be more skilled self-advocates, boundary-setters, and active agents of learning (Schussler et al., 2010). With this in mind, throughout the semester, teacher educators can provide opportunities for preservice teachers to reflect on and self-assess their understanding of course content, to demystify and name learning strategies that are working (or not working) for them, and to track and examine their emotional responses to class topics. As preservice teachers gain and share metacognitive awareness of their learning, motivation, and attitudes, teacher educators can respond with greater care to individual and class needs through their interactions and course design, modeling for preservice teachers the ways in which self-awareness and reflection can play a role in their future classrooms, as well.

Over time, this elevated self-awareness and reflection might awaken both the teacher educator's and preservice teachers' critical consciousness as they begin to consider who or what enables/disables or supports/undermines their capacity to act, to learn, and to be themselves (Gay & Kirkland, 2003). Indeed, it is the social, political, and cultural environments that shape an individual's agency, but with enhanced critical self-awareness, preservice teachers and instructors in teacher educator classrooms can together reshape these environments to (re)embolden individual agency (Gorski & Dalton, 2020). Exercises like Identity Mapping (Learning for Justice, 2018), in which preservice teachers name their identities and assess the privileges and disadvantages that go along with these identities, can deepen critical awareness of power dynamics within social and political structures. In developing critical consciousness, teacher education communities can then begin to reflect on institutionalized forms of oppression that preservice teachers encounter and discuss such issues as racial reckonings on university campuses with an understanding directed toward valuing their own and others' experiences, which in turn establishes emotional well-being for both those who are voicing their experiences and those who are listening to the experiences.

Positive Agency and Collaborative Relationships

Reflection on and awareness of the self is just one step—albeit an important one—in recognizing and supporting the ongoing struggles that many have faced and continue to face during the pandemic. As Freire (1970) notes, critical consciousness is based on reflection plus action. For us, too, critical care pedagogy develops reflection in preservice teachers for the purpose of caring for one another but also must strive to build systems of action in the teacher educator classroom. As an extension of developing self-awareness in preservice teachers, we turn to a discussion about meaning in positive psychology. Seligman et al. (2009) assert that "meaning consists in knowing what your highest strengths are, and then using them to belong to and serve something you believe is larger than the self" (p. 296). Through development of the preservice teachers' self-awareness and reflection, teacher educators can frame preservice teachers' awareness of their strengths to illustrate that they are serving something larger than themselves. In doing so, teacher educators support preservice teachers' development of collaborative relationship building and eventual action as a way to maintain "psychological well-being" (Osher et al., 2016, p. 652). Moreover, teacher educators can focus on building collaborative relationships with preservice teachers (Dallmer, 2004), which in turn models for preservice teachers how to build collaborative relationships within their own classes.

Through our conversations, we noted how meaningful and action-oriented teaching is but how often agency and voice are sometimes lost in the surrounding conflicts about education (Gratch, 2000) and, now, lost in the tensions of the pandemic. Making the purpose-filled nature of education visible for preservice teachers and empowering them to contribute to education in a collaborative environment can help ease the tension not just around the profession but around the pandemic and beyond. Bandura (2006) notes how agency and self-efficacy in individuals "provides the necessary staying power" (p. 176) to continue action even in the face of adversity. Additionally, teacher educators who allow for a collaborative relationship within their classes support preservice teachers "who voice their views and participate" (Bandura, 2006, p. 177) in developing action for positive change.

Furthermore, adding content-based projects to our curricula that are community-oriented and socially connected can help our preservice teachers practice taking collective action to impact society in positive ways. Mirra (2018) defines this as critical civic empathy because, as opposed to "false empathy" that utilizes empathy as a rhetorical device and "individual empathy" that "avoid[s] consideration of what it means to support" someone through social constructs that "redress past injustices to prevent future injustices," critical civic empathy is "oriented toward social/political action" and is "motivated by mutual humanization" (p. 11). By incorporating community-based projects like participatory action research (Duncan-Andrade & Morrell, 2008) or socially connected initiatives like "start[ing] a community garden or organiz[ing] a farmer's market to address access to fresh food in food deserts, protest[ing] a community-identified injustice, or partner[ing] with an organization to provide a service lacking in the community"(Simmons, 2019), preservice teachers and instructors together can enact Mirra's (2018) notion of empathy as one that actively seeks to take responsibility for the other, the ultimate form of care. For the preservice teachers in our classrooms, the possible implications of implementing community-oriented projects might reverberate into the future as they undertake the serious and loving work of educating citizens.

Conclusion

Our 2021 spring semester conversations created an ethos of community and caring for one another while unveiling steps that others could take and use in teacher education classrooms. There is little question that the experience of the pandemic will continue to color our perspectives and practices through the remainder of our careers; there is a sense that what is expected now is something deeper than simply identifying as a learner-centered teacher. Our discussions and reflection offer examples of caring classroom practices that teacher educators might implement in their classrooms or use as a springboard to discover their own methods of care, but they also point to the need for colleges of education to prepare preservice teachers to meet the complex realities of a changed world.

Beyond the classroom, colleges of education might also use these concepts to question how to enact a broader institutionalization of caring practices for teacher educators and preservice teachers. Critical consciousness and critical care pedagogy are languages that colleges of education can use to analyze the policies and procedures that manage the interactions between teacher educators, preservice teachers, and the college itself. Levett-Jones et al. (2009) draw the conclusion that "staff-student relationships are key to students' experience of belongingness" (p. 323). Our personal experiences as graduate students and teacher educators lead us to believe that this notion should be expanded. Staff-student relationships, staff-staff relationships, and student-student relationships are all key in creating the feelings of belonging necessary to build the lasting critical care pedagogy needed in colleges of education. An institutionalization of critical care pedagogy expands learning through considering the perspectives of others. Teacher education programs can lead by modeling the reflection and action needed to create a more compassionate environment that challenges preservice teachers to consider and expand their ideologies while acknowledging the difficulties of life after COVID-19.

References

Au, K. (2009). Isn't culturally responsive instruction just good teaching? *Social Education, 73*(4), 179–183.

Bandura, A. (2006). Toward a psychology of human agency. *Perspectives on psychological science, 1*(2), 164–180.

Cochran-Smith, M., Shakman, K., Jong, C., Terrell, D. G., Barnatt, J., & McQuillan, P. (2009). Good and just teaching: The case for social justice in teacher education. *American Journal of Education, 115*(3), 347–377.

Dallmer, D. (2004). Collaborative relationships in teacher education: A personal narrative of conflicting roles. *Curriculum Inquiry, 34*(1), 29–45.

Darder, A., Baltodano, M. P., & Torres, R. D. (2017). Critical pedagogy: An introduction. In A. Darder, M. P. Baltodano, & R. D. Torres (Eds.), *The critical pedagogy reader* (3rd ed., pp. 1–21). Routledge.

DeMink-Carthew, J., Netcoh, S., & Farber, K. (2020). Exploring the potential for students to develop self-awareness through personalized learning. *The Journal of Educational Research, 113*(3), 165–176.

Dewey, J. (1923). *Democracy and education: An introduction to the philosophy of education.* Macmillan.

Duncan-Andrade, D., & Morrell, E. (2008). *The art of critical pedagogy: Possibilities for moving from theory to practice in urban schools.* Peter Lang.

Freire, P. (1970). *Pedagogy of the oppressed: 50th anniversary edition* (4th ed.). Bloomsbury Academic.

Freire, P. (1985). Reading the world and the word: An interview with Paulo Freire. *Language Arts, 62*(1), 15–21.

Gay, G., & Kirkland, K. (2003). Developing cultural critical consciousness and self-reflection in preservice teacher education. *Theory into Practice, 42*(3), 181–187.

Gorski, P. C., & Dalton, K. (2020). Striving for critical reflection in multicultural and social justice teacher education: Introducing a typology of reflection approaches. *Journal of Teacher Education, 71*(3), 357–368.

Gratch, A. (2000). Teacher voice, teacher education, teaching professionals. *The High School Journal, 83*(3), 43–54.

hooks, b. (1994). *Teaching to transgress: Education as the practice of freedom.* Routledge.

Jeffrey, A. J., Auger, R. W., & Pepperell, J. L. (2013). "If we're ever in trouble they're always there": A qualitative study of teacher-student caring. *The Elementary School Journal, 114*(1), 100–117.

Jones, C. S., & Nangah, Z. (2021). Higher education students: Barriers to engagement; psychological alienation theory, trauma and trust: A systematic review. *Perspectives: Policy and Practice in Higher Education, 25*(2), 62–71.

Ladson-Billings, G. (1995). But that's just good teaching! The case for culturally relevant pedagogy. *Theory into Practice, 34*(3), 159–165.

Learning for Justice. (2018). How to be an ally. *Learning for Justice, 58.* www.learningforjustice.org/magazine/spring-2018/how-to-be-an-ally.

Levett-Jones, T., Lathlean, J., Higgins, I., & McMillan, M. (2009). Staff-student relationships and their impact on nursing students' belongingness and learning. *Journal of Advanced Nursing, 65*, 316–324.

Mahn, H,.,& John-Steiner, V. (2002). The gift of confidence: A Vygotskian view of emotions. In G. Wells & G. Claxton (Eds.), *Learning for life in the 21st century: Sociocultural perspectives on the future of education* (pp. 46–58). Blackwell Publishers.

Mirra, N. (2018). *Educating for empathy: Literacy learning and civic engagement.* Teachers College Press.

Newman, V. E., Yee, H. F., Walker, A. R., Toumbelekis, M., & Most, S. B. (2021). Out of fright, out of mind: Impaired memory for information negated during looming threat. *Cognitive Research: Principles and Implications, 6*(1), 1–11.

Osher, D., Kidron, Y., Brackett, M., Dymnicki, A., Jones, S., & Weissberg, R. P. (2016). Advancing the science and practice of social and emotional learning: Looking back and moving forward. *Review of Research in Education, 40*(1), 644–681.

Piorkowski, J. & Scheurer, E. (2000). "It's the way that they talk to you": Increasing student agency in basic writers through a social context of care. *Journal of Basic Writing, 19* (2), 72–93.

Rury, J. L. (2020). *Education and social change.* Routledge.

Schussler, D. L., Stooksberry, L. M., & Bercaw, L. A. (2010). Understanding teacher candidate dispositions: Reflecting to build self-awareness. *Journal of Teacher Education, 61* (4), 350–363.

Seligman, M. E., Ernst, R. M., Gillham, J., Reivich, K., & Linkins, M. (2009). Positive education: Positive psychology and classroom interventions. *Oxford Review of Education, 35*(3), 293–311.

Simmons, D. (2019, April 1). Why we can't afford white-washed social-emotional learning. *ASCD.* www.ascd.org/el/articles/why-we-cant-afford-whitewashed-social-emotional-learning.

4

NEW PATHWAYS IN TEACHER EDUCATION

Caring for the Self Post-COVID

Jennifer Baumgartner and Ingrid Anderson

COVID-19 created profound changes in classroom and teaching practices, as teaching was impacted by both the new safety constraints and the frequently changing rules around social engagement, both in and out of the classroom. While educators longed to return to in-person learning, the reality of the post-COVID classroom leaves many preservice teachers overwhelmed as they encounter a series of impossible dilemmas in which they are asked to hold spaces to support children's emotional health and well-being while trying to navigate their own emotional ups-and-downs (Jones & Kessler, 2020). Personal and professional well-being and self-care take on new meanings in this context of mutual vulnerability.

As teacher educators, we saw firsthand the need for our preservice teachers to be prepared with tools to support and sustain their emotional well-being during COVID teaching. The uncertainty surrounding teaching and learning in this new context is a continuing source of stress for teachers, administrators, and preservice teachers alike. Teacher stress and burnout are increasing and problematic trends in the field (Decker et al., 2002; Gokalp, 2012; Oberle & Schonert-Reichel, 2016; Whitaker et al., 2015). Teacher educators need to recognize that stress is more than a response to the environment or an environmental trigger (Holroyd & Lazarus, 1982); it also encompasses an individual's perception of the stress and the available resources. Here, we examine how teacher educators can care for preservice teachers by helping them to develop problem solving strategies that build self-care and coping skills.

Wellness and Resilience in Education

The mechanisms that served us in dealing with trauma and stress prior to the pandemic are now impacted by our new shared lived experience. Research into

DOI: 10.4324/9781003244875-6

disaster models provides an understanding of the emotional cycles experienced during the pandemic as well as the ebb and flow of resilience while working toward a new normal. To aid our conversation about the individual and collective impacts of trauma on those in education, we considered Doherty and Clayton's (2011) model to highlight the specific mediators and moderators impacting schools during and following a global pandemic. Societal mediators include changed views of the return to school, perceptions of risk and vulnerability, changed social narratives, and changes in social capital in educational settings. When these mediators engage, teachers experience acute, direct, and indirect psychosocial impacts from the collective trauma, highlighting sources of vulnerability or resiliency (Gartland et al., 2019; Mansfield et al., 2016; Sammons et al., 2007).

The direct and acute impacts of COVID—such as teachers' and children's mental health issues, physical fatigue, and emotional exhaustion—are subject to societal and school mediators, which result in impacts for teachers (bouts of anxiety and worry, depression and despair, burnout and attrition, grief and mourning, numbness and apathy) and the field (reduction in childcare programs, increased need for childcare and high-quality education, difficulty recruiting teachers).

Teacher educators, preservice teachers, and mentors experienced many emotional triggers during the pandemic that suggest the threatening impact of these imbalances. Emotional triggers from disaster related stress include difficulty communicating thoughts, sleeping, or maintaining balance, as well as somatic symptoms such as cold/flu symptoms, headaches, stomach problems, tunneled vision or muffled hearing (Federal Emergency Management Agency, 2020). Therefore, engaging in intentional and consistent wellness practices for self-care is critical.

School messages about teaching during COVID easily slipped to concern for children, excluding adults—including preservice teachers. Instead, there was an expectation that teachers would gladly sacrifice their well-being for the greater good of their students, overlooking the impacts on teachers' lives in and beyond the school (Osgood, 2011). These pushes, pulls, and tensions impacted teachers in unique ways, increasing the cumulative impact of the trauma (DeWolfe, 2000). Shared traumatic experiences—like the global pandemic—often shift professional boundaries, as the helper and helpee bond over shared trauma (Kerig, 2021). These shifted boundaries impact how we self-regulate (DeWolfe, 2000) and can lead to empathy without boundaries, as well as a lack of empathy, and higher levels of secondary trauma, compassion fatigue, and burnout (Maslach & Leiter, 2008).

This cumulative impact is of great concern as we work with preservice teachers. Preservice teachers are often unaware of societal mediators in education (Harmsen et al., 2018) so they were caught off guard by the mediators' impact on teaching during the pandemic, such as public shaming when schools closed and the lack of understanding of the pandemic's impact on teachers, their school day, and the readiness of children to learn. The various outcomes of the pandemic directly highlighted areas of preservice teachers' vulnerability, specifically their lack of experience and temporary position in classrooms.

Wellness practices become fundamental in addressing stress and creating positive coping strategies post COVID. Wellness is not just the opposite of injury (Stará & Charvát, 2013) but involves balance among all parts of the self: physical, social, mental, emotional, and spiritual (Myers et al., 2000). Self-care is a critical component of resilience. We define self-care as the practices that keep us physically, emotionally, mentally, socially, and spiritually whole, despite the numerous barriers experienced by teachers (Baumgartner et al., 2009; Baumgartner et al., 2021; Carson et al., 2016). In the post-COVID world, preservice teachers need new tools for decision making and building resilience as part of the new post-COVID normal.

The Self-Care Problem Solving Pathway

Solving problems is part of teachers' professional practice; yet, decision fatigue results from solving big and small problems on normal days, let alone the additional decision making required during the COVID-19 pandemic. Self-care and problem solving intersect when teachers consider how to make ethical decisions in professional practices. Understanding the decision-making process and the emotions that accompany those decisions will be of utmost importance in the coming years, given that emotional health and safety go hand in hand with learning. So, teacher educators need specific approaches to support preservice teachers' thinking about problem solving and care, since teachers who engage in self-care experience lower levels of stress, burnout, and compassion fatigue while increasing their compassion, self-compassion, and quality of life (Alkema et al., 2008; Shapiro et al., 2005; Thomas & Otis, 2010).

The Self-Care Problem Solving Pathway (Baumgartner & Anderson, 2022) provides a structure for teacher educators to address the complex feelings associated with the work of teaching with preservice teachers while building their skills to increase resilience. The Pathway's seven steps are outlined in Figure 4.1: identify the problem, identify feelings, reflect on feelings, identify barriers to wellness, plan for coping, identify resources, and develop a plan for self-care.

The Pathway builds on the foundation of the transactional model of stress (Lazarus, 1966; Lazarus & Folkman, 1984, 1987) that includes two central constructs: cognitive appraisal of an issue and coping. When preservice teachers experience an issue, they engage in appraisal to determine if it represents harm, challenge, threat, or benefit. This appraisal serves as a form of triage to consider what can be done to address the issue before determining what, if any, resources are required. Preservice teachers with more belief in their ability to solve problems would then be less likely to see issues as threatening, building the self-efficacy needed to minimize trauma and experience less stress (Lazarus & Folkman, 1987).

Step 1: Identify the problem
What is the problem? What are the ethical implications of the problem?

↓

Step 2: Identify feelings
How does the problem make me feel?

↓

Step 3: Reflect on feelings
What do I usually do to handle my feelings?

↓

Step 4: Identify barriers to wellness
What is stopping me?

↓

Step 5: Make a plan for coping
How do I move forward?

↓

Step 6: Identify resources
What skills/information, people or emotional support do I need to solve the problem and address the emotions that arise from problem solving?

↓

Step 7: Develop and implement a plan
How can I build my self-care decision making?

FIGURE 4.1 Self-Care Problem Solving Pathway

Step 1: Identify the Problem

The first step is to identify the problem. In doing so, preservice teachers first consider their professional code of ethics to ground the problem, asking the question, "What am I being asked to do?" Self-care is about understanding and addressing emotional wellbeing, so preservice teachers must understand that there is emotional involvement in all problem solving while considering the requirements, ideas, culture, and expectations that impact their work as teachers (Skovholt & Trotter-Mathison, 2016).

Step 2: Identify Feelings

After identifying the problem, preservice teachers must next identify feelings, asking, "How does the problem make me feel?" This is an oft missed step in the problem solving process but a critical one for supporting emotional well-being and increasing emotional wellness. We acknowledge that all problem solving decisions have emotional weight, whether positive, neutral, or negative. Positive feelings build a sense of agency, contribution, self-respect, and safety; negative feelings decrease the sense of contribution, self-respect, and security. Naming and recognizing these emotions can help preservice teachers move forward.

Step 3: Reflect on Feelings

At this stage, preservice teachers ask, "What do I usually do to handle my feelings?" in order to connect the problem with the feelings it evokes. Having preservice teachers acknowledge and openly address their feelings supports the professional practice of understanding the emotions and beliefs behind actions. In this way, they are able to build a bridge between the feelings that emerge from the problem and the feelings connected to an imagined resolution. As Mr. Rogers (2003) once said, "Confronting our feelings and giving them appropriate expression is a sign of strength" (p. 15).

Step 4: Identify Barriers to Wellness

Next, preservice teachers ask "What is stopping me?" to consider what is preventing them from resolving the problem; additionally, they must consider the feelings associated with solving the problem. In considering the problem's primary sphere of influence, they must consider whether the pressure is external or internal. External pressures, such as concern for psychological or physical safety, employment, or retaliation, might stop preservice teachers from addressing the problem; ethical dilemmas could also play a role. Internal pressures related to issues of professional skills (e.g., knowledge to solve the problem), reflective skills (e.g., ability to understand the beliefs at the root of our feelings), or emotional skills (e.g., resiliency to move the solution forward; Barbre & Anderson, 2022) might also create barriers.

Step 5: Make a Plan for Coping

In this step, preservice teachers identify the types of supports needed to address the problem, asking, "How do I move forward?" In doing so, they develop coping skills that help them to address the stressful situation (Lazarus, 1966). Coping skills are divided into three broad types of strategies: problem-based coping, emotion-focused coping, and avoidant coping (Carver & Scheier, 1999; Carver et al., 1989; Folkman & Lazarus 1980, 1985; Lazarus & Folkman, 1984). For example, preservice teachers might turn to someone to provide information and support that helps them better understand their abilities; they might realize they already possess the skills needed to move forward, or they might recognize specific systems or policies that will help them move forward. By matching potential resources to needed professional or emotional skills, preservice teachers are supported in appraising the situation, identifying and acknowledging feelings, and producing solutions.

Step 6: Identify Resources

Next, preservice teachers identify resources needed to solve the problem and address the emotions that arise from problem solving. They might consider specific information or skills needed before connecting with those who can provide the resources needed to develop those skills. They might identify allies, mentors, and friends who can help to address the issue at hand, personally or professionally. They might reflect on the negative feelings identified in Step 2 to determine what supports are needed to create positive feelings about the issue. Identified resources can be accessed in professional communities guided by ethical practices (Lazarus & Folkman, 1987), but these resources are only as strong as the professional community itself. Useful support comes from communities that create feelings of compassion, confidence, and hope.

Step 7: Develop and Implement a Plan

Lastly, preservice teachers create a plan for practicing self-care and developing skills to engage in that self-care (Skovholt & Trotter-Mathison, 2016) by answering the question, "How can I build my self-care decision making?". Whether written or digital, this plan can involve a mentor or colleague for accountability. The plan should address the following questions:

- How will I make sure I am open to new knowledge and skills?
- Who will I include in my inner circle to evoke positive emotions?
- How will I make sure that I stay in tune with my feelings, even and especially in the busyness of the day?

Self-Care Problem Solving Pathway Script

In highly stressful situations, the individual's ability to problem solve slows. Knowing this, teacher educators must work with preservice teachers to develop their ability to think when they are tired, and their resiliency is low. Here, we offer a possible scenario for using the Self-Care Problem Solving Pathway:

Alex is panicking. The demonstration of learning Alex planned for her practicum will not work and it is the final assignment needed to submit for licensure. Alex had planned a literacy lesson on the rug with a small group of children, incorporating movement and storytelling. Instead, due to COVID, she must work with a pod of four children at a single table. Two of the families have elected to keep their children home, so Alex now has only two children at the table. She is very worried about completing the assignment; when the stress becomes overwhelming, she asks to leave the classroom. The cooperating classroom teacher emails you, the teacher educator, to let you know Alex is struggling.

Using the Pathway's steps, teacher educators can help preservice teachers think through an issue and develop skills to address issues in the future. In Table 4.1, we offer an example script of a teacher educator using the Pathway to work through the scenario presented above.

TABLE 4.1 Problem Solving Pathway Script (Baumgartner & Anderson, 2022)

PATHWAY STEPS	DIALOGUE
Step 1: Identify the problem Help Alex think through the question, *"What am I being asked to do?"* in order to identify the problem.	**Teacher Educator:** *Let's look at what happened yesterday. Can you share what happened when you found out about the changes in the demonstration of learning?* **Alex:** *I just panicked. All I could think about was I am not going to graduate. I have worked so hard. This is out of my control.*
Step 2: Identify feelings To support Alex in regulating emotions, acknowledge Alex's feelings. For the teacher educator, the goal is to help Alex recognize if the experienced feelings are positive or negative.	**Teacher Educator:** *What are you feeling right now? Tell me about how you are experiencing this stressful moment.* **Alex:** *I am so stressed! I can't even think. I cry all the time. I really wanted this lesson plan to be great and now I am afraid it will fail and I won't get my license.* **Teacher Educator:** *I am hearing you say that you feel overwhelmed and afraid. Is that right?* **Alex:** *Yes.* **Teacher Educator:** *I also hear that you are very proud of your lesson and you are motivated to do a great job.*
Step 3: Reflect on the feelings As Alex begins to recognize the emotions, further scaffold emotional self-awareness and how the emotions impact the work in the classroom.	**Teacher Educator:** *When you started to feel this way, what happened? What did you do?* **Alex:** *I just couldn't keep going so I asked to leave the classroom. I didn't want to cry and fall apart in front of the class.* **Teacher Educator:** *How are you feeling now?* **Alex:** *Angry. And tired.*

PATHWAY STEPS	DIALOGUE
Step 4: Identify the barriers Help Alex identify the barriers to solving the problem, determining if it is an ethical dilemma or a matter of resources. This can be a complex problem that touches on emotional skills (Alex's resilience to self-direct problem solving), reflective skills (Alex's ability to understand the feelings that led to walking out of the classroom), or professional skills (Alex identifying who can answer whether the demonstration of learning will meet the state's requirement).	**Teacher Educator:** *Remember when we talked about the code of ethics? Do you think this issue is an ethical dilemma or something else? Let's start with the problem of meeting the requirements of graduation. Is there an ethical situation here?* **Alex:** *Well, no, not really. This was really all outside of anyone's control. I do wish that student teachers' situations were considered in the decision making and maybe the requirements could be changed though.* **Teacher Educator:** *I agree. We do need to think about how the current landscape impacts student teachers. You will still need to know and be able to do these things, but you also need opportunities to practice and demonstrate your skills. Let's work together to talk about that more. But before we do, can we talk about what happened? Leaving the classroom?* **Alex:** *Well, my response to the stress does impact me as the teacher, and walking out of the classroom impacted my mentor teacher and the children. I suppose my response might be an ethical situation. But I didn't know what else to do.* **Teacher Educator:** *You thought of the children and that is good. You were caring for yourself and that is good too. Let's talk about some other resources that might have been available to you that could have helped you make a different decision though that may not have been as disruptive.*
Step 5: Make a plan for coping Help Alex determine how to move forward and develop skills. In this example, we look at walking out of the classroom. Alex's emotional regulation did not allow for the identification of resources to solve the problem.	**Teacher Educator:** *So let's talk about when you felt overwhelmed in that room and made the decision to leave. You may have felt at the time that it was your only option. Let's think together and see if there was another possible response.* **Alex:** *I think I could start with a few deep breaths. I think, maybe, next time I will try to take a minute and organize my thoughts.* **Teacher Educator:** *Consider asking if this problem needs to be solved right now while I am with the children.* **Alex:** *I see, I can do that: Ask if this is a "now" problem or an "after class" problem.* **Teacher Educator:** *Yes, that's a good start. Now let's be more specific: What is at the root of emotions, the main problem?* **Alex:** *Oh, I see. It's knowing that I don't know if my demonstration of learning will meet licensing requirements.* **Teacher Educator:** *Let's finish this cycle of problem solving staying in the classroom and then we can address the issue of your demonstration lesson.*
Step 6: Identify resources Ask Alex to walk you through an alternative behavior pattern rather than walking out of the classroom. How could emotions be regulated? Work with Alex to plan the next steps.	**Teacher Educator:** *How can you approach a problem next time to stay in the moment and in the classroom?* **Alex:** *Well, I need to not panic. I want to work on a script to help talk myself through the problem. If I feel emotions rising, then I take three deep breaths. I ask myself, is this a problem that needs solving now with the children? If it is a later problem, I could write it down and work to set it aside for after school.* **Teacher Educator:** *Who is in your community to help you?* **Alex:** *I didn't think about that. I have you and my supervisor and all my friends in the program I could ask for help.*

PATHWAY STEPS	DIALOGUE
Step 7: Develop and implement a plan Help Alex make a plan to pause, recognize, and reflect on emotions when they occur.	**Teacher Educator:** *Do you remember how you feel inside when you start to feel overwhelmed? What are the signs to you?* **Alex:** *I have butterflies in my stomach and my head starts to spin.* **Teacher Educator:** *That is really good to recognize. Now let's talk about what you can do when you start to feel that way.* **Alex:** *Well, I will breathe, decide to focus on the children at the moment, and remember that I can call you later.* **Teacher Educator:** *That is a great plan.*

Conclusion

As teacher educators, we not only teach content, pedagogy, and instructional practices. We must also help preservice teachers gain skills in managing the emotional work of teaching. Brains that are triggered by trauma, like that experienced during the pandemic, struggle to process and respond to information. This is as true for children as it is teachers.

While COVID-19 has created a new normal, it will have long-reaching effects on our teaching practices. Rarely when dealing with educational crises do our own experiences parallel those of everyone around us. Teachers experienced disruption, as did preservice teachers, teacher educators, children, and families (Harvard Center for the Developing Child, 2020). This shared experience can create secondary trauma: As we try to support others, the trauma is compounded (The National Child Traumatic Stress Network, 2021). Building resilience capital is one way to mitigate the stress that is experienced in supporting others. In the act of nurturing resilience, we both practice acts of self-compassion and increase our ability to care for others. Developing an awareness of the emotional cost of teaching allows us to choose strategies to address the emotional labor of our work. The Self-Care Problem Solving Pathways invites us to build resilience and self-care through our everyday decision-making processes.

References

Alkema, K., Linton, J. M., & Davies, R. (2008). A study of the relationship between self-care, compassion satisfaction, compassion fatigue, and burnout among hospice professionals. *Journal of Social Work in End-of-Life & Palliative Care, 4*, 101–119.

Barbre, J., & Anderson, I. 2022 *Supporting children's mental health and well-being: A strength-based approach for early childhood educators.* Redleaf Press.

Baumgartner, J. & Anderson, I. (2022). The self-care problem-solving pathway. Childcare Exchange, *1*(263), 56-58.

Baumgartner, J., Carson, R., Apavaloaie, L., & Tsouloupas, C. (2009). Uncovering common stressful factors and coping strategies among childcare providers. *Child and Youth Care Forum, 38*(5), 239–251.

Baumgartner, J., Ota, C., DiCarlo, C., Bauer, R., & Carson, R. (2021). Using ecological momentary assessment to examine the relationship between childcare teachers' stress, classroom behaviors, and afterhours professionalism activities. *Child Care in Practice*, 1–20.

Carson, R. L., Baumgartner, J. J., Ota, C., Pulling Kuhn, A. C., & Durr, A. (2016). An ecological momentary assessment of burnout, rejuvenation strategies, job satisfaction, and quitting intentions in childcare teachers. *Early Childhood Education Journal, 45*(6), 801–808.

Carver, C. S., & Scheier, M. F. (1999). Stress, coping, and self-regulatory processes. In L. A. Pervin & O. P. John (Eds.), *Handbook of personality: Theory and research* (2nd ed., pp. 553–575). Guilford Press.

Carver, C. S., Scheier, M. F., & Weintraub, J. K. (1989). Assessing coping strategies: A theoretically based approach. *Journal of Personality and Social Psychology, 56*(2), 267.

DeWolfe, D. J. (2000). *Training manual for mental health and human service workers in major disasters.* US Department of Health and Human Services, Substance Abuse and Mental Health Services Administration, Center for Mental Health Services.

Decker, J. T., Bailey, T. L., & Westergaard, N. (2002). Burnout among childcare workers. *Residential Treatment for Children & Youth, 19*(4), 61–77.

Doherty, T. J., & Clayton, S. (2011). The psychological impacts of global climate change. *American Psychologist, 66*(4), 265.

Federal Emergency Management Agency. (2020, September). *Are you ready? An in-depth guide to citizen preparedness.* www.ready.gov/sites/default/files/2021-03/are-you-ready-guide.pdf.

Folkman, S., & Lazarus, R. S. (1980). An analysis of coping in a middle-aged community sample. *Journal of Health and Social Behavior, 21*(3), 219–239.

Folkman, S., & Lazarus, R. S. (1985). If it changes it must be a process: Study of emotion and coping during three stages of a college examination. *Journal of Personality and Social Psychology, 48*(1), 150–170.

Gartland, D., Riggs, E., Muyeen, S., Giallo, R., Afifi, T.O., MacMillan, H., Herrman, H., Bulford, E., and Brown, S. J. (2019). What factors are associated with resilient outcomes in children exposed to social adversity? A systematic review. *BMJ Open, 9*(4), 1–14.

Gokalp, G. (2012). Effects of stress on teacher decision making. In C. J. McCarthy, R. G. Lambert, & A. Ullrich (Eds.), *Research on stress and coping in education. International perspectives on teacher stress* (pp. 69–94). Information Age Publishing.

Harmsen, R., Helms-Lorenz, M., Maulana, R., & van Veen, K. (2018). The relationship between beginning teachers' stress causes, stress responses, teaching behaviour, and attrition. *Teachers and Teaching, 24*(6), 626–643.

Harvard Center for the Developing Child. (2020). *How to help families and staff build resilience during the COVID-19 Outbreak.* https://developingchild.harvard.edu/resources/how-to-help-families-and-staff-build-resilience-during-the-covid-19-outbreak.

Holroyd, K. A., & Lazarus, R. S. (1982). Stress coping and somatic adaptation. In Goldberger, L. & Breznitz, S. (Eds.), *Handbook of stress, theoretical and clinical aspects* (pp. 21–35). Free Press.

Jones, A. L., & Kessler, M. A. (2020). Teachers' emotion and identity work during a pandemic. *Frontiers in Education, 5,* 1–9.

Kerig, P. (2021, March 10). Why self-care isn't enough: Resilience for trauma-informed professionals. *Juvenile Justice Information Exchange.* https://jjie.org/2021/03/10/why-self-care-isnt-enough-resilience-for-trauma-informed-professionals.

Lazarus, R. S. (1966). *Psychological stress and the coping process.* McGraw-Hill.

Lazarus, R. S., & Folkman, S. (1984). *Stress, appraisal, and coping.* Springer.

Lazarus, R. S., & Folkman, S. (1987). Transactional theory and research on emotions and coping. *European Journal of Personality, 1*(3), 141–169.

Mansfield, C. F., Beltman, S., Broadley, T., & Weatherby-Fell, N. (2016). Building resilience in teacher education: An evidenced informed framework. *Teaching and Teacher Education, 54*, 77–87.

Maslach, C., & Leiter, M. P. (2008). Early predictors of job burnout and engagement. *Journal of Applied Psychology, 93*(3), 498–512.

Myers, J. E., Sweeney, T. J., & Witmer, J. M. (2000). The wheel of wellness counseling for wellness: A holistic model for treatment planning. *Journal of Counseling & Development, 78*(3), 251–266.

The National Child Traumatic Stress Network. (2021). *Secondary traumatic stress: A fact sheet for child-serving professionals.* www.nctsn.org/sites/default/files/resources/fact-sheet/secondary_traumatic_stress_child_serving_professionals.pdf.

Oberle, E., & Schonert-Reichl, K. A. (2016). Stress contagion in the classroom? The link between classroom teacher burnout and morning cortisol in elementary school students. *Social Science & Medicine, 159*, 30–37.

Osgood, J. (2011). *Narratives from the nursery: Negotiating professional identities in early childhood.* Routledge.

Rogers, F. (2003). *The world according to Mister Rogers: Important things to remember.* Hachette Books.

Sammons, P., Day, C., Kington, A., Gu, Q., Stobart, G., & Smees, R. (2007). Exploring variations in teachers' work, lives and their effects on pupils: Key findings and implications from a longitudinal mixed-method study. *British Educational Research Journal, 33*(5), 681–701.

Shapiro, S. L., Astin, J. A., Bishop, S. R., & Cordova, M. (2005). Mindfulness-based stress reduction for health care professionals: Results from a randomized trial. *International Journal of Stress Management, 12*, 164–176.

Stará, J., & Charvát, M. (2013). Wellness: Its origins, theories and current applications in the United States. *Acta Salus Vitae, 1*(2).

Skovholt, T. M., & Trotter-Mathison, M. (2016). *The resilient practitioner: Burnout and compassion fatigue prevention and self-care strategies for the helping professions.* Routledge.

Thomas, J. T., & Otis, M. D. (2010). Intrapsychic correlates of professional quality of life: Mindfulness, empathy, and emotional separation. *Journal of the Society for Social Work and Research, 1*(2), 83–98.

Whitaker, R. C., Dearth-Wesley, T., & Gooze, R. A. (2015). Workplace stress and the quality of teacher–children relationships in Head Start. *Early Childhood Research Quarterly, 30*, 57–69.

5

ENACTING CARE IN COLLABORATION DURING COVID-19 AS TEACHER EDUCATORS

Amanda Winkelsas, Tiffany Karalis Noel, Julie Gorlewski, and Elisabeth Etopio

Despite existing as a pre-pandemic need, the pandemic shed light on the importance of increasing attention to the diverse, and sometimes conflicting, emotions and life experiences of our preservice teachers (PSTs), teacher candidates, doctoral students, co-authors, and colleagues. At this transformative juncture, it is essential to foster a culture of care by refocusing on what is most important and redefining excellence in teaching and research (Corbera et al., 2020). Although we did not choose confinement during COVID times, we can choose how we adapt and respond to distressing and unavoidable circumstances. Corbera et al. (2020) discuss how confinement can help us reorganize our priorities and advocate for prioritizing collective, rather than individual, goals. While this involves remaining responsive and accountable to the university, it also means identifying opportunities to improve teaching, mentoring, and collegiality, and designing socially meaningful and environmentally sustainable research (Corbera et al., 2020):

> This should also involve prioritizing tasks where we can really make a difference, writing less but better, avoiding as much as possible a hectic race for new projects and articles, and engaging more seriously with knowledge transfer to civil society and policy change activities. (p. 3)

Just as we have needed to exercise flexibility with our PSTs, teacher candidates, and doctoral students, we must remember to be flexible with ourselves and be mindful of how our actions and behaviors model empathy for those who look to us for guidance.

DOI: 10.4324/9781003244875-7

Modeling Empathy

The global pandemic reminds us of the importance of demonstrating care by modeling the actions and behaviors we wish to cultivate in our students and professional communities. Warren (2014, 2018) describes empathy in the professional teaching context as an iterative process of acquiring knowledge and leveraging that knowledge to guide decision-making. In other words, empathy is the piece of the student-teacher interaction puzzle that connects what a teacher knows or thinks about students to what the teacher *does* when responding to students' needs (Warren, 2018). As the anchoring dimension of the application of empathy in social interaction, perspective taking is essential to establish empathetic concern (Warren, 2018): "Teacher education might not provide candidates all the pertinent knowledge they need...but teacher educators can model use of mechanisms such as perspective taking to engage teacher candidates in processes that broaden their professional understandings" (p. 7). As education leaders and teacher educators, we must be deliberate in modeling the caring practices we want students and colleagues to carry into their respective domains and communities.

Pedagogies of Connection

As we look ahead to the light at the end of the post-pandemic tunnel, we must remain both mindful of the connections that COVID-19 disrupted and committed to reconnecting with the relationships and communities that were at a distance for more than a year. Carter Andrews et al. (2021) discuss the utility of a *pedagogy of connection* in teacher education to ensure inclusive, culturally responsive, and socially just teaching. While much has been written about how to ensure education speaks to the diverse intellectual and cultural needs of students (e.g., Gay, 2018; Ladson-Billings, 2014; Paris & Alim, 2017), Carter Andrews et al. (2021) assert that in order to prioritize connection and connecting effectively, teachers must commit to humanizing pedagogies and practices.

Humanizing practice involves attention to and inclusion of multiple stakeholder voices and experiences (e.g., students, parents/guardians, teachers, school leaders) and centers care in maintaining positive relationships (Carter Andrews et al., 2021). Importantly, humanizing pedagogy has taken new form in the context of pandemic-prompted virtual learning environments. In the context of new learning environments where students, families, and educators are processing experiences and emotions,

> a humanizing aspect of connection is its focus on listening carefully, responding to students and families with cultural humility (Chang et al., 2012; Kumagai & Lypson, 2009; Lund & Lee, 2015), and understanding how to empathize with students (Warren, 2018) in ways that take sociocultural

context into consideration for how they learn amid new and persistent trauma resulting from the global pandemic. (Carter Andrews et al., 2021, p. 268)

The physical distance that emerged during the pandemic when remote teaching practices became much more common is, in many cases, a representation of the relational distance that exists in classroom interactions. Teaching and learning can feel remote even when embodied. The urgency to engage in humanistic, relational pedagogies was emphasized by the pandemic but it is a persistent matter that requires and benefits from attention to care.

Our Positionality

As four education professors in the Department of Learning and Instruction at a large public university in the northeastern United States, we regularly communicated, collaborated, and problem-solved throughout the pandemic. With the worst of the pandemic and 2019–2020 academic year behind us, we were intrigued by the opportunity to co-construct a narrative that synthesizes our unique and shared experiences as teacher residency director (Amanda), doctoral programs director (Tiffany), department chair (Julie), and assistant dean of teacher education (Beth). Recognizing our privilege as individuals in good health and with dependable jobs, our aim is to share honest experiences that humanize what it meant for us to enact care during a crisis and look towards the post-pandemic future of responsively and sustainably caring for our students, our colleagues, and ourselves.

Together, we discussed our desire and professional responsibility to enact care as department and program leaders, instructors, and advisors, yet acknowledged the simultaneous challenges of setting boundaries and attending to our own self-care. We also addressed the unique challenges that we face as women faculty who tend to disproportionately bear emotional labor relative to men (Shalaby et al., 2020). Importantly, Amanda punctuated the importance of ensuring faculty and staff are well-cared for "because that makes such a difference in how well they are able to care for students."

Co-Constructing Our Narrative

In and of itself, co-constructing narratives can serve as a form of enacting care, for it helps us to reflect on our experiences and the lived experiences of others while avoiding essentializing ways of speaking about students, colleagues, and communities. Through a collective process of listening to, responding to, and imagining one another's situations and conditions, we can build our capacity for empathy, perspective-taking, and new understandings of the human experience. Drawing from Cann and DeMeulenaere (2012), we used critical co-constructed autoethnography as a methodology for colleagues engaged in critical work to reflect together and more accurately represent the complexity of relationships. Incorporating aspects of critical theory, we used critical autoethnography to understand the lived experiences of our students, our colleagues, and ourselves, to examine social conditions influenced by the pandemic, and to fuse theory and action to challenge inequities and offer implications for navigating future care practices (Boylorn & Orbe, 2014).

One afternoon in June 2021, we rotated roles as interviewers and interviewees, responding to questions such as, "In what ways, if any, has your definition of care and caring shifted during the pandemic?" and "In what ways have you been navigating care for students? What successes are you celebrating? What challenges are you facing? What losses are you lamenting?" We discussed amplified tensions and silver linings that emerged from the challenges of the pandemic, all of which emboldened our commitment to continuously enact care, even in the aftermath of the pandemic and beyond. As we co-constructed the narrative, we organized our autoethnography by salient themes—such as *altered understandings of enacting care* and *enacting care in challenging circumstances*—which emerged through a dual in vivo and descriptive coding analysis. As we restoried by collecting stories, analyzing stories to better understand lived experiences, and rewriting the stories to form a coherent narrative (Ollerenshaw & Creswell, 2002), we used supporting quotes from our interview transcript to add richness to our narrative and honor our authentic voices.

Altered Understandings of Enacting Care

Collectively, we emphasized the importance of expressing care and empathy for individuals, such as students and colleagues, even before the pandemic. As Amanda explained, "My definition of care pre-pandemic was just a general sense of compassion and attempts at empathy, and trying to understand PSTs as whole human beings who are balancing multiple demands on their time and attention."

While consistently demonstrating care in our communications and dispositions emerged as a common pre-pandemic theme, the pandemic pushed us each to recognize and respond to isolated traumas, some of which were only unearthed when we analyzed the subtext. "Care seems to emerge most when you experience a student who's had trauma," Beth said, supporting Carter Andrews et al.'s (2021) discussion of humanizing connections in the face of trauma. Beth continued,

> I had an incident last week with a PST, where I was getting a lot of words, really trying to understand what the underlying issue is...[eventually], I found it. The PST's partner is disabled and lost their job during the pandemic, requiring full-time work on top of coursework. That makes you think about the human experience of what the PST is going through, and how do we demonstrate care?

Similarly, Tiffany valued opportunities to substitute typical email correspondence with Zoom or phone conversations as an approach to demonstrating care: "Some doctoral students would tell me that scheduling live meeting time made them feel like I truly cared about them...I found we could also problem solve much quicker through those conversations."

Shifting to defining care from a systemic perspective, Julie expressed that, while care and empathy for individuals is critical, ensuring all students have equal opportunities to be successful is essential: "That means we have to look at systems and structures to ensure they demonstrate care; sometimes they have the opposite effect." Resonating with all of us, Julie further explained that we lost some of the invaluable aspects of enacting care because of the pandemic: "I can't give you a hug, I can't bring you a coffee. So things that would have demonstrated care when people needed it most became restricted." In relation to modeling care in the context of teacher education, this means that efforts to demonstrate empathy had to be intentionally reconsidered and enacted.

This absence of the ability to model caring behaviors in person had multi-dimensional implications. In remote settings, teacher educators had to model empathy for PSTs; mentor teachers had to model care for P-12 learners and teacher candidates; teacher candidates had to practice enacting care in virtual classrooms; and teacher education programs were tasked with predicting and evaluating candidates' ability to demonstrate empathy in their future classrooms, whether or not they had interacted with P-12 students in person during their placements. The challenges inherent in these experiences were significant but they also represented opportunities to reimagine empathy and care in those learning environments. As we reflected on our altered understandings of enacting care, we lamented the loss of physical presence and visceral affect during the pandemic but we celebrated how the universal experience fostered relatedness and empathy for the human experience.

Enacting Care in Challenging Circumstances

Despite having shared responsibilities, our distinct roles elicited new challenges to enacting care throughout the pandemic. For Julie, the greatest pre-pandemic challenge involved finding ways to care effectively for particularly disgruntled individuals. For example, "when a faculty or a student is having an experience where they feel unsupported, then they lash out and they need your support, even as they are taking action against the unit," commitments can feel conflicted. It can be difficult to serve as the representative of an institution which is perceived as cold, indifferent, and unfeeling, especially when you are closely connected to the people who constitute the institution. Therefore, empathy for those who believe they have been treated unfairly is a critical form of care—and perhaps one of the most difficult to enact. Despite these challenges, Julie viewed the role of care during the pandemic as having a positive impact on inevitable challenges in complex educational environments: "I think faculty and students were more forgiving to one another, and to the system, because they felt cared for."

In Beth's experience as a liaison among the university, local schools, and school communities, one of her primary challenges involved communicating with parents of P-12 students who were participating in a tutoring outreach program: "I took phone calls from frustrated parents...I felt for [them]." Like Julie, Beth viewed care as an approach to easing concerns and creating connections with members of the school community:

> I told one of the women, I'm also a mother of a teenage son...just being able to relate to one another around common concerns was one way that care emerged for me during the pandemic. We need to model listening, empathy, understanding, and perspective taking, and help students develop [those skills] as well.

One of Amanda's and Tiffany's consistent approaches to enacting care in the classroom involved asking students how they were feeling at the start of each class. Amanda explained,

> At the beginning of any of our class sessions, one of the first things I say to PSTs is that I realize that this is an exceptionally challenging year and a challenging time. I can't imagine all of the things that you've been managing this year. So, let's just start with that.

The impact of opening this space of empathy was powerful, as Amanda noted: "There were a couple of times where people would be crying as they explained how they were feeling." Inviting PSTs' emotions into class spaces became an opportunity to model a practice that was also commonly taking place in P-12 classrooms through community circles. When PSTs openly shared difficult emotions, this became an opportunity to discuss how to handle situations when P-12 students share difficult emotions; we then discussed when to follow-up with students one-on-one, when to reach out to a guidance counselor or school social worker, or how to ensure you are engaging in self-care after listening to students share traumas or other struggles.

Some unexpected technological possibilities were generated by the confinement of the pandemic. Both Amanda and Tiffany discussed the value of Zoom's chat and breakout room features, as they created spaces for students to connect with and comfort each other in ways that might otherwise be challenging in an in-person environment. Amanda explained that her facilitation of Zoom breakouts ensured a consistent culture of caring in the classroom and helped her PSTs release their frustrations. Furthermore, both Amanda and Tiffany enjoyed the use of Zoom's chat feature to check in with students and colleagues. Amanda appreciated the temporal flexibility of chat in offering support when PSTs shared vulnerabilities, noting that it can be tricky to figure out how to address a difficult issue shared in a group. As she explained,

> There's a lot more that you can do when someone is talking and you can express your care for another person [in the chat] …When they do finish sharing something that's really hard, they see all of those messages.

Tiffany expanded on the utility of chat to establish or extend personal connections, especially when she sensed tensions: "I appreciated that it was a private way to check in with somebody and let them know you're there for them…it felt like a more caring approach to human interaction than talking over email." Beyond the pandemic, many PSTs and teacher candidates expressed a desire to continue using technology for check-ins with P-12 students, given the private interactions that can sometimes follow more easily. As we reflected on enacting care in challenging circumstances, we acknowledged the negative impact of isolation on heightened tensions among our students, our colleagues, and ourselves, yet we appreciated new opportunities to share and validate each other's experiences during a time when everyone was managing their own forms of trauma. Once again, these experiences offer important implications for teacher education, as teacher educators engage in explicit efforts to model empathy and enact strategies for cultivating and sustaining caring relationships.

Preparing for the Rebuilt P-12 Classroom

In preparation for the post-pandemic, rebuilt P-12 classroom, we focused on the necessity of self-care, collaboration, and fostering global connections through enhanced technological capabilities. For example, Amanda described being more intentional about connecting content to a culture of learning:

> I think there's so much going on in attending to social-emotional learning, that [the teacher candidates] are really at the forefront. I think the more they learn about each other's classrooms, the better off they'll be. They have something to offer each other that's exciting and new, and that they're proud to share.

However, Amanda also noted some of her concerns related to the future of P-12 education: "The more you listen, the more you take in… this is exactly what's happening for P-12 teachers who work in communities where there's tremendous trauma. You experience secondary trauma, and you need care yourself." Amanda's point might be especially true for women in education who tend to bear a disproportionate share of care labor, which only increases during times of crisis (Shalaby et al., 2020). Tiffany added, "Throughout the pandemic, I explained to my husband that whenever a man makes himself emotionally unavailable to students, there's usually a woman who overextends herself to ensure the necessary care is provided." Aligned with Corbera et al.'s (2020) suggestions for prioritization, emotional labor challenges present a direction for shared improvements across teaching, mentoring, and collegiality domains. For example, for teacher candidates, there was tremendous value in being able to debrief with their mentor teachers, who were able to share strategies for supporting students or engaging in self-care.

Supported by Warren (2014, 2018), Julie discussed the value of modeling co-teaching at both the P-12 and university levels. Despite what was initially viewed as a concerning email from university leadership to designate a backup instructor for every course, Julie was able to perceive potential value in the unusual request: "What it symbolized was a collaboration that would be really beneficial at both the university and P-12 levels. The idea of having someone you can count on to reduce the isolation and to jump into your classroom if needed." Relatedly, Beth appreciated the enriched experiences that an established co-teaching model could provide to schools: "I think we'll get there with co-teaching, which is children benefiting from having two very capable adults working together in the classroom." The notion of embracing the collaborative nature of true co-teaching aligns with collaborative professionalism and the ideal that there is a collective responsibility to help each other and serve the students (Hargreaves & O'Connor, 2018). While promoting self-responsibility for teacher education students and faculty is necessary, it is also important to emphasize the criticality of collaboration to learn from each other and further the belief that, together, we can better demonstrate care to the students that we teach.

Supporting innovative approaches to instruction, such as co-teaching, Tiffany focused on the pre-, during-, and post-pandemic importance of keeping up with technology trends: "Since a lot of the doctoral students I work with are classroom teachers, I saw the pandemic as an opportunity to model and enact care using new types of technology that can help us teach more effectively and create opportunities for [global] connection." For example, Tiffany described how she engaged in writing projects with students in Beijing, Sydney, and Tokyo, since online collaboration had become commonplace during the pandemic. She also envisioned an education future that is highly reliant on technology and asynchronous learning to meet the growing demand for flexible, affordable, and remotely accessible degree programs (Witherow, 2020):

> For me, a silver lining was the opportunity to connect and collaborate with online students in ways that I may not have otherwise thought about pre-pandemic. It pushed me to be a more inclusive and responsive educator in meeting the needs of our online doctoral student population, which I think serves as an important model for the future of education.

Collectively, we discussed the role of P-12 school leaders in understanding how to demonstrate their commitment to care in ways that support teachers, foster positive relationships, and encourage transparent dialogue. There is a need to consider supportive structures in university and P-12 settings to help faculty and staff balance care of others and mindful self-care practices (Cook-Cottone & Guyker, 2018). Amanda added, "I feel there's something that needs to be done to sustain the people who are sustaining everybody else, and to help people understand boundaries...you know your relationships with people are really important because they get you through, but where are those lines drawn?"

Navigating Future Care Practices

As we reflected on navigating future care practices in a post pandemic world, we smiled and nodded in affirmation as Amanda spoke to the necessity of time in sustaining care: "I think that we all just need more time, more support, and figuring out how to have productive and supportive relationships that don't become so draining that it's hard to keep up with other components of the work we all need to be doing." Amanda further emphasized the importance of addressing structural challenges and inequities that result in unsustainable and reactive care practices:

> How do you spend time putting band-aids on wounds, but not too much time that you don't have any effort or energy left to address the things that caused the wounds? I don't want to lose sight of the structural problems that are causing some of us to take on a really huge burden, which many of us are absolutely willing to do...but then that detracts from the need to make systemic changes, because we've got a bunch of people who are putting band aids on things all over the place and helping people make their way—which we need—but we also need a longer term, more sustainable solution.

Beth expressed that she was beginning to think about the strengths and assets that PSTs and teacher candidates who experienced COVID-19 would have to offer classrooms and communities. However, she also considered the losses that would need to be compensated for in new ways:

> Even if [PSTs and teacher candidates] probably aren't going to need support as much with technology, they sure are going to need it with classroom management. So, how do we inform those structures that can be responsive to first-year teachers who haven't gotten the same types of experiences, but on the other hand have gotten other valuable kinds of experiences that are going to make them more flexible and more responsive in other ways?

In response, Amanda suggested teaching future teachers to care for each other and "being really intentional about how you're trying to cultivate a community and network of people who can sustain each other." Tiffany envisioned continuing to encourage doctoral students to utilize newly accessible technologies as a way to stay connected and form new connections with peers and faculty across countries and time zones: "Doctoral students who were online pre-pandemic and who felt like they were going through coursework alone finally felt stronger connections, because everyone else was experiencing the program the same way they were... that was powerful, and I hope we don't lose that."

Related to Amanda's and Tiffany's suggestions around sustaining caring learning environments, in her leadership role as department chair, Julie spoke of continuing to model care practices that foster community beyond COVID times. For example, Julie created an every-other-week standing meeting for junior faculty to informally discuss how they were professionally and socially transitioning to academic life in a new university context. She also built in time at every monthly department meeting for faculty to share their experiences as a large group and in small breakout sessions: "Our first fall department meeting was no business at all, it was entirely just reconnecting and hearing from everyone about how everyone was doing. As much as it was hard for me to do, I think it was really important to set that tone." Supported by Corbera et al. (2020), Julie's approaches aimed at fostering collegiality and collective support demonstrate prioritization of building community and working together towards common goals.

Conclusion

Conceptualizations of care and caring are generally perceived and experienced largely as individual, and it is natural to understand care in this way. However, critical to meaningful enactments of care in institutions is the cultivation of a culture of care, an endeavor that is necessarily collaborative and intentional. Building on personal examples shared by Beth and Amanda, Julie explained,

> I'll shift to defining care from a more systemic perspective because of course caring for people and having empathy for the individuals and their situations is central to how we would define care pre- and during the pandemic. But thinking about it from a systemic perspective, the larger definition of care would be to ensure that all of our students have equal access to opportunities to be successful and to achieve whatever their career goals and personal goals are. So that means we have to look at systems and structures to ensure that they also demonstrate care because systems and procedures can have the opposite effect if we're not careful.

Humanistic, relational pedagogies cultivate communities that center care. Common experiences of the chapter authors are captured in the principles of these approaches, which build learning on relatedness, connection, and empathy for human experiences. Although the authors' institutional roles differed, the centrality of these aspects, which contribute to a culture of care, persisted.

Like curriculum, systems and institutions—and the policies that shape them—are constructed by individuals and driven by decisions made by those individuals. This means that the extent to which institutional procedures reflect care can be evaluated and transformed, an endeavor that is also collaborative. Such an effort would involve prioritization of institutional purposes and goals and determination of accountability: To whom are we ultimately answerable? Beth recounted her son's recent observation: "My 13-year-old reminded me yesterday, 'Mom, you know your job isn't to give us what we want, it's to give us what we need.'" The truth that this young person articulated resonates with what care can mean in collaboration toward systemic change. Julie, considering the intersection of education and care from both systemic and personal perspectives, noted that "care doesn't always feel good. Care can feel like struggle, it can feel like suffering," but as Hillary Clinton (2011) reminds us, "Caring for others is an expression of what it means to be fully human."

References

Boylorn, R. M., & Orbe, M. P. (Eds.). (2014). *Critical autoethnography: Intersecting cultural identities in everyday life.* Left Coast Press.

Cann, C. N., & DeMeulenaere, E. J. (2012). Critical co-constructed autoethnography. *Cultural Studies ↔ Critical Methodologies, 12*(2), 146–158.

Carter Andrews, D. J., Richmond, G., & Marciano, J. E. (2021). The teacher support imperative: Teacher Education and the pedagogy of connection. *Journal of Teacher Education, 72*(3), 267–270.

Clinton, H. (2011, December 6). *International Human Rights Day address at Palais des Nations.* Address presented at Palais des Nations in Geneva, Switzerland.

Cook-Cottone, C. P., & Guyker, W. M. (2018). The development and validation of the Mindful Self-Care Scale (MSCS): An assessment of practices that support positive embodiment. *Mindfulness, 9*(1), 161–175.

Corbera, E., Anguelovski, I., Honey-Rosés, J., & Ruiz Mallén, I. (2020): Academia in the time of COVID-19: Towards an ethics of care. *Planning Theory & Practice, 21*(2), 191–199.

Gay, G. (2018). *Culturally responsive teaching* (3rd ed.). Teachers College Press.

Hargreaves, A., & O'Connor, M. T. (2018). *Collaborative professionalism: When teaching together means learning for all.* Corwin.

Ladson-Billings, G. J. (2014). Culturally relevant pedagogy 2.0: a.k.a. The remix. *Harvard Educational Review, 84*(1), 74–84.

Ollerenshaw, J. A., & Creswell, J. W. (2002). Narrative research: A comparison of two restorying data analysis approaches. *Qualitative Inquiry, 8*(3), 329–347.

Paris, D., & Alim, S. (2017). *Culturally sustaining pedagogies: Teaching and learning for justice in a changing world.* Teachers College Press.

Shalaby, M., Allam, N., & Buttorff, G. (2020, December 18). Gender, COVID and Faculty Service. *Inside Higher Ed.* www.insidehighered.com/advice/2020/12/18/increasingly-disproportionate-service-burden-female-faculty-bear-will-have.

Warren, C. A. (2014). Towards a pedagogy for the application of empathy in culturally diverse classrooms. *The Urban Review, 46*(3), 395–419.

Warren, C. A. (2018). Empathy, teacher dispositions, and preparation for culturally responsive pedagogy. *Journal of Teacher Education, 69*(2), 169–183.

Witherow, K. (2020, April 27). *Demand for online studies skyrockets, but here are students' biggest concerns.* https://institutions.educations.com/insights/demand-for-online-studies-skyrockets-but-here-are-students-biggest-concerns.

6

PUTTING THE MASK ON FIRST

Resilience and Wellness in Post-COVID Teacher Education

Jeff Spanke, Devon Lejman, and Kathryn Parthun

Ever since Congress declared the 1990s as the Decade of the Brain, millions of published studies on brain science (Elsevier, 2014) have challenged long-held beliefs about brain-behavior relationships and their influence on classroom performance (Bowers, 2016; Fischer et al., 2010; Howard-Jones et al., 2016). Still, despite the constant fascination with brain science and education, there remains a "separation of related lines of inquiry" (Gabrieli, 2016, p. 617) within the two fields. Harrison (2019), for instance, found that 61.54% of teacher educators "reported limited knowledge of cognitive neuroscience and its effect on pedagogical practice" (p. xiv). While "brain literacy, like all literacy, requires exposure, explicit instruction, knowledge translation, practice, and continuing education" (Walker et al., 2019, p. 3), most teacher education programs do not address brain literacy or mind, brain, and education science in their curricula (Coch, 2018). Even though research has demonstrated that "children's [Social Emotional Learning] is directly influenced by teachers' own social emotional competence" (Waajid et al., 2013, p. 33), teacher preparation programs are unlikely to stress the neurological origins of this competence.

We argue that this dearth of neurological emphasis in teacher education, coupled with a curriculum of care that seems almost unilaterally focused on student behavior and learning outcomes, contributes to the increasingly problematic rates of teacher attrition and burnout that have raged since the COVID pandemic began in March 2020:

> As of October 2020, about one-quarter of respondents…said that they were likely to leave the teaching profession before the end of the 2020–2021 school year, a majority of whom said that they were not likely to leave the profession before the [pandemic]. (Diliberti et al., 2021, p. 2)

DOI: 10.4324/9781003244875-8

This current exodus marks an addition to the 8.5% of teachers who leave the field annually and the estimated 40–50% of those who leave the profession within their first five years (Ingersoll et. al., 2018).

Thus, in order to combat this increasing threat to the American teacher workforce, we believe programs should foreground holistic and sustainable teacher wellness education as a more prominent fixture in their curricula to curve the frightening yet predictable rates of teacher attrition. Preservice teachers learn, for instance, that *students* are indeed whole people with individual needs and complicated, diverse backgrounds and identities. *Teachers,* however, are rarely portrayed as anything other than monolithic functions tasked with the education of those nuanced individuals (Shoffner, 2016). While teachers at all levels face increased pressure to address students' various traumas in their instruction, they are seldom afforded sustainable tools or institutional support to monitor their own wellness.

For many teachers, this feeling of operating merely as *functions* charged with the education of otherwise whole, young, and traumatized students has only amplified in the wake of our current pandemic. Certainly, COVID has disrupted— derailed, destroyed, decimated—much of our various states of being. As our narratives below attest, in our respective capacities as an administrator, novice teacher, and teacher educator, COVID has dramatically influenced how we each view the linked but inherently distinct notions of social emotional learning (SEL), neuroscience, and teacher education. While we recognize and appreciate the considerable strides that teacher education has made in terms of preparing preservice teachers to care for students (Weissberg et al., 2015), COVID has confirmed for us that without first preparing teachers to care for themselves through an understanding of their own brain-states, their efforts to care for others will likely remain either superficial or unsustainable. If, however, preservice teachers could emerge from their preparation programs having triangulated their practice firmly in content, methods, *and* an operational neuroscientific understanding of their own emotional/cognitive well-being, they could not only cultivate greater purpose and fulfilment in their careers but more healthily navigate the inevitable disruptions to their pedagogical, professional, or personal equilibria. We offer our stories in the spirit of that pursuit.

Through the unique perspectives and experiences offered below, we begin this chapter by examining teacher education through a lens of social emotional learning before narrowing our scope to focus more specifically on Mind Brain and Education Science (e.g., Sousa, 2010; Tokuhama-Espinosa, 2010). Jeff is a teacher educator and assistant professor of English. His former student, Devon, had her student teaching abruptly terminated because of the COVID-19 pandemic and currently teaches English at a midsized, lower-middle class, Midwestern high school. Like Jeff, Kathryn earned a bachelor's degree in behavioral neuroscience and, as a former high school science teacher, now develops programs geared toward helping K-12 teachers implement SEL into their curricula.

In our opening narrative, Kathryn highlights the difficulties of administering district-wide SEL curricula without a corresponding emphasis on the neurological origins of student and teacher emotions. Devon expands upon Kathryn's experience by drawing attention to the imbalance between SEL initiatives that focuses on students and similar programs geared toward teachers. Against our current COVID backdrop, both Kathryn and Devon speak to the debilitating struggles of trying to care for students-in-trauma when teachers themselves lack either the resilience or skills to self-regulate or do not feel supported by their schools and communities. We conclude our chapter by tethering Kathryn's administrative and Devon's pedagogical struggles to Jeff's role as an English teacher educator.

Ultimately, we contend that stressing the longitudinal benefits of teacher wellness (Boogren, 2019) leads to an increased focus on connection over compliance (Desautels, 2020), resilience and self regulation, and neuroscientific approaches to teaching and learning. If teacher education can empower preservice teachers with an operational understanding of their own brain-states, then these future educators might grow to cultivate a stronger, more sustainable sense of fit and purpose in their relationships with students and schools. Teacher education is right to emphasize the role of relationships in teaching. But as we hope to demonstrate in this chapter, any successful and sustainable relationship must begin with a healthy acknowledgment of the unique identities and wellness of all parties involved.

Compliance At Best: Kathryn's Story

A year before COVID-19 hit, I was offered the grant-funded position of Director of Social and Emotional Learning for my district. Given that we had a ready plan in place to address the emotional needs of our students, I thought we would be prepared to respond to the mental health and behavioral needs that COVID revealed in our students and staff. After all, when done effectively, SEL gives individuals the skills to learn about themselves, understand and respond to their emotions, regulate when feeling dysregulated, and develop empathy and relationship skills. I soon learned, though, that the SEL program my district endorsed was really nothing more than cognitive behavioral therapy slapped in a box, wrapped in a bow, and packaged for consumption. Not *bad,* necessarily, but not what it needed to be in a pandemic world.

Our current SEL program frames emotions as either positive or negative, the former leading to good decisions, and the latter leading to bad ones. While I don't necessarily disagree with this logic, I do find fault in our SEL program's assumption that shifting from negative to positive emotions is as simple as flipping the switch. This is where our SEL curriculum falls flat.

I wish our program stressed that emotions are physiological and psychological responses to our environments rather than things we can just switch on and off. Emotions are neither good nor bad; they just *are.* Instead of demanding that students flip the switch and take control over their emotions, we must prioritize the self-awareness of how emotions feel in our bodies. In doing so, we can recognize and identify when we are feeling big emotions and, therefore, learn to understand what we need in those moments to feel more regulated. Instead of feeling guilty for having big emotions, we can embrace that our nervous system is trying to communicate to us that we have an unmet need and give ourselves more grace with how we respond to our emotional energy.

Unfortunately, for stressed-out educators who already have way too much on their plates, SEL gets diluted into an *addition* to the curriculum. We do math, then we do science, then we read Shakespeare, *and then* we pause everything to do SEL before going back to the "real learning." And this, of course, is a really tough sell for anyone, especially stressed-out teachers.

But real SEL isn't about programs; it's about people. It should never just be *adding more to the plate*; it's the plate itself. And since the educator is the most influential brain state in the room, teachers should understand and reflect on their own socio-emotional health so that they can lead SEL through their modeling, classroom management, and teaching. If a teacher is well-regulated, they are more likely to have well-regulated students and be able to assist a student who is not. The reverse is also true: A dysregulated adult cannot regulate a dysregulated child.

This is why teacher wellness is imperative. When our staff practice *real* self-care (not Instagram-self-indulgence), they are more resilient and better able to handle the demands of caring for their students. I used to see kids misbehaving and automatically think, "Wow, they must have a bad teacher." But now I find myself wondering, "Hmm, what does that teacher need? Why are they stressed? What's their nervous system uncomfortable with and how can I help?" And, frankly, it all starts with neuroscience! We need to support teachers who are stressed about teaching groups of unvaccinated kids during a pandemic. They should know the science of what happens in their brains when they experience dysregulation, that their anxieties have neuroscientific origins, and that through understanding these origins, we can develop empathy for all stakeholders.

Without framing these conversations in neuroscience terms, SEL will never be anything more than worksheets and lesson plans that students don't buy into because teachers can't sell them. If we ignore the evidence that *our* self-wellness must come first and that, only after we're regulated, can we develop positive connections in our classroom, we'll never maximize student learning. We'll only ever have compliance at best. Ultimately, that's what COVID's shown. Lives have been lost, privileges exposed, traumas inflicted, and we can't go back to normal.

Normal is teacher education that doesn't educate teachers about *their* brains. Normal is thinking that SEL is just about having a good day today or a bad day tomorrow or doing fifteen minutes of monthly circle time to let kids point to their emotions on a picture chart. Normal is hearing "schools" and only thinking "kids" because they're the "product." Normal is burnout and normal is dysregulation. Normal doesn't put teachers' wellness first.

Disappointed Beyond Measure: Devon's Story

"How are you, Devon?"
"That's a loaded question."

The question, spoken with genuine curiosity, concern, and interest; the response, mine, delivered throughout college with just enough sarcastic irony to avoid any stressful digging. Being asked to look closely at ourselves is inherently uncomfortable but these were also the moments during college when a genuinely caring person asked me to examine myself.

Nearly all of my methods classes began with "icebreakers"—go around the room, share your name, year, major, and one fun, school appropriate (ugh) fact about yourself. And there's nothing wrong with that, really—as a new teacher myself, I understand the need to fall back on familiarity, even if that strategy isn't necessarily the best tool. Objectives be damned, comfort tends to trump effectiveness in the end.

But especially now, among COVID-19's incalculable losses—between the grief and fear and uncertainty and anger and the perpetual *discomfort* it has ignited—one aspect, one feeling, stands out: I am disappointed beyond measure. I have been let down as a student, a teacher, and a young person, begging my predecessors for some semblance of care, concern, or concession of fault without placing more burdens and blame on my peers and me. For all that we call this pandemic unprecedented, the responses from those with the power (and salaries) to enact change has been underwhelming, to say the least.

My teaching career began not "in the field" but in a virtual reality. My first year, I met my students over Zoom (if I was lucky), got to "know" them through writing prompts, and spent my first seven weeks sitting behind a blank screen in an empty classroom. We were told we'd slowly reopen with less than half of kids present at any time. We were issued one bottle of disinfectant and sanitizer and enough masks and reusable water bottles to last most mornings. They gave us maps to the cafeteria, guidelines for making seating charts, and vague but insistent reassurances that "we'll be okay." But beneath this big push to somehow get back to normal, everybody knew that nothing would be the same. Things were changed. We all had changed. The students who eventually returned were different from the ones who'd left six months earlier. I was in the same boat, drowning in my own wake of COVID-19.

I never finished student teaching, the thing that everyone always said would set me up for my career. I didn't have a graduation. My friends all moved out, away, or back home. I felt isolated, exhausted, and jaded like never before, and I knew that these feelings/responses were not compatible with a classroom and career that demands energy and enthusiasm. Sure, I always expected to spend my first year staying at school ridiculously late, never sleeping or socializing, and generally dissolving myself into my job. I won't pretend those things did n't happen—they did—but I needed to work to put a stop to them a lot sooner than I would have under typical circumstances. Teaching didn't fulfill me; I wasn't forming relationships; I didn't get any lightbulb moments or teacher highs—pretty much any of those major "little things" that make teaching worth it.

So, I set boundaries: turned off my notifications, stopped Zooming at night, never stayed at school past 4:00 pm, kept at least Saturdays for myself. I wasn't willing to give more than the situation already demanded, especially when I knew my extra efforts wouldn't likely deliver any major gains. Self-care turned out to be incidental, a mere byproduct of my situation, and in that sense, it wasn't too different than college.

As an undergrad, I received instruction ad nauseum on writing lesson plans, grading, and analyzing; I was taught what a teacher is not; I was plopped in front of people (colleagues, not students) and told to "teach" "lessons." I was fed strategies for trauma-informed teaching and preached to about my students' individual needs and creating a "safe" learning environment. But my program never taught me that I was also, first, a human.

We were warned against the banking model of education by investors who treated us like empty vessels. The goal was always more about molding us through teacher preparation than preparing us for lives as teachers. We were taught the complexities and nuances of students but were never treated as complex, nuanced students ourselves —and we were kids, too. We loved talking about our students—our future, hypothetical, inherently fictional students—and we wrote and planned and stressed and cried for *them* but never felt like anyone fought for us.

It was a shit show. And as the scales fell from my eyes, I realized that we were being taught how to do things for strangers by experts who never embodied those things themselves. They told us not to worry, but we did; even though a lot us were n't fine, we were assured that *it* would be, as if our personhood was somehow divorced from our reality.

I remember learning that my students' brains would not fully develop until around age 25 and that I should keep that in mind as a teacher. At the time of writing this, I'm still apparently two years out, just shy of being complete. The only times I felt that my individual wellness mattered were in those brief, extracurricular interactions that I often sought for myself during office hours or after class. Otherwise, I learned about healthy, actualized teaching from my social circles, clubs, or the randomness of class scheduling and individual professors, the kind who sincerely wanted to know how I was when they asked me how I was.

I never felt like a person in my program. A teacher, yes. Human, not so much. Don't get me wrong: I did have access to genuine mental health support; I utilized the Counseling Center throughout college, and I'm grateful that such a resource was available for "free." But that center in particular, by no fault of its own, was a small boat in a very big ocean of deeply rooted, systemic toxicities created and inadequately addressed by the university—and frankly, by the institution of American higher education.

"Maybe If We Learned This Stuff in College": Jeff's Story

The day after we finished the first draft of this chapter, I went to dinner with a couple of former students who had just begun their third years as middle school English teachers. They had met in my class four years prior, started dating shortly thereafter, and had recently gotten engaged. Needless to say, we had a lot to talk about that night. After we found our seats and ordered our drinks, I asked them each how they were doing, teaching in a pandemic. Their initial responses echoed pretty much everything I'd gathered from former students over the last year. Words like *crazy, mess,* and *empty* fell in the wake of other, more physiological signs of fatigue and futility: sighs, aggressive exhalations, snorts, dismissive laughter bordering on the maniacal, eyes rolling and the like. As one vented,

> I mean, we're miserable. Our kids are miserable—they're *crazy,* seriously, these behaviors are *horrendous*—our administration has no clue what the hell they're doing, nobody does, and on top of everything, they now make us all do these 'workshops' where somebody with no experience comes in and talks to us about SEL or some shit and shows us PowerPoints about our brains and gives us more work to do. I hate it. It sucks…I mean, this stuff is *interesting,* I guess, but it doesn't really help us now, right?! Like, maybe if we woulda learned this stuff in college…but doing it *after* we're already struggling doesn't make sense!

"It's just too late," her fiancé offered in solidarity. "We really shoulda gone over this stuff earlier. Somebody shoulda taught us this in college." After an awkward pause, we smiled and toasted to our silent consensus that if anyone should've taught them "this stuff in college," it should've been me…or, at least, some manifestation of the collective Us.

Cheers.

The next day in my upper-level methods course, I shared some of the details of the conversation from dinner and asked my students for their proverbial thoughts. A resounding chorus of pleas and desperation cut me off before I finished my question. My students' responses, though admittedly anecdotal and informal, further supported a sneaking suspicion that had been brewing ever since Kathryn, Devon, and I first started collaborating on this chapter. Yes, COVID has changed, perhaps irrevocably, several aspects of how we teach and learn. But in addition to shifting the ways we now conceptualize care in education, what COVID has also done is expose particular fissures in our practices that have gone unchecked since well before we donned our masks and went virtual.

Much like my two former students-now-teachers, my methods students collectively groaned that, just weeks shy of student teaching, they still did not feel as though their preparation program had encouraged them to foster their own teacher identities or offered strategies to regulate their emotions or maintain a holistic sense of health and wellness in teaching. They did recall going over work-life balance in some courses but many said that it was often reduced to conversations about having an occasional glass of wine, taking bubble baths, or making time to see friends. "It's not wrong," one student conceded, "but it's kinda the same thing as putting a band-aid on someone with a cold."

For the most part, these students reported knowing nothing of brain literacy, social emotional learning, trauma-informed pedagogies, or resilience and boundaries in teaching. As they spoke freely, I couldn't help but notice the similarities between how my current students bemoaned the lack of institutional emphasis on teachers-as-people and Devon's experience from two years prior. While COVID certainly contributed to fundamentally different preparatory experiences, it didn't seem to alter too dramatically the overwhelming perception that teacher education doesn't regard teachers with the same holistic sense of care and well-being as it does students. And much like my former students from dinner, these current students on the verge of their final semester all expressed a seemingly unrequited desire to have "gone over this stuff" somewhere earlier in the program.

When I asked them how, specifically, they imagined this could happen, it didn't take long for them to curate a robust list of suggestions:

> It has to start at the beginning, in the intro courses. Everything needs to start with identity. Methods, content, classroom management—all of these things depend on who the teacher is, how they work, what their skills are, and all the unique things that they bring to the table. The whole program really needs to be grounded in figuring out who we all are. Everything else builds off that.

From there, we got more particular, ultimately compiling a list of ways to improve teacher education. Our list of programmatic and personnel considerations included

- more proactive—not *reactive*—publicizing of university mental health services. If possible, have those services specifically catered to educators, in the same way that other professions have specialized therapists.
- requiring a specific course (or course sequence) that focuses on teacher wellness through a neuroscientific lens, instead of discussing work-life balance tangentially or extracurricularly. In other words, design a brain-literacy curriculum in the same fashion that many programs have implemented content-area literacy courses.
- emphasizing and incentivizing sustained programmatic mentorship, either student-student or faculty-student. My students noted that these initiatives

already exist for practicing novice teachers but are not prevalent fixtures in teacher education.

- earlier, more frequent, and more purposeful collaborations with local schools and community partners. Among other obvious benefits, this, my preservice teachers argued, would help reiterate the notion of teaching being a kind of relationship with a school/community, as well as help illuminate the idea of fit when it comes to choosing a school.
- an increased overall curricular/programmatic emphasis on "curiosity, creativity, exploration, and experimentation" over "regimentation, mechanization, memorization, and recitation." And yes, each of these words was actually said.

In addition to our list of suggestions and specific programmatic ideas, my preservice teachers generated a variety of metaphors to illustrate their case. For example, studying brain-literacy was akin to learning about automotive repair alongside driver's education, studying anatomy if you're a body-builder, learning physics and chemistry in architecture school, or brushing up on finance during marriage counseling. Just like Kathryn's and Devon's stories attest, my preservice teachers felt as though teacher education programs, replete as they admittedly are with content and methods instruction, aren't complete without a triangulated emphasis on other, seemingly tangential, elements of the teaching profession. Teacher wellness *matters,* in very much the same way that knowledge of the body matters to a weight-lifter. You don't need to know how an engine works in order to get a driver's license but it sure comes in handy when your 15-year-old Honda Civic breaks down.

The teaching profession has always been rife with stories of struggle and hardship. These didn't begin with COVID. But if our current pandemic has highlighted anything, it's that teacher attrition will likely never be mitigated solely through reactionary, superficial measures or by applying a proverbial band-aid to injuries that are more than skin deep. Much of teacher education relies on preparing preservice teachers to teach students standards-based skills for future success. Perhaps it's time to start infusing our programs with similar skills aimed at helping our preservice teachers succeed in ways that exceed planning, instruction, and assessment. While these skills certainly involve methods of content instruction and classroom management, they also more broadly include ways of regulating ourselves, reading our brains, understanding and controlling our emotions, and thriving within the boundaries we set for ourselves.

This is where care should begin in teacher education post-COVID, with a concerted and consistent focus on individual teacher identities, the social/emotional manifestation of those identities, and an understanding of their neuroscientific origins. Before we can teach our preservice teachers how to care for others, we must first share with them how to know and care for themselves—and that means helping them put on their own masks first, breathing strong and bracing for whatever turbulence might lie ahead.

References

Boogren, T. H. (2019). *180 days of self-care for busy educators.* Solution Tree Press.

Bowers, J. (2016). *Psychology,* not educational neuroscience, is the way forward for improving educational outcomes in all children: Reply to Gabrieli (2016) and Howard-Jones et al. (2016). *Psychological Review, 123*(5), 628–635.

Coch, D. (2018). Reading from a mind, brain, and education perspective. In M. S. Schwartz & E. J. Paré-Blagoev (Eds.), *Research in mind, brain, and education* (pp. 97–132). Routledge.

Desautels, L. (2020). *Connections over compliance: Rewiring our perceptions of discipline.* Wyatt-MacKenzie Publishing.

Diliberti, M. K., Schwartz, H. L., & Grant, D. (2021). *Stress topped the reasons why teachers quit even before COVID-19.* RAND Corporation.

Elsevier Research Intelligence Analytical Services. (2014). *Brain science: Mapping the landscape of brain and neuroscience research.* Elsevier.

Fischer, K. W., Goswami, U. C., Geake, J. G., & Task Force on the Future of Educational Neuroscience. (2010). The future of educational neuroscience. *Mind, Brain, and Education, 4,* 68–80.

Gabrieli, J. (2016). The promise of educational neuroscience: Comment on Bowers. *Psychological Review, 123*(5), 613–619.

Harrison, C. (2019). *Including cognitive neuroscience content in the core curriculum of teacher-education programs: A phenomenological study of California teachers' conceptions*[Unpublished dissertation]. Pepperdine University.

Howard-Jones, P. A., Ansari, D., Smedt, B., Laurilland, D., Varma, S., Butterworth, B., Goswami, U., & Thomas, M. (2016). The principles and practices of educational neuroscience: Comment on Bowers (2016). *Psychological Review, 123*(5), 620–627.

Shoffner, M. (Ed.) (2016). *Exploring teachers in fiction and film: Saviors, scapegoats, and schoolmarms.* Routledge.

Sousa, D.A. (2010). *Mind, brain, and education: Neuroscience implications for the classroom.* Solution Tree Press.

Tokuhama-Espinosa, T. (2010). *Mind, brain, and education science: A comprehensive guide to the new brain-based teaching.* W. W. Norton and Company.

Waajid, B., Garner, P. M., & Owen, J. E. (2013). Infusing social emotional learning into the teacher education curriculum. *The International Journal of Emotional Education, 5*(2), 31–48.

Walker, Z., Hale, J. B., Chen, S. H. A., & Poon, K. (2019). Brain literacy empowers educators to meet diverse learner needs. *Learning, Research, and Practice, 5*(2), 174–188.

Weissberg, R. P., Durlak, J. A., Domitrovich, C. E., & Gullotta, T. P. (2015). Social and emotional learning: Past, present, and future. In J. A. Durlak, C. E. Domitrovich, R. P. Weissberg, & T. P. Gullotta (Eds.), *Handbook of social and emotional learning: Research and practice* (pp. 3–19). The Guilford Press.

7

SEEING BEYOND THE PLEXIGLASS

Enacting a Vision of Caring During COVID

Catherine M. Scott and Melony H. Allen

As teacher educators, we aim to develop early childhood and elementary teacher candidates' abilities to enact caring pedagogy by intentionally embedding elements of care into their coursework that they then enact in their own teaching. However, the onset of the COVID-19 pandemic significantly changed the ways in which teaching and learning occurred, leading us to wonder what the nature of our teacher candidates' enacted ways of caring would be, what barriers they would encounter, and to what extent they would be able to enact their notions of caring. Understanding these unique experiences provides opportunities for teacher educators to better enact care in response to teacher candidates' expressed needs. This understanding can also be harnessed to further develop candidates' conceptions and practices of care.

Conceptual Framework

Teaching is a highly relational activity and building positive relationships is at the core of caring pedagogy (Moen et al., 2020; Noddings, 2012). Velasquez et al. (2013) point out that caring pedagogy involves practices that recognize a symbiotic relationship between student and teacher and helps "educators nurture students socially, intellectually and morally at the individual and community level" (p. 182). Noddings (2012) provides us with practices that establish and maintain "relations of care and trust which include listening, dialogue, critical thinking, reflective response, and making thoughtful connections among the disciplines and to life itself" (p. 771). Involving both cognitive and affective dimensions, these practices can be viewed in the ways that teachers provide engaging and meaningful instructional experiences for students, encourage dialogue, and recognize student needs (Goldstein & Lake, 2000). These practices involve both cognitive and affective dimensions.

DOI: 10.4324/9781003244875-9

Receptive listening, as an act of caring, is the conduit for understanding the thinking and feelings of students in order to best meet their expressed needs (Noddings, 2012). This sort of listening can occur when both the teacher and student engage in dialogue around content, feelings, or thoughts. While this dialogue occurs, a caring teacher will think critically about what the student is expressing and provide a reflective response to meet their communicated needs, whether that is directly related to the subject at hand or to an expressed emotional need. The teacher will also work with the student to verify that their needs are being met and to teach them how to provide care for others (Velasquez et al., 2013).

As noted by Goldstein and Lake (2000), caring can be a demanding task, particularly with limited experience and a lack of understanding of how to make the exchange symbiotic. For most teacher candidates, the ideas of caring and teaching are often built on persistent paradigms that associate women with caring and teaching (Goldstein & Lake, 2000). When using these paradigms to shape their own views of caring (particularly due to their lack of experience), they might sometimes find that their own views of how to enact care diverge from the realities of classroom practice. As a result, teacher candidates' definitions of caring could be essentialized, oversimplified, or too idealistic (Goldstein & Lake, 2000), romanticizing assumptions that caring is an instinctual, simple notion. With the challenges of COVID-19 adding to an even less certain classroom setting, understanding how to enact care might be even more difficult.

Methodology

This qualitative study attempted to address three research questions: (1) What do teacher candidates believe about ways of caring?; (2) What barriers exist for teacher candidates to enact care?; and (3) To what extent are teacher candidates able to enact the ways they envision care? The study was exploratory in nature; the ways in which participants made meaning of their experiences, and the ideas that they had regarding enacting care in the classroom, were unknown before the study began. Multiple data sources were collected from teacher candidates across a semester-long seminar course, where candidates met to reflect and engage in discussion about their internship placement.

This study used a case study approach as the site was bound by place, length, and activity (Creswell & Poth, 2016). Only candidates in the early childhood and elementary program internship courses participated. Candidates were bound by participation in their specific seminar course, which was required for all candidates completing a culminating internship. Although the candidates are in two separate programs, they were required to complete the same class and internship requirements. Both courses lasted one semester, and data were collected only during this 16-week timeframe, as candidates simultaneously completed their internships.

Context and Participants

This study took place at a mid-sized liberal arts institution in the southeast United States. Teacher candidates in the early childhood and elementary education programs spend the first two years of their academic program completing university-required coursework and program prerequisite courses. For the latter two years of the four-year program, candidates complete methods courses and spend increased time in field experiences for three semesters, with a culminating semester-long internship placement and seminar course. Candidates in early childhood education are certified for grades pre-kindergarten through third, and candidates in elementary education are certified for grades two through six.

Fifty-eight teacher education candidates participated in the two sections of the internship seminar course offered during the spring 2021 semester, 33 from early childhood education and 25 from elementary education. Fifty-six candidates were women, and three were men (see Table 7.1). Typically, early childhood candidates met for class on Thursday evenings and elementary education candidates met for class on Tuesday evenings; however, there were three nights when both cohorts met together to discuss care and their classroom experiences.

TABLE 7.1 Candidate demographics

Early Childhood Education	31 white women
	2 African-American women
Elementary Education	20 white women
	2 African-American women
	1 African-American man
	1 Latino man
	1 white man

Data Collection and Analysis

At the beginning of the semester, candidates completed a survey identifying their placement grade level and location, what they were most looking forward to, and what they were most concerned about for the semester. They then read *Teaching and the Balancing of Round Stones* (Duffy, 1998), which explains the art of teaching. In the first two weeks of class, candidates completed a video response where they identified the "stones" that they were balancing in their field experiences, what was important to their vision of teaching, and how they would balance these stones and ensure alignment with their vision. Finally, they were asked to identify the supports they needed to enact care in the classroom.

Candidates also participated in three classroom discussions and one Jamboard response focused on care in the classroom and COVID. Each 40-minute in-class discussion and the Jamboard focused on three topics: (1) how candidates defined and were enacting care in the classroom, (2) what challenges they were dealing with regarding care, and (3) how they worked around these challenges and the resources utilized to do so. These data were coded and analyzed for themes across candidate responses.

Throughout the semester, candidates engaged in literature circles using the text *I Wish My Teacher Knew* (Schwartz, 2016). The text focuses on areas of concern when working with students, including moving, abuse, grief, and trauma. Literature circles met eight times, once per chapter. For each meeting time, one candidate was responsible for engaging their colleagues in discussion about the chapter and considering the ways in which they could enact care for their students in the classroom. Candidates' responses to these questions (both oral and written) were coded and analyzed for themes related to enacting care and challenges with enacting care.

Qualitative data were collected during the internship seminar course, which met twice a month on Zoom due to COVID safety protocols. Data came from a variety of sources, including teacher candidates' literature circles, classroom discussions, FlipGrid and Google form responses, and Jamboard responses. The data were analyzed by chunking into coding categories based on the three research questions and current literature on care-based practice in the classroom. Data were reviewed by each researcher independently, who developed tentative codes for patterns in conversation topics and responses. Coding categories were developed using themes from across each of the data sources (Yin, 2003). Then, the researchers checked for agreement in coding patterns and revised codes as needed. The reviewers reduced the number of coding categories to hone in on themes (see Table 7.2 for examples).

Once the set of themes was agreed upon, data were reviewed once again to confirm the findings. The initial 11 themes were condensed to six, based on similarities across candidate responses. The final themes for candidate responses were naïve views of care, receptive engagement, COVID-19 protocols, resources to guide pedagogical practices, finding their "teacher" voice, and shifting pedagogical practices.

TABLE 7.2 Coding categories and examples

Initial Codes	Examples	Final Code
Academic needs	"We're trying to help students each meet their goals while also rushing through the curriculum."	**Naïve views of care**
Social needs	"How to develop their social and emotional skills and teach them to work with peers when we have to be distanced."	
Emotional needs	"I want my students to feel confident and loved."	
Relationship Building	How do I get them to see me as a teacher, not a student?	**Receptive Engagement**
Student autonomy	Engaging students in choice	

Initial Codes	Examples	Final Code
Physical health concerns	Parents and teachers worried about sick kids at school.	**Covid-19 Protocols**
Social distancing concerns	Need to use a pointer to highlight items on a student's worksheet, rather than crouch down next to them, so as to maintain distance.	
Emotional health concerns	"We can't hug or give a high five."	
Who is helping?	"I'm collaborating with my CT (cooperating teacher) and the cohort."	**Resources to guide pedagogical practices**
Teacher versus friend	"Sometimes I am so worried about classroom management that these aspirations get lost in fear of my inability to manage the classroom."	**Finding their "teacher voice"**
Changes in thoughts	"We have to adapt" and be creative	**Shifting pedagogical practices**

What Teacher Candidates Believe About Ways of Caring

Our findings from working with teacher candidates show a shift in their views of enacting care during COVID. In this section, we address each research question and the ways in which participant responses changed over the course of their internship experience.

Naive Views of Care

At the onset of the semester, candidates displayed fairly similar views of how to show care in the classroom. Based on written responses, the majority of candidates indicated "naive views of care": the idea that by helping students, candidates were thus enacting care in their classrooms. Of the responses, half (50%) focused on meeting students' academic, mental, emotional, and social needs. Twenty-one responses (35%) focused on loving the student and putting their best interests before teaching; nine (15%) focused on relationship building and showing students that they cared about students' interests. Four candidates (7%) also mentioned the importance of setting high expectations for students, both in and out of the classroom. Finally, two candidates (3%) noted the importance of showing empathy in the classroom, with only one response directly related to COVID:

> As a teacher, to care means to express empathy to your students especially considering during these unique times. We are all trying to balance these new restrictions, but for young minds it's harder to accept and understand so providing them that extra support and love.

Early in the semester, the data revealed that many candidates were knowledgeable about specific ways to encourage and engage in receptive listening. For example, candidates discussed how they would routinely use intentional sharing time, as well as one-on-one conversations, as opportunities to learn more about students and families in order to best meet their needs. At this time, most candidates focused on students' emotional needs, and as noted by the data, they focused entirely on what the teacher was doing in the relationship rather than a reciprocity between teacher and students.

Limited Receptive Engagement

As the semester progressed, candidate views of how to show care shifted. At the end of the semester, they discussed how providing students choice, and helping them to build self-efficacy by involving them in decision-making, was an important part of care. In addition, they shared that it was critical to adjust the curriculum to meet student interests. Finally, showing students how to develop "grit" was an aspect of care that they felt addressed students' academic, mental, emotional, and social needs. As one candidate explained,

> Grit is important for students because they are always going to face challenging things in all areas of life. If we teach them at a young age to push through hard times and stick to challenging tasks, even when they are hard, we will set them up to be successful academically, socially, mentally, and physically.

Interestingly, although candidates discussed the value of providing choice, and the importance of engaging students in decision-making, they did not provide any examples of times when they had allowed such opportunities to occur in their classrooms.

COVID-19 Protocols as Barriers to Enacting Care

Initially, the majority of candidates shared barriers related directly to pandemic safety protocols. Fifty-four participant responses (90%) focused specifically on COVID. Twenty-six candidates (43%) explicitly stated that they were upset to not give hugs or high-fives to their students. In the districts where the candidates interned, schools created plexiglass "cells" around all student desks in the classrooms in an effort to reduce the spread of germs. Fifteen teacher candidates (26%) expressed concern over the plexiglass, noting that it made both hearing and seeing the student difficult (and vice versa), and that it added an additional challenge when trying to help students one-on-one with their work. In one class discussion, participants detailed the difficulty of keeping the plexiglass clean and preventing students from getting markers, food, and other debris on it. The candidates also commented on the challenges of navigating around the classroom due to the amount of space the plexiglass took up in the floor plan. As one elementary education candidate noted, "The plexiglass has made it harder to interact with my students. I am not able to reach over their desk and help them with their work. I have to physically walk all the way around them to help."

While offering their concerns regarding the lack of physical contact due to social distancing protocols and plexiglass, candidates also discussed three additional concerns. They worried that masks would inhibit students from understanding their instruction or seeing their expressions (12%). They also expressed concerns that coronavirus was preventing "regular" classroom activities, including circle time and small group instruction (12%), and transitions were challenging between virtual, hybrid, and in person instruction (8%). Teacher candidates all felt that these obstacles would challenge them during the semester as they tried to build a sense of classroom community and care.

Teacher Candidates Enacting Their Visions of Care

Guiding Pedagogical Practices

At the beginning of their internship, candidates provided written responses explaining how they thought they would demonstrate care for their students during COVID safety protocols. Candidates largely felt that they would brainstorm with their cooperating teachers and peers to determine how they would show students that they cared. They shared that being flexible, getting to know their students, and figuring out ways to work together despite social distancing would be how to enact care.

As the semester progressed, candidates' views on how they were able to enact care shifted. For example, one discussion with both cohorts offered insights into the ways they were finding to enact care in the classroom. In early February, candidates had been asked what resources they needed from us, as instructors, to help them enact care. The majority of candidates responded by indicating that they were using the internet, their cooperating teacher, or other sources to find what they needed, and no help was necessary. Curious about the resources that they were using, we followed up with candidates to see how their search was going (and thus, to determine if they needed help). One candidate shared that there were thirty minutes in the morning, prior to the day starting, that her students came in and talked with her. She laughed, sharing, "They ask me a lot of questions, too. They want to know where I live. Do I live with my parents or do I live at school? Am I a grown up? So I ask them questions too." Another candidate, who was in a completely virtual classroom, wrote postcards to all of her students. Others shared that they were working to integrate topics of interest to the students, as well as tools which the students enjoyed, such as TikTok, to make instruction more meaningful.

Finding Their "Teacher Voice"

One issue that many candidates shared was the challenge of "finding their teacher voice": being supportive, yet firm, as classroom leaders. Candidates were trying to determine how they could find the balance between being a "fun" teacher (e.g., a "friend") and a respected teacher. While this is not an atypical challenge for new teachers, for some it was exacerbated by virtual instruction. One candidate shared that her struggle did not come from trying to be assertive with the kids but from the parents sitting directly next to the child during virtual instruction and turning into "mama bear" when the child was asked to correct a behavior.

Shifting Pedagogical Approaches

At the end of the semester, candidates solidified some of the ways in which they had enacted care in the classroom. In an April 2021 class discussion, the candidates noted that "trial and error" and "adapting to student needs and school culture" were needed to enact care. When asked how they enacted care and helped develop students' character, and if COVID were a challenge in doing so, only one candidate shared that COVID impacted their abilities to enact care. In fact, some transitioned away from the expectations that providing hugs and physical contact were the only way to show that they cared: "With children there is no faking, they can see right through it. I feel that it can be more than just hugs, it can be showing them you care about their lives." Another student shared, "I feel like coronavirus has given me more opportunities to show my students I care." She explained that, because children had to learn about and experience illness, death, sadness, and isolation as a result of COVID, compassion and empathy became critical, teachable moments.

In the class discussion, candidates spoke less about "things I can't do because of…" and instead switched to "I'm doing this…" One candidate noted that, to enact care, she spent a great deal of time talking about feelings with her class, and that doing so helps students to become empathetic adults. Candidates said that just showing up and being present in the classroom allowed for the opportunity to build relationships, and that things were falling naturally into place. Morning greeting and time on the playground allowed chances to talk with students and learn more about them. Another agreed, sharing that coronavirus had thrown so much at them, too, that a change in mindset was necessary: "It all just clicked." From the candidates' perspectives, the opportunity to spend time in the classroom and be open to new experiences paid off.

Discussion

At the start of the semester, teacher candidates held views of caring that were one sided; their focus was on the ways in which they could help students, without considering the ways in which students could contribute to the relationship. These naive views of care align with Nodding's ideas of motivational displacement (Velasquez et al., 2013); by ensuring that they were helping the children in their class, our teacher candidates thought that they were enacting care. As with Goldstein and Lake's (2000) study of teacher candidates, our candidates also held essentialized, oversimplified, and idealistic views of teaching. Many felt that showing students they cared equated to showing physical signs of affection (e.g., hugs), and that it was their job to bestow this care upon the children by meeting this need. Although they noted that they were concerned about the academic, social, emotional, and moral development of students, candidates focused heavily on student emotions. Discussions in schools and on the news about "what students were missing" or how hard the pandemic was for everyone's mental health transferred to candidate concerns in the classroom (Elliliom, 2020; St George & Strauss, 2021; Schwartz et al., 2021). While teacher candidates were limited in their views of how to enact care, they did recognize and utilize commonly expected methods for enacting care in the classroom by engaging in dialogue to learn about their students (Noddings, 1992).

However, as the semester progressed, we saw shifts in the ways in which candidates enacted care. As they began to spend time in the classroom and learn about their students, they focused on tasks such as developing students' self-efficacy and providing opportunities for student choice, both steps towards valuing reciprocity in the act of caring. They also discussed adjusting the curriculum to meet students' interests and needs and using explicit strategies for fostering their students' moral development through building students' character, all important facets of enacting care in the classroom (Velasquez et al., 2013).

While candidates were successful with some aspects of enacting care, such as identifying ways to show care, engaging in dialogue with their students, and recognizing the concerns that COVID brought in dealing with students' emotional well-being, other areas needed further development to implement caring pedagogies. Candidates did not provide opportunities for students to demonstrate care for others or to engage in work of personal interest, despite noting the value of doing so to build self-efficacy. Lastly, none of the candidates acknowledged actually checking with students to see if their needs were being met, thus limiting aspects of responsiveness (Velasquez et al., 2013).

Implications

As teacher educators, our time with candidates during COVID brought about opportunities for reflection. We believe that candidates' caring pedagogies can be further developed by providing a space for them to connect and reflect upon their experiences and practices through the lenses of both students and teachers.

Once candidates know students' interests and areas for support, how do they transfer that information into actionable steps? We believe a practical way to accomplish this is by requiring candidates to provide evidence of students' work where they have incorporated students' interests and addressed their learning needs. While we heard from our candidates about what their students were interested in and what they needed to propel their learning forward, we made assumptions that candidates would use this knowledge to inform their teaching. Our study revealed that this rarely happened. In the future, we must hold candidates accountable for receptive listening by incorporating opportunities for them to critically analyze work samples that incorporate student interests compared to tasks that do not. We envision this occurring in an ongoing fashion, where pairs share throughout the semester in a whole group setting followed by small group discussions on the question, "In what ways did you listen and respond to your students this week by incorporating some aspect that you learned from them?" This approach better supports our candidates' pursuit of caring pedagogy.

While we recognize that our candidates know how to establish relationships with students, they lacked implementable steps for enacting all aspects of care in the classroom. It is our responsibility to help candidates develop clarity and focus in determining how they will do things, such as provide students with choice and using strategies to show care. While COVID certainly amplifies concerns for students' emotional well-being, we must also take care to address all aspects of students' well-being with our teacher candidates, so we can ensure that student needs are met with an implementable plan. Finally, we must work with teacher candidates to recognize the reciprocity in establishing a caring relationship. Students must be participatory in the experience, so that candidates are not the only ones "delivering" care to others. In these ways, we can position candidates to see beyond the plexiglass (and other barriers) to enact a vision of care, no matter the circumstances.

References

Creswell, J. C., & Poth, C. N. (2016). *Qualitative inquiry and research design* (4th ed.). Sage Publications.

Duffy, G. D. (1998). Teaching and the balancing of round stones. *Phi Delta Kappan, 79*(10), 777–780.

Einhorn, E. (2020, December 15). COVID is having a devastating impact on children - and the vaccine won't fix everything. *NBC News.* www.nbcnews.com/news/education/covid-having-devastating-impact-children-vaccine-won-t-fix-everything-n1251172.

Goldstein, L. S., & Lake, V. E. (2000). "Love, love, and more love for children": Exploring preservice teachers' understandings of caring. *Teaching and Teacher Education, 16*(8), 861–872.

Moen, K. M., Westlie, K., Gerdin, G., Smith, W., Linner, S., Philpot, R., Schenker, K., & Larsen, L. (2020). Caring teaching and the complexity of building good relationships as pedagogies for social justice in health and physical education. *Sports, Education, and Society, 25*(9), 1015–1028.

Noddings, N. (1992). *The challenge to care in schools: An alternative approach to education.* Teachers College Press.

Noddings, N. (2012). The caring relation in teaching. *Oxford Review of Education, 38*(6), 771–781.

St. George, D., & Strauss, V. (2021, January 21). Partly hidden by isolation, many of the nation's school children struggle with mental health. *The Washington Post.* www.washingtonpost.com/local/education/student-mental-health-pandemic/2021/01/21/3d377bea-3f30-11eb-8db8-395dedaaa036_story.html.

Schwartz, K. (2016). *I wish my teacher knew: How one question can change everything for our kids.* Da Capo Press.

Schwartz, K. D., Exner-Cortens, D., McMorris, C. A., Makarenko, P. A., Van Bavel, M., Williams, S., & Canfield, R. (2021). COVID-19 and student well-being: Stress and mental health during return-to-school. *Canadian Journal of School Psychology, 36*(2), 166–185.

Velasquez, A., West, R., Graham, C., & Osguthorpe, R. (2013). Developing caring relationships in schools: A review of the research on caring and nurturing pedagogies. *Review of Education, 1*(2), 162–190.

Yin, R. K. (2003). *Cases study research: Design and methods.* Sage Publications.

PART II

Care in the Content Areas

8

ENACTING AN ETHIC OF CARE AS A TESOL TEACHER EDUCATOR

Pedagogical Practices During and After the COVID-19 Pandemic

Ekaterina Koubek

Scholars have long advocated for the importance of care in teaching in all educational settings, including teacher education (Goldstein & Freedman, 2003; Noddings, 2005; Thayer-Bacon & Bacon, 1996). As Goldstein and Freedman (2003) postulate, "To prepare teachers who will be able to draw on caring to build a strong foundation for their professional practices, we must create teacher education programs specifically focused toward this goal" (p. 441). Furthermore, they emphasize that teacher educators need to assist preservice teachers in understanding the role of caring in teaching. However, O'Connor (2008) warns educators that caring teaching can be an exhausting endeavor, as "being able to act as a professional and still sustain a sense of self within the [teaching] role has emotional implications for teachers" (p. 122).

The need for care is perhaps the greatest during this time of disruption caused by COVID-19. Building and rebuilding teacher-student relationships is of utmost importance as anxieties and uncertainties have eroded "the bedrock" of education (Noddings, 2005). The purpose of this chapter, then, is to examine the role of care and its enactment by one teacher educator in a Teaching English to Speakers of Other Languages (TESOL) program. As a teacher educator with 15 years of experience, I wondered in what ways I enacted care in my teaching during COVID and how my preservice teachers perceived these practices.

Theoretical Background

Noddings (2005) defines care as "the very bedrock of all successful education" (p. 27), although as an approach to moral philosophy, care ethics has been widely recognized in various contexts beyond education (Noddings, 1994, 2012). At the foundation of this approach lies the relationship of the carer and cared-for, a

DOI: 10.4324/9781003244875-11

relationship that is ontologically and ethically basic (Noddings, 2012). Grounded in the belief that "every human life starts in relation and it is through relations that a human individual emerges" (Noddings, 2012, p. 771), care ethics emphasizes genuine relationships in which, over time, the carer and cared-for exchange positions and exhibit caring relationships toward one another, thus further promoting moral development. In the educational context, the carer—the educator—strives to create a classroom climate for the cared-for—the students—that is based on care and trust.

Noddings' (1984) characteristics of care include the concepts of engrossment and motivational displacement. According to Noddings (2005), engrossment is "an open, nonselective receptivity to the cared-for. Other writers have used the word 'attention' to describe this characteristic" (p. 15). Engrossment occurs when a teacher establishes a caring relationship by accepting and valuing student feelings and experiences. Motivational displacement, on the other hand, is "the sense that our motive energy is flowing toward others and their projects" (p. 16). By focusing on student needs, teachers become engrossed in their students, which leads to the motivational displacement of shifting their focus from self to students in order to support student motivation and connection of content to their lives.

My Context

I joined James Madison University (JMU) in 2014 as an associate professor and TESOL coordinator. The TESOL program offers a major and a minor at the undergraduate level. Two graduate programs are also offered: an MAT in TESOL focused on K-12 English as a Second Language licensure and an MEd in Equity and Cultural Diversity focused on educational theories and practices that emphasize equity and diversity.

I am a white cisgender female who was born outside of the US and retained my home language accent. My teaching includes both undergraduate and graduate courses in second language acquisition, TESOL methods, and language assessment, with occasional responsibility for field supervision; my class sizes range between three and 22 preservice teachers. When I joined at JMU, I wondered whether my preservice teachers would trust me as an educator, given my accent and origin (Herget, 2016; Matthews, 2017), but I embarked on the challenge of preparing them to work with multilingual learners while sharing my journey as an English language learner.

According to JMU's 2021 census, the university enrolls over 21,000 students, with 78 percent of students identifying as white; women make up 58 percent of the student body while men make up 42 percent. In the College of Education, these percentages are even higher, since most K-12 teachers are white women (National Center for Educational Statistics, 2021). The TESOL programs are no exception, attracting a small, dedicated group of students eager to engage in equity, diversity, and social justice issues.

Methodology

Through action research (Kemmis & McTaggart, 1988), I sought to understand the role of care and its enactment in my teaching during the COVID pandemic. According to Kemmis and McTaggart (1988), action research is "a form of self-reflective enquiry undertaken by participants in social situations to improve the rationality and justice of their own practices, and the situations in which those practices are carried out" (p. 162). As Leitch and Day (2000) postulate, "The ways in which the reflective inquiry processes within action research are framed and interpreted, however, relate to the underpinning epistemology of the action research model being employed" (p. 183). Here, practical action research was employed for the purpose of improving "practice through the application of practical judgement and the accumulated personal wisdom of the teacher" (Leitch & Day, 2000, p. 183). By utilizing Elliott's (1991) steps of observe-reflect-plan-act-evaluate with introspective, self-reflexive inquiry, I probed into my values for enacting care in my teaching context before and during COVID-19 to better understand what I was doing and why in order to address care post-pandemic.

Since action research is often carried out through qualitative means (Leitch & Day, 2000), data for this study consisted of qualitative responses on student course evaluations, anonymous qualitative student survey responses, and my reflective journals. Data were analyzed using thematic analysis (Merriam & Tisdell, 2016) by first reading and rereading the data in their entirety to develop preliminary notes that were then used to formulate initial codes. Upon rereading all data again, revised codes emerged that were later aligned with Noddings' (1984) characteristics of care, such as engrossment and motivational displacement. These codes were used to make sense of my practice before, during, and beyond the pandemic. Critically reflecting on my current practices of enacting care during COVID necessitated a closer analysis of my past practices in order to take an introspective look at what worked, why, and how to move forward post-pandemic.

The Role of Care Pre-Pandemic

Engrossment

Throughout my teaching career, I have often prioritized preservice teachers and their needs above other responsibilities. To create caring relationships pre-pandemic, I focused on learning about my preservice teachers and establishing a community of learners based on mutual trust and understanding. By establishing a caring and trusting environment in which they were challenged to take risks to openly share their ideas, I worked to foster critical thinking and learning. Implementing structured introductory activities at the beginning of each semester and having unstructured conversations before or after each class were instrumental in fostering a sense of community, which in turn contributed to preservice teachers' sense of belonging, as they shared in their course evaluations: "She stressed the importance of building a community in the classroom and wanted us all to feel comfortable to participate in class" (Spring 2015) and "She created a relaxed and trusting classroom environment where students could speak openly and respectfully about the content and about personal lives" (Spring 2016).

Showing care for preservice teachers as human beings, first, and learners, second, required establishing classroom norms based on dialogue and active listening. To build caring relationships, I needed to learn about my preservice teachers, their needs, and interests by actively listening to their stories and contributions. In addition, establishing class norms for dialogue was of paramount importance to foster a diversity of ideas and points of view. This, in turn, supported their sense of belonging, as echoed in one preservice teacher's course evaluation:

> I also appreciated the fact that [she] really listened to us and facilitated effective discussions. I've traditionally been shy in classes, but I found it easy to talk in this class—from the very first class [she] established a warm, supportive space in which to learn, and I really credit that environment for helping me to have a successful learning experience (and an enjoyable time) in that class. (Fall 2014)

Motivational Displacement

To view the world through my preservice teachers' eyes, I needed to experience a motivational shift from a focus on myself to my students. By putting myself in their shoes, I was reminded of my struggles as a college student and what I would have appreciated my instructors doing to support my learning.

Making myself available to address preservice teachers' needs and questions was recognized as beneficial to their learning, as their course evaluations evidenced: "[She] was always available to help us in any way she could, including answering emails, meeting in office hours, and letting me borrow her books whenever I needed" (Spring 2015) and "She is a very busy woman who still makes you feel like she always has time for you and whatever help, questions, or input you may want from her" (Fall 2017). Holding high but realistic expectations and believing in preservice teachers' success was also perceived as a sign of care:

> [She] encourages students to do their best but doesn't make it too easy. She very obviously cares about her students, and holds them to a high standard, pushing them to do their absolute best, but reminding them that tests and grades are not the defining factor of a student. (Fall 2017)

Additionally, providing clear course organization and structure with appropriate scaffolding was connected to the preservice teachers' success: "Her course is designed to make you work hard but in a way that is manageable and orga-nized and will truly make you learn something" (Spring 2018). Holding high expectations without appropriate support could potentially discourage them from doing their best and therefore undermine the feeling of trust previously established.

The ways I enacted care pre-pandemic demonstrated that, for preservice tea-chers to trust me and develop a caring relationship, I needed to establish a com-munity of learners, listen to and believe in them, be available, and provide a clearly organized and scaffolded course to support their learning. My fear of not being valued or trusted by my preservice teachers due to my accent and country of origin was not substantiated. On the contrary, they appreciated my experiences as a language learner and educator, as echoed in this course evaluation: "I felt that she cared about me personally and was willing to let me learn from her own journey as an educator and language learner" (Spring 2015).

The Role of Care During the Pandemic

Due to the outbreak of COVID-19 during Spring 2020, JMU shifted courses online with minimal time to prepare, which caused tension for faculty, as many needed to simultaneously attend to their families with no childcare, elder care, or appropriate workspaces. Despite struggling with similar emotions as my preservice teachers and being apprehensive about these changes as mother of two K-12 students, daughter of elderly parents in Eastern Europe, and partner to a spouse who could not work from home, I attempted to learn about my preservice teachers' circumstances to address their immediate needs. Exercising cognitive reframing (Morin, 2020) enabled me to shift my focus from negative outcomes of the pandemic to more positive consequences, thus allowing me to address the teaching-learning process more rationally.

Later that year, as it became apparent that fall classes would resume in person without the availability of COVID vaccines, students and faculty alike, while excited to see one another in person, experienced anxiety and stress related to the opening of schools. Following health and safety guidelines (i.e., mandatory mask-wearing, no consumption of liquid or food in classroom), accommodating through the Hyflex mode of instruction (in which some preservice teachers came in person while others simultaneously attended online), and going back and forth between in-person and online teaching mandates took a toll on my ability to be an effective educator. Faculty in my college were also asked to teach additional classes while maintaining their research and service agendas, in addition to managing their personal circumstances. Having my children participate in remote learning from home full-time while trying to navigate changing teaching demands felt like a never-ending shift, which further contributed to feelings of stress and anxiety.

Engrossment

Despite having a community of learners established at the beginning of Spring 2020, it was necessary to re-establish it that semester due to the sudden shift to remote learning. Utilizing technological affordances, I aimed to rebuild our community, and preservice teachers believed I was successful in my efforts: "[She] worked so hard to create a safe learning community in our classroom and demonstrated exactly how to teach through her teaching" and "We did Flipgrid, peer review, and discussions for collaboration, so it still felt like we had a little classroom community" (Spring 2020).

Through surveys, I gathered that preservice teachers preferred asynchronous instruction due to the inequities of resources, such as the lack of reliable internet and electronic devices, textbooks, and study spaces. Moreover, the anxieties and uncertainties about COVID-19 made preservice teachers focus on safety and security, which caused me to first address Maslow's needs before Bloom's (Koubek, 2021). In addition to implementing asynchronous instruction, regular virtual office hours and individual check-ins with preservice teachers, through either WebEx or phone calls, became my standard practice. Learning about each preservice teacher's circumstances and checking in on them were fundamental aspects of enacting care in my courses, as was echoed in a preservice teacher's course evaluation:

> I also want to say that [she] went above and beyond to communicate with all her students after the COVID situation and set up personal WebEx conferences with each of her students to check in with them and get feedback on the transition to online. (Spring 2020)

Despite the changing demands during the 2020–2021 academic year, preservice teachers witnessed my attempts to mitigate their anxieties, stress, and uncertainties while providing structure, care, and advocacy. Utilizing one of the strategies from Spring 2020, I continued checking in with them the following semester: "[She] checked in on us pretty much every class. She would ask how we were doing/ feeling, and she would ask us to share any kind of positivity to lift our spirits during stressful and overwhelming times" (Fall 2020).

My commitment to preservice teachers and their needs was also demonstrated through multiple layers of formative feedback. Pre-pandemic, I provided feedback on final drafts of assignments instead of all drafts, as I did during COVID. Not only did preservice teachers notice this feedback, they appreciated it because it was timely, specific, and non-evaluative, which in turn helped them refine their misunderstandings prior to submitting their work for a final grade: "She went above and beyond to offer personalized and detailed feedback for every assignment, which really helped me to succeed in her class" and "She gave so much feedback and I know that took a lot of her time. All of the feedback was so helpful, and I appreciate that so much. [She] cares so much about her students and their learning" (Fall 2020). The pandemic has taught me that this type of feedback, albeit time-consuming, is essential for preservice teachers' growth. Furthermore, if we desire preservice teachers to provide effective feedback to their students, we need to model it for them, so they have sufficient time and practice to learn from it.

During Spring 2021, I attended a virtual TESOL convention where I learned about mindfulness practices to mitigate student anxiety (Zadina, 2021), which I began implementing in early April. At the beginning of each class, I would use four steps to bring preservice teachers' attention back and help them focus: (1) playing 60-beat instrumental music as students came to class; (2) exercising a 4–7–8 breathing technique six times; (3) breathing naturally for several minutes; and (4) writing up three private gratitude notes. Implementing mindfulness exercises is believed to instill predictability and help rewire the brain, which in turn could promote student learning and academic engagement (Zadina, 2021). Preservice teachers expressed their gratitude for making this a priority in each class, as one stated on a mindfulness survey: "It helped me reduce stress, especially if I was stressed before the class. It boosted my interest in the lesson more. I also felt that it gave me more cognitive flexibility" (Spring 2021). While new to mindfulness, I witnessed firsthand the benefits for preservice teachers and myself as we became more at ease when interacting with one another. Although not directly connected to content, preservice teachers valued these mindfulness practices because they assisted in lowering anxiety and staying focused.

Motivational Displacement

The pandemic taught me that, when educators genuinely believe in students, students can develop resiliency and a growth mindset. To shift focus from myself to my preservice teachers, I regularly affirmed them and their contributions: "She really cares about us and what she teaches. She told us on multiple occasions she was proud of us, and we don't usually hear that from professors" (Spring 2020). This affirmation, in turn, contributed to preservice teachers' increased engagement and achievement, as evidenced in the quality and quantity of peer feedback, submitted assignments, and collaborative work in and outside of class.

At the onset of COVID, when pivoting to remote asynchronous learning, I also focused on providing weekly schedules with objectives, tasks with deadlines, expected performance levels and assessment procedures, suggested preparation times, and locations for submitting assignments. Not only were these schedules posted in Canvas, our university learning management system, they were also sent to preservice teachers' emails. This type of organization and support helped to reduce preservice teachers' anxiety: "In the online section of the semester, I had more work in this class than other classes, but it was the least stressful because the schedule was so clearly defined" (Spring 2020).

Although I did not implement these schedules during the 2020–2021 academic year, I continued to provide scaffolding and support, including dividing a final project into manageable parts, which preservice teachers very much appreciated: "Because of the way she structured the course, it never really felt like anything overwhelming. The whole course was scaffolded to build up to our final projects" (Fall 2020). The ultimate sign of my care was my flexibility with deadlines and choices of assignments. Flexibility was necessary to maintain a positive learning environment and support preservice teachers' learning: "[She] was very supportive as always and was flexible and understanding when it came to outside factors that influenced classwork/attendance" and "[She] was very understanding about personal issues due to COVID" (Fall 2020).

As I reflected on my efforts to enact care during COVID, my preservice teachers' feedback highlighted their experiences with my efforts. Not only did it demonstrate their satisfaction with my attempts to support them in various ways, it also provided me with an indication of a mutually caring relationship. Reading this preservice teacher's course evaluation statement gave me hope that my efforts as an educator had not gone unnoticed: "She goes above and beyond for her students and knows how to truly care for them. She has really been a light in this year of darkness" (Spring 2021). As the year came to a close, emails and cards of gratitude from my preservice teachers left me proud of my students who will one day enact care with their own students.

The Role of Care Beyond the Pandemic

Over a decade ago, O'Connor (2008) warned that caring teaching has emotional implications and can be exhausting for educators; now, more than ever, educators' roles need to be reevaluated in light of our pandemic experiences. The general public has witnessed what educators did to change their instruction overnight after the outbreak of COVID-19. However, the commitments and sacrifices made to meet students' needs seemed to be shortly forgotten. As Jones and Kessler (2020) suggest, "It is time now to take a step back and reassess how mounting pressures have not attended to teachers' humanity" (p. 2).

Buckley-Marudas and Rose (2021) posit, "One of the most critical lessons to carry forward from teaching in this global health crisis is a renewed commitment to understanding and enacting education as a human endeavor" (para. 13). They further argue, "The quality and depth of relationships with students has surfaced as an essential element of teaching in the pandemic" (para. 13). Since the ethics of care approach is based on having a mutually caring relation between the carer and cared-for (Noddings, 2012)—in this case, teacher educators and preservice teachers—how this relation is developed and maintained in the post-pandemic world is yet to be seen (Buckley-Marudas & Rose, 2021). To move forward, Berry (2020) advocates that all stakeholders work together to "address the challenges they face and the innovations they seek" (p. 17).

As we move forward, I plan to continue "being engrossed" in my preservice teachers by learning about them as individuals with unique needs, interests, talents, and aspirations in order to establish and maintain a caring relationship. By exercising the motivational displacement (Noddings, 2012) that shifts focus from myself to my preservice teachers, I aim to validate their diverse identities and rich contributions while making meaningful connections to their lives and future profession. I will also continue to capitalize on successful strategies that have proven effective in my teaching, such as creating a community of learners, actively listening, providing formative feedback, scaffolding courses with clear organization, and fostering mindfulness practices.

However, I hyflex instruction is not a suitable option for properly enacting my caring teaching on a long-term basis. Students and educators need to be present in person to better address misunderstandings and questions. As Jones and Kessler (2020) argue, moving instruction online "hamper[ed] many teachers' capacities to each day realize their sense of self as mentor, helper, and nurturer of students" (p. 7), which was also supported by this preservice teacher's course evaluation: "This class being in–person with half the class coming online was very difficult. It was difficult to have discussions and to still feel in–person with the instructor when she also had to attend to students on Zoom" (Spring 2021).

Additionally, by tapping into the benefits of mindfulness practices, my hope is for my preservice teachers and me to employ a regimen of healthy strategies in our daily lives. By incorporating these practices in each class, I will hopefully help to establish a routine that preservice teachers can eventually apply in other settings. Emphasizing Maslow's before Bloom's needs, my ultimate sign of care is to help preservice teachers reduce their anxiety and increase their self-efficacy, which might in turn help to retain and sustain them in the teaching profession (Sainato, 2021).

Conclusion

In this chapter, I applied a self-reflective inquiry within action research to examine the role of care and its enactment in my TESOL courses during COVID-19 and how my preservice teachers perceived these practices. Noddings' (1984) characteristics of engrossment and motivational displacement were employed to analyze the values and practices carried out to enact care in my teaching. My inquiry revealed that my use of specific practices, such as creating a community of learners, actively listening to students, believing in student potential, providing formative feedback and appropriate scaffolding, clearly organizing the course, and fostering mindfulness practices, contributed to my preservice teachers' feelings of being cared for during the pandemic.

However, as Buckley-Marudas and Rose (2021) argue, "It is evident that the relational work of teaching and learning is something that must be prioritized in a postpandemic era" (para. 12). We will see how and to what extent teacher educators enact care to support the relational teaching and learning process in post-pandemic times. I believe caring has never before been more at the heart of education as during these unprecedented times. Utilizing Noddings' (2012) care ethics prioritizes the relationship between teachers and preservice teachers, with an ultimate goal of establishing mutually genuine caring relationships.

References

Berry, B. (2020). Teaching, learning, and caring in the post-COVID era. *Phi Delta Kappan*, *102*(1), 14–17.

Buckley-Marudas, M., & Rose, S. E. (2021). Collaboration, risk, and pedagogies of care: Looking to a postpandemic future. *The Journal of Interactive Technologies & Pedagogy, 19*.

Elliott, J. (1991). *Action research for educational change*. Open University Press.

James Madison University. (2021). *Facts and figures. Enrollment*. www.jmu.edu/about/fact-and-figures.shtml.

Goldstein, L. S., & Freedman, D. (2003). Challenges enacting caring teacher education. Journal of Teacher Education, *54*(5), 441–454.

Herget, A. (2016, August 18). Foreign-born faculty face challenges. *Higher Education Jobs*. www.higheredjobs.com/articles/articleDisplay.cfm?ID=1012.

Jones, A. L., & Kessler, M. A. (2020). Teachers' emotion and identity work during a pandemic. *Frontiers in Education, 5,* 1–9.

Kemmis, S., & McTaggart, R. (Eds.). (1988). *The action research reader* (3rd ed.). Deakin University Press.

Koubek, E. (2021). (Re)Imagining remote teaching and learning: Meeting students where they are. In J.Davis & C. Irish (Eds.), *Lessons from the pivot: Higher education's response to the pandemic* (pp. 56–62). Education Faculty Articles. https://scholar.umw.edu/education/11.

Leitch. R., & Day, C. (2000). Action research and reflective practice: Towards a holistic view. *Educational Action Research, 8*(1), 179–193.

Matthews, D. (2017, November 16). Fear of accented English. *Inside Higher Education*. www.insidehighered.com/news/2017/11/16/study-finds-student-distrust-those-who-are-not-native-speakers-english.

Merriam, S. B., & Tisdell, E. (2016). *Qualitative research* (4th ed.). John Wiley & Sons.

Morin, A. (2020, February 26). *Using cognitive reframing for mental health*. www.verywellmind.com/reframing-defined-2610419.

National Center for Educational Statistics. (2021). *Teacher characteristics and trends*. https://nces.ed.gov/fastfacts/display.asp?id=28.

Noddings, N. (1984). *Caring: A feminine approach to ethics and moral education*. University of California Press.

Noddings, N. (1994). Conversation as moral education. *Journal of Moral Education, 23*(2), 107–118.

Noddings, N. (2005). *The challenge to care in schools: An alternative approach to education*. (2nd ed.). Teachers College Press.

Noddings, N. (2012). The caring relation in teaching. *Oxford Review of Education, 38*(6), 771–781.

O'Connor, K. E. (2008). "You choose to care": Teachers, emotions and professional identity. *Teaching and Teacher Education, 24*(1), 117–126.

Sainato, M. (2021, October 4). 'Exhausted and underpaid': Teachers across the US are leaving their jobs in numbers. *The Guardian.* www.theguardian.com/world/2021/oct/04/teachers-quitting-jobs-covid-record-numbers.

Thayer-Bacon, B. J., & Bacon, C. S. (1996). Caring in the college/university classroom. *Educational Foundations, 10*(2), 53–72.

Zadina, J. N. (2021, March 26). *The pandemic brain: Science and strategies for optimal learning* [Keynote address]. TESOL2021 International Convention & English Language Expo, virtual.

9

BUILDING CARING COMMUNITIES IN MATH METHODS

COVID and Classrooms in Teacher Education

Jennifer A. Wolfe

Mathematics teacher educators continue to grapple with systemic issues of inequity, made hyper visible by the COVID-19 global pandemic and the long, painful history of racial unrest in the United States, and the move from face-to-face mathematics instruction to remote online learning brought these long-standing issues of equity, access, and inclusion to the forefront. As Aguirre et al. (2013) argue, "equity demands responsive accommodations be made as needed to promote equitable access, attainment and advancement in mathematics education for each student" (p. 9). As such, mathematics teacher educators' teaching practices needed to shift to *care for*, not just *care about*, preservice teachers (PST) in mathematics (Noddings, 2002; Venet, 2021) in order to co-create a sense of belongingness that is "fostered through authentic connections—seeing our students for who they are, their strengths, their challenges, and accepting and embracing both as we work with them and help them grow" (Horn, 2017, p. 29). We must ask ourselves, then, how to shift mathematics teacher preparation towards enacting caring practices that will foster the development of students' sense of belongingness. How do we cultivate collaborative learning environments that center on building authentic, caring relationships with and between students? As bell hooks (1994) contends, "Seeing the classroom as a communal place enhances the likelihood of collective effort in creating and sustaining a learning community" (p. 8) grounded in an ethic of care (Noddings, 2002), where "learning how to be cared for and learning how to care for others are central tasks of education" (Venet, 2021, p. 100).

In considering what we have learned about ourselves, our students, and our communities as we navigate the pandemic, we must consider how to build upon our learning in ways that center an ethic of care. In this chapter, I share practices for enacting care in mathematics teacher education courses during and "post"

DOI: 10.4324/9781003244875-12

COVID-19 centered on (1) building relationships and trust through identity exploration and positioning within and outside the classroom; and (2) co-creating communal spaces with a shared vision of collective responsibility for one another's learning. I begin by sharing my identities in relation to building caring communities. Next, I offer what guides my understanding of care and how my notions for enacting care shifted during and after the first year of COVID-19. Finally, I provide examples of my classroom practices for creating and sustaining caring learning environments.

A Piece of Me

I am a biracial Asian American female and mathematics education scholar. I am a first-generation college graduate, daughter of a Thai immigrant, and the oldest of three. Like many historically and presently excluded folx, I know how it feels to be pushed to the margins and silenced. I grew up in a rural town where I experienced otherness and racism that fueled my lack of self-confidence, leaving me untrusting of others. I clung to the myth of meritocracy: If I just worked harder, did more with less, I could survive, and maybe thrive. Lacking a sense of belongingness and navigating a systemically oppressive educational system that actively spirit-murders (Love, 2019) people of color has influenced my relationships, my views on my own capabilities, and my voice in advocating for myself and others. An unconditional positive regard for my humanity and a non-transactional ethic of care did not exist. While I might have had educators who cared *about* me, I did not feel cared *for*.

So, as a kid, I sought refuge in the world of mathematics. I loved solving puzzles, developing patterns, and getting lost in a place where I did not have to defend my existence. Within the mathematics classroom, however, processes and paths of knowing were narrow, with no room for collaboration and exploration. The idea of developing positive mathematics identities and cultivating a sense of care, belongingness, and collective responsibility were nonexistent. These experiences drive my work as a mathematics teacher educator to enact care and collaboration to change the narrative of mathematics learning. I want to co-construct a learning environment where we can experience love, joy, healing, vulnerability, and care (Wolfe, 2021). I am an educator-in-progress, and through purposeful reflection and community care, I seek to grow in my teaching practices.

Positive Mathematics Identity

Identities are the ways we see ourselves and how we see ourselves in relation to others; they can "…emerge in the form of *stories* that announce to the world who we think we are, who we want to become, or who we are not" (Aguirre et al., 2013, p. 14). Our identities are not fixed; they are fluid and influenced by our teachers, peers, mentors, guardians, chosen family, society, and personal choices. Mathematics identity can be defined as

> the dispositions and deeply held beliefs that students develop about their ability to participate and perform effectively in mathematical contexts and to use mathematics in powerful ways across contexts of their lives...a key consideration about mathematics identities is that they are strongly connected with the other identities that students construct and view as important in their lives, including their racial, gender, language, cultural, ethnic, family, faith, and academic identities. (Aguirre et al., 2013, p. 14)

Thus, to work towards building positive mathematics identities and collective care for one another's learning, we must examine how our identities are positioned both within and outside the classroom. As Gutiérrez (2013) argues, "All math teachers are 'identity workers', regardless of whether they consider themselves as such or not" (p. 11). Students' identities make up who they are and if those identities aren't cared for and validated in the classroom space, their participation in a collective effort to learn mathematics will be impacted. To care for one another, we need to examine privilege, oppression, intersectional identities, and interrogate the work we do in mathematics classrooms that undermine collective efforts to dismantle systems that spirit-murder (Love, 2019) historically and presently excluded and marginalized groups. As Jewell (2020) contends,

> Knowing who we are, where we hold agency, how our identities come to be, and how they determine our roles in society helps us to understand ourselves and how we can change a system where some folx have privilege and power, and some folx are under-resourced and oppressed to one where we are all liberated. (p. 22)

To better understand how our preservice teachers show up to our classrooms, we have to work together to unpack how our identities impact the way we come to think about who can do mathematics and what it means to do mathematics. We have to examine our own identities and share our stories of who we are and how we came to be. Thus, a critical component to building positive mathematics identities is through active non-judgmental listening. As Jansen (2020) argues, "Really hearing our students not only helps them learn but also makes them feel valued as people...Listening to our students is not only productive for their learning but also powerful for developing their identities as learners" (p. 17). When we listen to our students with curiosity rather than judgment, we are saying you matter, your multiple intersectional identities matter, and what you share in our community matters. Through listening and taking collective action to build identity-affirming classrooms, we are engaging in unconditional positive regard and care for one another's mathematics learning.

Unconditional Positive Regard

Much of my work during the pandemic has been shaped by Venet's (2021) equity-centered trauma-informed education. She describes *unconditional positive regard*—a term coined by the psychologist Carl R. Rogers—as being in relationship with students where she *cares for* them, not just *cares about* them. She contends that the message of unconditional positive regard is one of "I care about you. You have value. You don't have to do anything to prove it to me, and nothing's going to change my mind" (p. 98). As Venet (2021) explains,

> Caring *for* students means being in relationship with them, whereas caring *about* students allows us to keep our distance. If we commit to an ethic of care, building relationships and caring for our students aren't strategies in the name of increasing academic achievement but the actual goal itself. (p. 100)

During and "post" COVID-19, my notions of care shifted in response to the inequities and trauma experienced by PSTs. I began to see more clearly how academia and society were responding to the pandemic in dehumanizing ways that perpetuated patterns of violent invisibility (Jessup et al., 2021) and video-classism (Jackson, 2020). I learned to take a moment to pause, breathe, and extend grace and patience to myself and others and became more transparent and trusting of others and my PSTs. I shifted my practices to ground my teaching values in care and held space for my PSTs to unpack events that might have caused harm. These priorities were constructed through an ethic of care (Noddings, 2002) and an unconditional positive regard (Venet, 2021) for engaging PSTs in communal mathematics learning. Collective responsibility and care are critical for opening up identity-affirming spaces where PSTs feel empowered to bring their whole selves to the classroom.

Many of my PSTs shared how mathematics professors in other courses and/or mentor teachers in field placements were controlling students' bodies in the virtual classroom by requiring cameras to be on and raised virtual hands to be called upon while privatizing the chat feature to deny student-to-student interactions. In contrast, I centered an ethic of care through co-creation of community agreements for interactions with my PSTs shaped by a lens of unconditional positive regard and caring. I now begin my methods courses by co-creating community agreements with PSTs to establish how we can best learn together. These agreements are intended to build both personal and community accountability in caring for another's learning.

In co-creating community agreements, teacher educators are explicitly stating that we trust PSTs to know how they learn best. We are sending the message that we are in a collective effort of caring *for* one another, not just *about* one another, because this is *our* learning community. Caring for PSTs means that teacher educators open up space for them to take collective ownership in community learning, becoming invested in developing and shaping identity affirming strengths-based learning spaces where we hold one another accountable for each other's learning. This caring requires shifting our practices towards shared authority and power in learning spaces and co-constructing community agreements for interactions so that all voices have space to be shared, valued, and honored. As O'Connor (2021) states, "The process of building community agreements communicates to students that even if we've just met, I trust them to know themselves best—as learners, as people, and as participants in the space where we will treat each other with dignity" (para 3). The process of co-constructing community agreements is an actionable, intentional shift of power towards dismantling hierarchies of who gets cared for.

Enacting Unconditional Positive Regard in Math Methods

In 2020, I taught a secondary mathematics methods course for PSTs the semester before their student teaching. Most of my PSTs were full-time students, new to online learning, taking both synchronous and asynchronous courses, and navigating multiple new platforms. Some had reliable internet access; others did not. Some were working multiple jobs while simultaneously caring for loved ones, grieving for those who had passed, navigating isolation from in-person contact, processing traumatic events, and engaging in movements to fight anti-Black racism, all while facing the uncertainty of when and if we would experience an end to the pandemic.

The distinction between caring for and about PSTs guided the pedagogical and relational shifts I made in my teaching during COVID-19; below, I describe several instructional practices I found helpful in cultivating this shared responsibility for care. We learn mathematics through actively participating in a community effort for thinking, creating, and connecting mathematical ideas. For collaborative groups to function, there must be a collective view that everyone has something to contribute and a strength to offer. PSTs must care for each other, be invested in one another's learning, and recognize that our collective efforts and caring for one another's ideas lead to richer learning for all.

Flipgrid Introductions

Before the semester, I sent out a Flipgrid video sharing a bit about myself, an email describing my commitment to unconditional positive regard and support for students, and a survey to identify accessibility to resources and needed supports for online learning. I sought to build relationships and trust with my PSTs by creating a space where they felt they could advocate for their needs while making a commitment to them and their well-being by conveying, "I care about you." This approach can be viewed as resistance toward an academic system that often puts content before students and where unconditional positive regard is rarely put into action.

After the first day of class, I asked students to record a Flipgrid video introducing themselves, modeled on an activity described by de Araujo (2018), in which they read an excerpt and watched an embedded video from her blog. Since our names are part of our identity, I ask them to include their first, last, and preferred names and invite them to share their pronouns. I then ask them to respond to two questions: (1) What do you know enough about that everyone else in the class, including the instructor, could learn from you? (2) What are three things you hope to learn in this course? They record their Flipgrid video and then respond to at least two peers that they have not yet met. I encouraged PSTs to use the sentence stems from the *learning to listen and listening to learn* protocol (Burkhalter et al., 2020; Jansen, 2020; Wolfe, 2021) in their responses. I then watched the videos, taking notes on what each PST shared in preparation for my one-to-one chats. In doing so, I am actively caring for my PSTs by reflecting upon their identities; I am also able to capitalize on unplanned classroom moments where I am able to explicitly build upon what they share in their videos.

Digital Storytelling

Next, PSTs engaged in a digital storytelling assignment (Chao, 2014) by creating a Google Slide (filled with images, photographs, texts, gifs, and memes) that best represented their identities and experiences learning mathematics. I shared my own digital storytelling Google slide (Wolfe, 2021) since sharing is an act of care and vulnerability that humanizes our learning spaces. Teaching is a listening profession (Hintz et al., 2018; Jansen, 2020) so after PSTs created their stories, they engage in a *learning to listen and listening to learn* protocol (Burkhalter et al., 2020; Jansen, 2020; Wolfe, 2021), the purpose of which is to create a space to become better at listening, talking in depth, and building community. The guidelines for the protocol are as follows:

1. Each PST is given equal time to talk (three minutes).
2. The listeners do not interpret, paraphrase, analyze, give advice, or break in with a personal story.
3. After the timer goes off, each listener has two minutes to speak that begins by thanking their peer (by name) for sharing their story.
4. The listener uses the following sentence stems to communicate what they heard their peer share and what they learned from listening: "What I heard you share was…" and "When you shared…it made me think about…"

Before PSTs shared their stories, I explained that storytelling can bring up very vulnerable and personal spaces. "I asked them to consider what they can learn about their peers' identities and the ways in which their peers represent themselves as mathematicians in their digital stories, since by sharing our stories, we can begin to build a caring mathematics learning community." In listening without judge-ment, PSTs can begin to see the humanity in one another and the ways their identities have been shaped and influenced within and outside the mathematics classroom, which supports collective movement towards caring for one another.

Identity Maps

PSTs next created identity maps. They were provided with a piece of paper with a circle in the center and invited to write in their name and pronouns. They then drew line segments to other circles where they would fill in identity markers, reflecting upon everything they could think of that makes them who they are (e.g., race, gender, language, ethnicity, sexuality, spirituality, citizenship, and other identities; Jewell, 2020). Once PSTs created their maps, we engaged in conversation through the following prompts (Jewell, 2020; Kleinrock, 2021):

- Are there parts of you that hold power and privilege within your community?
- Which identity markers are the most important to you?
- Which identity markers were the most validated by your teachers and schools?
- What do you notice about the two groups?

By focusing on identity work through an ethic of care, I was able to "reflect upon the ways in which I see and value my students in class, as well as where I might hold biases or preferences, and how I can become more aware in order to dismantle them" (Kleinrock, 2021, p. 4).

One-on-One Chats

After PSTs shared their digital stories and identity maps with one another, I had them sign up for a one-on-one Zoom chat with me. I started our chat by asking how they were doing, mentioned something they shared in their Flipgrid intro-duction videos, and found ways to connect it to a shared experience. I invited them to discuss their digital storytelling slide and asked about their interests, past experiences learning mathematics, and hopes for the class. Finally, I asked if there was anything they would like to share to help me best support them. I kept a live Google doc that I revisited periodically as I learned more about each PST.

Through these activities, I was better positioned to enact care for my PSTs. The surveys, digital stories, Flipgrid videos, identity maps, and one-on-one chats allowed me to consider what I had learned about each of their identities, how they represented themselves as mathematical thinkers and doers, and what impli-cit biases I needed to break in order to find, name, and leverage PSTs' strengths for learning mathematics. My answers helped me engage in active caring for PSTs as we transitioned into "post-pandemic" learning.

Community Agreements

In the methods class, I co-constructed community agreements with PSTs to build both personal and community accountability for one another's learning. I asked a series of questions that focused on what the PSTs needed to feel heard, cared for, and safe in our classroom. I de-identified all responses, compiled them anonymously into a single Google doc, and had PSTs look for common themes. They then worked in pairs to unpack and describe these themes before group discussions focused on what the themes meant and what they might look and sound like in the classroom. For example, PSTs noticed the theme of "care about one another's ideas," so we talked about the meaning of caring and worked together to provide explicit examples of what caring about one another's ideas would sound like and look like in our classroom.

Through co-construction, I made transparent my commitment to caring for their learning by providing classroom time and space for PSTs to express what they needed to feel cared for. Caring for PSTs meant that I opened up space for them to take collective ownership in our community learning. We became invested in co-developing and shaping identity affirming strengths-based learning spaces (Kobett & Karp, 2020; Seda & Brown, 2021). I sent the message of a collective effort for caring for one another, not just about one another, and this was not my learning community but ours.

I now begin all of my math methods courses with co-creating community agreements to establish how we can collectively learn together. Such co-constructed agreements are one way teacher educators can engage in equitable teaching practices and, in doing so, model intentionally shifting power, resources, and influence in the classroom to students who are historically and presently excluded and/or marginalized (Learning for Justice, 2016).

Supporting the Mathematics Learner

Torres' Rights of the Learner (2021) was developed with the vision of a democratic classroom empowering students to take collective responsibility for communal learning. These rights are foundational and reinforce that learning is not linear. While these rights have been interpreted, described, and adopted by others (e.g., Jansen, 2020; Kalinec-Craig, 2017), I integrated the following rights of the learner in my methods courses:

- the right to be confused
- the right to claim and make mistakes
- the right to only say (or write) what makes sense to you
- the right to revise your thinking
- the right to share your unfinished thinking and not be judged

Mathematics is a subject that carries with it high status in our society. Students who are "good" at math are often positioned and perceived by their peers as more competent. However, notions of what constitutes being "good" at math are usually narrowly focused on speed and efficient use of procedures and less about conceptual understanding. By taking up the rights of the learner in our class-rooms, we experienced mathematics learning as a process, not just a product. We learned mathematics through sharing our unfinished thinking and approaching one another's ideas with curiosity, not judgement. I chose to integrate the rights of the learner into math methods to promote more democratic ways of mathe-matics learning that also provide access and opportunity to build upon one another's rough draft thinking.

I also integrated Jansen's (2020) work on rough draft math as a form of equity pedagogy and care for PSTs. By tagging our mathematical ideas as rough drafts, my PSTs felt safer in taking risks to share their in-progress thoughts and were more receptive to listening to others' ideas:

> If we invite rough draft thinking, we are likely to have more opportunities to disrupt students' assumptions about who is an is not good at math. We can point out many more ways of being smart in math, like posing a helpful question, and more students can see mathematical strengths in their peers and in themselves. (Jansen, 2020, pp. 15–16)

Rough draft talk helps PSTs see the power in collectively encouraging and caring about one another's ideas, shifting the mathematics learning culture from one of performing to one of communicating. Engaging in rough draft math honors and centers the power of learning through both reflection and revision. My PSTs observed that revising their work led to greater understanding and increased comfort in sharing their in-progress thinking with their peers. They appreciated feedback on their work that was grounded in what they were able to do as a starting point for revision, rather than the often deficit views they experienced that focused on what they got wrong. By taking up these rights and holding one another accountable, we created and sustained a community effort for engaging in mathematics thinking and learning for all.

Conclusion

As we consider math education practices and priorities for enacting care post-pandemic, I am reminded of Khodai's (2021) quote on social emotional learning in mathematics education: "Belonging is not bestowed, it is created. Safety is not guaranteed, it is negotiated" (p. 556). Prior to the pandemic, my enactment of care was focused more on caring about my PSTs than caring for them. I didn't fully understand the distinction until faced with a pandemic that demanded more of me and my PSTs. To enact care, I had to interrogate, problematize, and revise my current practices and policies. I had to rethink what it meant to be in relationship with—to truly know—my PSTs and approach every teaching decision and interaction with PSTs from a position of unconditional positive regard for their whole being, their identities. Through an ethic of care and unconditional positive regard, I enacted and modified the activities shared in this chapter (e.g., Flipgrid introductions, digital storytelling, identity maps, one-on-one chats, and co-constructed community agreements) to better position myself to center and build upon PSTs' identities and create more identity affirming and liberatory mathematics learning spaces. My hope is that, in sharing these priorities and providing these activities, mathematics teacher educators can begin to shift their teaching practices in "post-pandemic" teacher education to center care and unconditional positive regard to care for and empower their PSTs.

References

Aguirre, J., Mayfield-Ingram, K., & Martin, D. (2013). *The impact of identity in K-8 mathematics: Rethinking equity-based practices*. National Council of Teachers of Mathematics.

Burkhalter, K., Blackburn, S., & Brown, V. (2020, August 4). *Let's Talk* [Webinar]. Learning for Justice. www.learningforjustice.org.

Chao, T. (2014). Photo-elicitation/Photovoice interviews to study mathematics teacher identity. In J. J. Lo, K. Leatham, & L. Van Zoest (Eds.), *Research trends in mathematics teacher education* (pp. 93–113). Springer.

de Araujo, Z. (2018, August 9). 180 Ideas #7: See them say it. Mathematical Educated. https://mathematicallyeducated.com/2018/08/09/180-ideas-7-see-them-say-it.

Gutiérrez, R. (2013). Why urban mathematics teachers need political knowledge. *Journal of Urban Mathematics Education*, *6*(2), 7–19.

Hintz, A., Tyson, K., & English, A. R. (2018). Actualizing the rights of the learner: The role of pedagogical listening. *Democracy and Education*, *26*(2), 1–10.

hooks, b. (1994). *Teaching to transgress*. Routledge.

Horn, I. (2017). *Motivated: Designing math classrooms where students want to join in*. Heinemann Publications.

Jackson, T. (2020, March 27). *COVID-19 and videoclassism: Implicit bias, videojudgment, and why I'm terrified to have you look over my shoulder* [Post]. LinkedIn. www.linkedin.com/pulse/covid-19-videoclassism-implicit-bias-videojudgment-why-jackson.

Jansen, A. (2020). *Rough draft math: Revising to learn*. Stenhouse.

Jewell, T. (2020). *This book is anti-racist: 20 lessons on how to wake up, take action, and do the work*. Francis Lincoln.

Jessup, N., Wolfe, J. A., & Kalinec-Craig, C. (2021). Rehumanizing mathematics education and building community for online learning. In K.Hollebrands, R.Anderson, & K. Oliver (Eds.), *Online learning in mathematics education* (pp. 95–113). Springer.

Kalinec-Craig, C. A. (2017). The rights of the learner: A framework for promoting equity through formative assessment in mathematics education. *Democracy and Education*, *25*(2), Article 5.

Khodai, H. (2021). Belonging through social emotional learning. *Mathematics Teacher: Learning and Teaching PK-12*, *114*(7), 556–558.

Kleinrock, L. (2021). *Start here start now: A guide to antibias and antiracist work in your school community*. Heinemann.

Kobett, B. M., & Karp, K. S. (2020). *Strengths-Based teaching and learning in mathematics: 5 teaching turnarounds for grades K-6*. Corwin.

Learning for Justice (2016). Critical practices for anti-bias education. www.learningforjustice.org/frameworks/critical-practices.

Love, B. (2019). *We want to do more than survive: Abolitionist teaching and the pursuit of educational freedom*. Beacon Press.

Noddings, N. (2002). *Educating moral people: A caring alternative to character education*. Teachers College Press.

O'Connor, C. (2021). Using community agreements to start the year strong. Edutopia. www.edutopia.org/article/using-community-agreements-start-year-strong.

Seda, P., & Brown, K. (2021). *Choosing to see: A framework for equity in the math classroom*. Dave Burgess Consulting, LLC.

Torres, O. (2020, August 13). Equity in education series-rehumanizing schools: Rights of the learner. [Webinar]. Todos Live! https://vimeo.com/447665338.

Venet, A. S. (2021). *Equity-centered trauma-informed education*. W. W. Norton & Company.

Wolfe, J. A. (2021). A journey in becoming. *Mathematics Teacher: Learning and Teaching PK-12, 114*(3), 258–261.

10

MODELING CARE AND COMPASSION FOR STUDENT TEACHERS DURING AND AFTER COVID

MinSoo Kim-Dossard, Lauren Madden, Stuart Carroll, Louise Ammentorp, and Tamara Tallman

The COVID-19 pandemic created an upheaval in the field of education. Many practicing teachers left the profession because of concerns over their own safety (e.g., Will et al., 2020) or because they were not interested in teaching remotely (e.g., Reilly, 2020). "The whole idea of being remote and disconnected was equally daunting as the fear of not being safe," said a teacher quoted in *Time* magazine (Reilly, 2020). Even prior to the pandemic, a report entitled *Teacher Stress and Health Effects on Teachers, Students, and Schools* (Greenberg et al., 2016) stated that teaching is one of the most stressful occupations in the United States. This report outlined findings on the negative impact teacher stress has on students' social adjustment and academic performance, while finding that mentoring, workplace wellness, social emotional learning, and mindfulness programs improve teacher well-being and student outcomes.

Over the past 20 years, the field of teacher education has focused on issues of accountability, certification, and accreditation. However, as Rogers and Webb (1991) emphasize, "To develop caring teachers, teacher educators must model caring relationships with preservice students" (p. 178). The reality of the pandemic required the prioritization of care and social emotional learning (SEL). The importance of SEL for teachers is often underestimated. As Jones et al. (2013) point out,

> In the current national focus on teacher quality, the essential role of teachers' social and emotional competencies is often overlooked. But ask educators when they need those competencies and they'll likely respond "every day"… Social and emotional competencies influence everything from teacher-student relationships to classroom management to effective instruction to teacher burnout. (p. 1)

DOI: 10.4324/9781003244875-13

In particular, student teachers completing the last phase of their preparation program sit in a vulnerable and unique position, even in the absence of a pandemic and its disruptions to school systems. As Delamarter and Ewart (2020) observed, "For many of our candidates, the normal fears and anxieties that surround student teaching have been magnified to the point that even our most promising student teachers feel overwhelmed and panicked" (p. 1). Student teachers are teaching and learning in uncharted waters, navigating in person, hybrid, and virtual settings that did not exist prior to March 2020.

Student teachers need to develop SEL-related skills and strategies for themselves and for the students they will be teaching in their future post-pandemic classrooms. Through the purposeful integration of a care approach in their program, student teachers learn the value of self-care and the importance of creating environments for their students to develop socially and emotionally. A caring relationship between teachers and students is established through teachers accepting and acknowledging student experiences, prioritizing and committing to meeting student needs, and recognizing what motivates and matters to students (Noddings, 1984, 1992, 1996; Owens & Ennis, 2005). Not only does this provide a strong foundation for learning, it also functions as an impetus for promoting a classroom culture where students value themselves and others. Grounded in Noddings' (1984) notion of the ethic of care, which argues that caring must serve as the core of the education system, we perceive student teachers as situated in a unique position. They provide care to their students and, simultaneously, they are cared for by their mentor teachers and college faculty.

In this chapter, we reflect on the ways in which we modeled and implemented a care-based approach to supporting student teachers during the 2020–21 academic year. The author team consists of faculty members in a small public college in New Jersey. We each taught sections of the senior capstone course for elementary and early childhood student teachers. Our instructor team represented varied disciplinary backgrounds, experiences, and approaches in our planning, instruction, assessment, and adjustment of the course. The team's combined experience allowed us to meet our students where they needed us. Having each worked with the students prior in other capacities (e.g., academic advising, teaching methods courses), we were able to home in on students' specific needs and build community quickly.

Although our department typically uses a collaborative approach to planning and teaching the capstone course, given the unique context of the 2020–21 academic year, we purposefully structured and planned the course to allow for regular instructor team meetings for our collective reflection, revision, and idea sharing. The process of reflecting on our teaching was iterative: Individuals reflected personally (through internal thoughts or written teaching journals) then collaboratively with the instructor team through regular planning meetings. As we were navigating uncertain terrain ourselves while planning and teaching the course, this individual and collective reflection provided us with opportunities to examine our assumptions, expectations, and priorities during the pandemic.

The course typically includes topics such as connecting theories to practice, assessment, communication with families, and reflective practice. However, the pandemic transformed the course, bringing care to the forefront of our work with students. By prioritizing the mental health and wellbeing of our students, we used a care-based approach to make purposeful changes to our course. The three themes examined in this chapter reflect the significant changes that took place over the course of the academic year: (1) changes to the curriculum and course assignments; (2) building relationships with, and among, students; and (3) supporting student advocacy. Our reflections are included to explain the ways care shaped our work.

Changes to the Curriculum and Course Assignments

The senior capstone course focuses on opportunities for student teachers to reflect on their student teaching experience and prepare themselves for the next chapter after graduation as inservice teachers. Throughout the semester, there are various assignments deliberately designed for these purposes, including an interview portfolio, "musings," and a family engagement project. The content of the course is front-loaded, with a two-day boot camp followed by bi-weekly meetings for the remainder of the semester. These class meetings are divided into whole group activities, including guest lectures or logistical information for course assignments or the licensure process, and meetings of individual sections. The course setup purposefully allows student teachers to reflect in small and large groups to maximize the opportunity to share ideas and offer advice to peers in similar situations.

The team of instructors modified the course assignments in preparation for (and during) the 2020–21 academic year. For example, we significantly adapted assignment requirements so that student teachers could focus on emerging needs in their field experiences and dedicate more time and energy to planning effective lessons and addressing the needs of students in their classroom. Some student teachers experienced multiple changes in the mode of instruction (e.g., going back and forth between online and hybrid) due to exposure to COVID-19 and periodic, unplanned deep cleaning at their schools, while some school districts did not permit student teachers to teach in person in an effort to limit the number of people coming into the school building. All of these factors demanded flexibility, resourcefulness and responsiveness by the student teachers. The capstone team, in turn, prioritized meeting the needs of student teachers to provide as much support as possible.

We also modified the schedule and structure of class meetings in the Fall 2020 semester. In place of the two day in-person boot camp, we offered shorter whole group and individual section meetings synchronously over Zoom along with asynchronous activities to complete outside of scheduled class time. We found that the every-other-week class meeting schedule wasn't quite enough support for many of our student teachers. Yet, we also needed to find a balance between frequency and duration of class meetings. Many student teachers spent an entire six- to seven-hour school day logged into video conferencing software with their classes (sometimes while simultaneously teaching in-person children), and a three-hour class meeting in the evening was simply too much. So, we purposefully limited our synchronous meetings to 60–90 minutes. Instead of a three hour class, we increased the frequency of the meetings and varied the structure.

For example, in each of our sections, we offered extended office hours, "drop-in" meeting times, and optional small-group sessions during the non-class weeks where faculty and students could troubleshoot teaching dilemmas, offer academic support, or simply serve as sounding boards. We found that groups of three student teachers allowed for personalized conversation without putting students on the spot. We also provided opportunities for both required and optional individual check-in meetings to discuss successes and concerns; this allowed for tailored support based on students' unique circumstances. Regardless of format, the student teachers appreciated these sessions and attended many of them. This flexibility in the meeting format is a key takeaway as we move forward. We realize we can better differentiate our support of student teachers by providing options for how we meet with them, so we will continue to offer online conferencing, which is also extremely helpful for those who commute longer distances.

In addition to adapting the structure of the course, we revised our assignment expectations. For example, we modified one of the signature assignments for the course, the family engagement project, to correspond to the evolving circumstances in and outside of student homes. In typical semesters, the project requires student teachers to learn more about their classroom and local communities, identify an existing need, set goals, plan a project that includes all families, implement it by facilitating on-going communication between school and families, and assess the effectiveness of the project. COVID-19 eliminated various ways that families participated in their children's learning, such as attending events like back-to-school nights. We were also aware of the stress the pandemic put on families as they juggled working from home, managing multiple children learning virtually, and/or addressing emerging needs related to the pandemic, such as ill family members or job losses. Young children, in particular, required more guidance through various virtual learning platforms and tools. The capstone team revised the assignment to highlight the most salient aspects: identifying a family engagement related problem or concern in the classroom, designing a project with practical and deliberate steps, and reflecting on the implementation of the project. While the assignment was previously graded based on various elements, like the number of participants and the multiple methods student teachers utilized to reach family members, the limiting factors during the pandemic led us to consider successful implementation of the project differently.

We guided student teachers to use the family engagement project as an opportunity to get to know their students and their family members, incorporate ways for family members to participate virtually in synchronous and/or asynchronous ways (e.g., uploading videos on Flipgrid) and/or maximize any contact they had with families, including virtual parent-teacher conferences and supply pick up/drop off events. The turn-out rate varied greatly from classroom to classroom, however, the project resulted in quality conversations with family members, creative solutions for the limitations the pandemic imposed on technology, and in-depth reflections that served as the foundation for implementing the family engagement projects effectively in various circumstances. Moving forward, we will highlight the importance of engaging families where they are and using online resources and formats to better support families.

The challenges COVID-19 imposed on student teachers and the team of capstone instructors led us to consider different ways to format in-class discussion-based course assignments, as well. For example, our "musing" assignment provides time and space for student teachers to present an issue or concern from their classroom and solicit suggestions and feedback from the rest of the class. During the pandemic, the musings became repetitive; many of the shared concerns traced back to pandemic-related circumstances no one had any control over. Additionally, a similar group of student teachers frequently voiced their input in response to peers' musings during our synchronous virtual class sessions. To energize the discussions, we decided to create a discussion board where presenters would create a short video elaborating on specific issues and ask the rest of the class to respond to the video asynchronously by providing comments. This unplanned change allowed more student teachers to give and receive individualized feedback and enabled them to pace themselves after long hours of teaching online. The pandemic reminded us that, just as we encourage flexibility in our students, we as teacher educators need to continuously adapt our instruction and assignments to meet the needs of our students. The purposeful integration of technology, such as Flipgrid and online discussions, is something that will augment our practice post-pandemic.

In addition to the adaptations and revisions of existing course assignments, we developed instruction and workshops on mindfulness, mental health, and support for children's SEL and development. We included resources (e.g., readings, videos, websites) by experts in these areas and guest lectures from practicing teachers experiencing the changes in the COVID-19 era educational landscape. We discussed the CASEL (Collaborative for Academic, Social, and Emotional Learning) Framework and how it relates to their students and themselves (Schonert-Reichl et al., 2017). Student teachers also learned about the Substitution, Augmentation, Modification, and Redefinition, or SAMR (Fastiggi, 2019), model so they could make informed decisions regarding the different ways technologies can enhance teaching and learning experiences. Lastly, we shared lessons, activities, and resources that worked in hybrid and remote settings, which were then shared by pre- and inservice teachers who had to quickly adapt to the sudden, unexpected changes caused by the pandemic.

Building Relationships With and Among Student Teachers

We realized early on in the academic year that we had to center care and relationships in our course. Noddings (2013) notes that care is essential in relationships: "If we want to produce people who will care for another, then it makes sense to give students practice in caring and reflection on that practice" (p. 191). The challenges that emerged during the pandemic often meant that the needs of teachers, including student teachers, and their students were not fully met (Cristol & Gimbert, 2021; Gueldner et al., 2020). We recognized that creating a community of care was necessary for the well-being of our students and ourselves. Coming together as a team to discuss our experiences made everyone feel less isolated while providing a place to work through challenges.

As an instructor team, we made deliberate efforts to support the mental health and well-being of our student teachers. For example, we had them create personal mental health plans with check-ins on one another's progress, choosing from a list of options. They then shared their progress and commitment (e.g., "I went for a walk every day this week after school") and supported each other in finding opportunities for rest and reflection. We began to start classes with various check-in questions (e.g., What would you tell yourself today, if you were your own best friend? What are your "rose" and "thorn" for today?), sharing of a self-care/compassion plan and reflection (e.g., fun activity, meal plan, relaxation strategy), and/or various visuals (e.g., an emoji rating scale, memes) to engage student teachers in conversations and encourage them to decompress after a demanding day. Through this process, they expressed empathy for one another, which provided a solid foundation for building relationships and supporting each other throughout the challenging semester. We also included more SEL-inspired community building activities led by the student teachers, serving the dual purpose of building relationships among their classmates while providing the opportunity to share activities and resources for their own classrooms. Lastly, we incorporated "social" gatherings as part of the course, setting up get-togethers over Zoom for student teachers to listen to music and chat with each other, completely outside of class time and devoid of the instructor. This offered time to simply be with one another and decompress.

After intentionally incorporating more care-based learning into our instruction, we noticed a notable shift in the types of interactions student teachers had during synchronous class meetings. For example, we noticed they developed a loving-kindness approach in their comments, as evidenced by compassionate comments and descriptions of one another's character and contributions. After one student teacher would share, others would compliment them with specific and detailed praise, both about the comment itself (e.g., What a creative way to engage your students with physical activity at home!) and about the speaker (e.g., You are always so thoughtful to others.). By the end of the semester, in one section, the student teachers often called one another King or Queen in a way that initially felt silly but later felt like a true appreciation of one another.

This positive support system impacted their attitude towards student teaching. We saw this in our musings activity. In the beginning of the semester, some student teachers discussed their frustration regarding the lack of participation from many of their students and the apathy which they perceived from their students and families. Over the course of the semester, their mindsets began to shift as they realized they needed to be flexible and caring towards their students and their families and creative in their instruction. They began to see student difficulties as an opportunity to refine and improve communications, to adhere to expectations and keep students accountable, and to help maintain forward progress.

As they practiced self-care, they also encouraged their students to do the same, just as we had done for them. Many of them led mindfulness and other SEL activities with their students, such as mini-yoga sessions and guest speakers on self-care and self-management. Our student teachers positively influenced student engagement and intellectual curiosity through their active interest and passion for teaching, just as we did for them. This is perhaps one of the greatest lessons from our experience. As we put care in the forefront of our teaching, so did our student teachers, ensuring that we will embrace this a care-based approach post-pandemic.

Supporting Student Advocacy

During the student teaching semester, student teachers in New Jersey are required to complete the edTPA performance assessment. Even during non-pandemic times, many consider the edTPA a subtractive experience that reduces the quality of student teaching (Clayton, 2018). Test requirements are onerous and confusing, and even with support, students struggle to interpret its multiple demands (Paugh et al., 2018). The value of the edTPA has been called into question by external psychometric analyses revealing that the exam is neither reliable nor valid (Gitomer et al., 2021).

The edTPA requires student teachers to demonstrate deep knowledge of their students' prior knowledge and cultures, in part by creating a videotape of classroom teaching that satisfies a wide range of rubric requirements. It is difficult to satisfy edTPA demands as a student teacher in someone else's classroom in a "regular" semester; it becomes near impossible when that classroom is virtual, hybrid, or a mix of modalities during a pandemic semester. In some cases, student teachers were at home, virtually teaching children who were "live" in a classroom, something that the creators of edTPA had never contemplated.

In Spring 2020, our state waived the edTPA requirement for certification and indicated that this waiver would hold through the duration of the public health emergency. Then policies shifted, and the guidance around the testing requirement changed, with "flexibility" based on individual circumstances replacing the blanket waiver. The state's final position on this was not revealed until late November (with student teaching ending in early December), so uncertainty about the exam loomed over the entire semester. Our response as capstone instructors was to encourage our student teachers to apply for flexibility waivers, even though there were concerns that other colleges were pushing student teachers to complete the remote learning version of the edTPA promoted as an acceptable substitute. Instructors received only one hour of training on taking the test in a virtual learning environment, and we were convinced that it was wholly inappropriate as an assessment of teaching or certification requirement. The lack of timely guidance by the state added to the tremendous amount of stress for our student teachers and ourselves.

We banded together with our student teachers to lobby our representatives, governor, and the New Jersey Department of Education to continue the full waiver policy, supporting them in the initiation of petitions, social media campaigns, and other advocacy efforts. We found that working together against edTPA developed a sense of agency in our student teachers and community of purpose between faculty and students. Many of our student teachers were able to take advantage of flexibility rules and be certified without completing the edTPA; our college had the highest percentage of flexibility recipients in the state. We also supported our student teachers who were required to take the test because no flexibility rule would apply, by offering whole group presentations on weekends, holding individual working sessions, sharing tutorial videos and other resources, and helping them to organize their submissions.

Many of those who did not qualify for the narrowly defined flexibility rules had terrible circumstances: cooperating teachers with COVID-19, their own COVID-19 diagnoses, family members who were ill or who had passed away. They greatly appreciated our help in navigating a bureaucratic requirement with no practical merit. We also shared scholarly research on the edTPA's ineffectiveness to ensure students' arguments were data driven and mathematically sound. The fight against edTPA developed the sense of agency and community among student teachers. Post-pandemic, we will continue to support our student teachers as we fight against this costly, invalid, and unnecessary requirement by supporting and sharing petitions and awareness campaigns led by students and faculty.

Conclusion and Implications

Our care-centered approach to teaching and learning remains central to our teaching, collaboration, and reflection. We continue to prioritize care and compassion and advocate for our student teachers. Our instructor team is committed to the purposeful integration of care in our courses. We encourage student teachers to make self-care/compassion plans and keep each other accountable throughout the week. We offer opportunities for in-person and remote conferences and meet-ups. We incorporate community building activities. Finally, our support for student activism, particularly with regard to the harmful edTPA exam, is ongoing.

As we consider the implications of our work post-COVID-19, a few things are clear. Student teachers are entering a workforce full of uncertainty and new challenges. While there is strong evidence and recognition of the impact and benefits of SEL programs in K-12 settings (Mahoney et al., 2020), teachers and student teachers often are not provided such support for their own well-being. Teacher educators must assist student teachers in developing strategies for managing anxiety and stress that they can use throughout their career. The central role of care, compassion, and community is perhaps the most important takeaway of the COVID-19 pandemic.

References

Clayton, C. D. (2018). Voices from student teachers in New York: The persistence of a subtractive experience of the edTPA as a licensure exam for initial certification. *Education Policy Analysis Archives, 26*(27), 1–35.

Cristol, D., & Gimbert, B. (2021). Preservice teachers' self-awareness needs post-pandemic. *Academia Letters*, Article 256.

Delamarter, J., & Ewart, M. (2020). Responding to student teachers' fears: How we're adjusting during the COVID-19 shutdowns. *Northwest Journal of Teacher Education, 15*(1), 1–10.

Fastiggi, W. (2019). The SAMR model. *Technology for Learners*. https://technologyforlearners.com/the-samr-model.

Gitomer, D. H., Martínez, J. F., Battey, D., & Hyland, N. E. (2021). Assessing the assessment: Evidence of reliability and validity in the edTPA. *American Educational Research Journal, 58*(1), 3–31.

Gueldner, B. A., Feuerborn, L. L., & Merrell, K. W. (2020). *Learning in the classroom: Promoting mental health and academic success*. Guilford Publications.

Greenberg, M. T., Brown, J. L., & Abenavoli, R. M. (2016). Teacher stress and health effects on teachers, students, and schools. *Edna Bennett Pierce Prevention Research Center, Pennsylvania State University*. www.prevention.psu.edu/uploads/files/rwjf430428.pdf.

Jones, S. M., Bouffard, S. M., & Weissbourd, R. (2013). Educators' social and emotional skills vital to learning. *Kappan, 94*(8), 62-65.

Owens, L. M., & Ennis, C. D. (2005). The ethics of care in teaching: An overview of supportive literature. *Quest, 57*, 392–425.

Noddings, N. (1984) *Caring: A feminine approach to ethics & moral education*. University of California Press.

Noddings, N. (1992). *The challenge to care in schools: An alternative approach to education*. Teachers College Press.

Noddings, N. (1996). The Cared-for. In S. Gordon, P. Benner, & N. Noddings (Eds.), *Caregiving: Readings in knowledge, practice, ethics, and politics* (pp. 21–39). University of Pennsylvania Press.

Noddings, N. (2013). *Caring: A relational approach to ethics and moral education*. University of California Press.

Paugh, P., Wendell, K. B., Power, C., & Gilbert, M. (2018). "It's not that easy to solve": edTPA and preservice teacher learning. *Teaching Education, 29*(2), 147–164.

Reilly, K. (2020). With no end in sight to the Coronavirus, some teachers are retiring rather than going back to school. *Time.* https://time.com/5864158/coronavirus-teachers-school/.

Rogers, D., & Webb. J. (1991). The ethic of caring in teacher education. *Journal of Teacher Education, 42*(3), 173–181.

Schonert-Reichl, K. A., Kitil, M. J., & Hanson-Peterson, J. (2017). *To reach the students, teach the teachers: A national scan of teacher preparation and social and emotional learning*. A report prepared for the Collaborative for Academic, Social, and Emotional Learning. University of British Columbia.

Will, M., Gewertz, C., & Schwartz, S. (2020). Did COVID-19 really drive teachers to quit? *Education Week.* www.edweek.org/teaching-learning/did-covid-19-really-drive-teachers-to-quit/2020/11.

PART III
Care and Teacher Educators

11

AUTHENTIC CARE AND TEACHER EDUCATION

A Self-Study of Buddhist Compassion from the Pandemic

Nozomi Inukai and Melissa Riley Bradford

The COVID-19 global pandemic quickly changed the landscape of teaching and learning. At our institution, all classes became virtual, making it difficult to form the personal connections that naturally arise through informal, face-to-face conversations. After a year of teaching online, in the Winter 2021 quarter, we each struggled with a difficult student, which manifested in harsh feedback on course evaluations. While this experience is nothing new to us as teachers, we realized that it was harder to ascertain student circumstances and, thus, we felt compelled to examine our online pedagogy.

In addition to the global pandemic, political division and systemic racism have also weighed heavily on student minds, leading them to yearn for care and compassion more than ever. If our students in teacher education felt that way, students in K-12 schools must have also required as much, if not more, care and compassion. Yet, at least in the official curriculum, the cultivation of dispositions such as care and compassion is often not considered as important as the teaching of knowledge and skills in teacher education (Schubert & He, 2020). Given these circumstances, as faculty, we were compelled to bring care and compassion to the forefront of our teaching practices, not only to respond better to our students' needs, but also to demonstrate the importance of care and compassion in their teaching.

In this chapter, we explore our enactment of care through self-study (e.g., LaBoskey, 2004) by drawing on the Buddhist notion of compassion as articulated by Japanese educator Daisaku Ikeda (e.g., Ikeda, 2010). Ikeda is a global peacebuilder, Buddhist philosopher, and the founder of 12 Soka schools from kindergarten to graduate school (Goulah, 2021). The past decade has seen rapid growth in scholarship in the field of Ikeda/Soka Studies in Education, including educational leadership, K-12 teaching, and teacher education (Inukai, 2021). As a

DOI: 10.4324/9781003244875-15

relational way of knowing, being, and doing, Buddhist compassion as articulated by Ikeda can bring new perspectives to our understanding of care and caring.

At the DePaul University College of Education, Nozomi teaches undergraduate and graduate students seeking state licensure in elementary and secondary education, while Melissa teaches master's and doctoral level students in educational leadership and curriculum studies. We came together because we share a scholarly interest in Ikeda/Soka Studies and have applied Buddhist principles to our teaching and our lives. Based on these shared interests, we chose to use the Buddhist notion of relationality and interdependence (e.g., Ikeda, 2017, 2010) and the concept of human revolution (e.g., Goulah, 2012; Ikeda, 2010) as foundational frameworks to guide our reflections and our practice as teacher educators in order to more closely personify the ideals of Buddhist compassion. Specifically, we asked: What does it look like when two instructors use Buddhist compassion as a guiding ethos? Using Schubert and He's (2020) assertion that care and compassion are both disposition and action, we examined both our values/ attitudes and our practice in the classroom. This study has helped us improve our ability to care for our students and we hope that by embodying compassion and modeling care as teacher educators, we can help them do the same in their respective contexts as teachers and educational leaders.

Buddhist Compassion and Education

Interdependence of All Living Beings and Imaginative Empathy

The concept of compassion has deep significance in Buddhism. Ikeda explains the origin of the Buddhist notion of compassion, from the Sanskrit, as "containing two aspects: the desire to share a friendship with others and the desire to embrace the suffering of others as one's own. Thus, it originally means supreme amity for people without discrimination of any kind" (Unger & Ikeda, 2016, p. 45). In Buddhism, compassion is comprised of two Chinese characters—*ji* (慈) and *hi* (悲)—and has come to mean to relieve people from their sufferings and give joy and happiness (Gu & Ikeda, 2012). This sympathy and sharing of pain indicate a horizontal relationship based on respect rather than a hierarchical relationship in which someone superior "saves" suffering people. In the Lotus Sutra, the Buddha's compassion is likened to a room where all people are warmly embraced to sit down to discuss life as equals, learn from each other, and strive to improve their lives together (Ikeda et al., 2000).

Underlying such Buddhist notions of compassion is the belief that the Buddha, or enlightened, nature is inherent in all phenomena and that all living beings in the cosmos emerged and exist in interdependent and mutually supporting ways (*engi*, in Japanese). Because all living beings have the Buddha nature within, everyone is fundamentally equal, endowed with inherent dignity, and can contribute to the harmony of all other living beings. Moreover, in the Buddhist ontology of relationality, all phenomena exist within mutually supportive relationships, forming a living cosmos. As Ikeda (2010) writes, "Nothing and nobody exists in isolation. Each individual being functions to create the environment that sustains all other existences. All things are mutually supporting and interrelated, forming a living cosmos" (p. 173). Because each of us is an inseparable part of an interconnected cosmos, one's own happiness cannot be separated from the happiness of others. Thus, we are called to bring out compassion, which Ikeda explains as an act of empathy "to feel others' suffering as our own" (Ikeda et al., 2000, p. 210). Ikeda (2012) writes that, beyond all the borders and differences, the deepest and the most fundamental root of our identity as a human being is that of a bodhisattva, one who cares and works for other people's happiness. Buddhists who are awakened to their identity as a bodhisattva "take a vow to have concern for the welfare of all beings, not just a specific group or themselves" (Thayer-Bacon, 2003, p. 158).

Ikeda goes so far as to assert that the universe itself is the embodiment of compassion and that human beings have been entrusted by the cosmos with becoming aware of and fulfilling the mission of leading all life toward happiness and creative evolution. He states that we live "to be active participants in the compassionate workings of the universe, enriching and enhancing its creative dynamism as we live out our lives to the very fullest" (Ikeda, 2010, p. 182). From a Buddhist perspective, therefore, enacting compassion can be perceived as a cosmic mission of human beings.

From an educational perspective, the interdependence of all living things in the cosmos instructs us "to give the utmost consideration to how to enable others to reveal their potential, how to establish better human relations, and how to create the greatest possible value" (Ikeda, 2017, p. 164). Someone aware of the dignity of their own life respects the lives of others and enacts compassion by working together with them to manifest individuality and create value. The process of value creation (*sōka,* in Japanese), or creating positive outcomes that benefit oneself and others, is, for Ikeda, a contributive life of fundamental happiness, which is the ultimate goal of education. Compassion is also an essential component in the student-teacher relationship. To enact compassion in our classrooms, we must have imaginative empathy. Because "the first step toward compassion is to put ourselves in the place of others, empathetically acknowledging the reality of their existence" (Ikeda, 2010, p. 184), we as teachers are compelled to imagine the struggles of our students and have empathy as the basis of our relationships.

Human Revolution and Mutual Growth

However, establishing this compassion within our lives is not an easy task. Thus, Ikeda (2010) posits that "the establishment of a firm and unshakable self is the necessary basis for true compassion" (p. 183). In order to build this life state, especially when interacting with people who are difficult to work with, we do human revolution, a continuous and volitional process of inner transformation of one's own mindset and attitude (Goulah, 2012). In other words, one must cultivate what Ikeda refers to as the greater self, in which we view all our interactions with others as sources of our own growth and development. Ikeda (2021) clarifies,

> Compassion in Buddhism does not involve the forcible suppression of our natural emotions, our likes and dislikes. Rather, it is to realize that even those whom we dislike have qualities that can contribute to our lives and can afford us opportunities to grow in our own humanity…Compassion consists in the sustained and courageous effort to seek out the good in all people, whoever they may be, however they may behave. It means striving, through sustained engagement, to cultivate the positive qualities in oneself and in others. (pp. 7–8)

From the Buddhist perspective, therefore, enacting compassion is not just for the other; it is also for our own growth. In fact, striving to enact compassion for others, especially in the face of difficulty, provides us with a great opportunity to grow as human beings. Ikeda uses the example of Sadāparibhūta Bodhisattva (Bodhisattva Never Disparaging) from Buddhist scripture to communicate the perseverance one must develop in order to embody compassion:

> [Bodhisattva Never Disparaging] paid reverence to the supreme value—that is, the Buddha nature—inherent in everyone. Ironically, unaware of this Buddha nature within themselves, the very people he revered despised and persecuted him. Nonetheless, he persevered in revering them until ultimately they were enlightened to their own supreme dignity. (Unger & Ikeda, 2016, p. 31)

The model of Bodhisattva Never Disparaging inspires us to never give up on anyone, not just because it is a good thing to do, but because when the Buddha nature in ourselves bows to the Buddha nature in the other, the other's Buddha nature bows back, just like a mirror image, which ultimately is the path to our own happiness and growth.

Extending this type of mutual growth to education, this means that student-teacher relationships should be reconceptualized as mutually supporting each other's growth. As Goulah's (2018) bilingual analysis reveals, Ikeda coined the term *kyōiku* (mutual fostering, 共育), a homophone of *kyōiku* (education, 教育), which emphasizes "fostering" over "teaching" and denotes a "two-way vector of influence between teacher and student" (p. 67). This way of thinking signifies the attitude that I can grow as a teacher and as a human being thanks to my students. In such a relationship, the hierarchy between the teacher and student is flattened, and both become indispensable to each other's growth. Further, the inner growth of the teacher will lead to creating a better educational environment, thereby contributing to students' wellbeing (Ikeda, 2021). Based on shared value creation between teacher and student, even the students who are difficult to deal with become indispensable to our growth as teachers and human beings, and reciprocally, the inner growth that is sparked within us allows us to better carry out our mission as teachers.

Self-Study Methodology

Our desire to further our growth led us to employ self-study, a methodology borne out of teacher education research. Self-study methodology (LaBoskey, 2004; Samaras, 2011) is a collaborative approach to research that positively impacts our teaching and our students' learning while also generating knowledge about teaching and learning (Samaras, 2011). In self-study of teacher practice, teacher educators examine whether their practices align with their beliefs and values (LaBoskey, 2004). To critically reflect on our beliefs and practices aligns with our guiding ethos of human revolution, or inner transformation, in Buddhist philosophy.

As a personal inquiry situated in a teacher educator's lived practice, self-study is a transparent and systematic research process that involves critical collaborative inquiry. Data collection methods primarily consisted of journal entries, stories, and dialogic reflections with each other as critical friends, meaning colleagues who enhance each other's research through constructive feedback, asking provocative questions, and helping each other dig beneath the surface of our inquiries (Samaras, 2011).

Before our Spring 2021 courses began, we reflected on our previous quarter's teaching and how we hoped to better enact compassion in our courses. Once the quarter began, we wrote reflective journal entries after class sessions in a shared document. Then we posted comments to each other's journal entries, creating a written dialogue. In addition, we discussed our journal entries via video conferencing to probe each other for deeper reflections, during which we took notes and used the auto transcription feature of the software for reference.

To analyze our data inductively, we used thematic analysis (Braun & Clarke, 2006), looking for repeating patterns of meaning in our journals and transcripts. We began by taking turns reading through our transcripts and journals and, using the commenting feature, labeling parts we found descriptive and meaningful with preliminary, exploratory codes such as *trying new strategies* and *soliciting critical feedback*. Then we discussed together the commonalities in these exploratory codes and began to identify ideas that fit together as themes. Using a recursive process, we reviewed and refined the themes we identified and then looked for explicit connections to the Buddhist perspective of compassion. Finally, we revisited our data with a deductive lens, scanning for anything we might have missed and checking for data that best encapsulated the themes.

Findings

Based on the thematic analysis of our data, three major themes emerged: (1) self-study as self-care; (2) a caring relationship starts with our own inner change; and (3) practical expressions of care. We represent our data in the form of journal entries and quotes from our transcripts.

Self-Study as Self-Care

Although the study was focused on how we worked to embody Buddhist compassion with our students, we quickly and rather unexpectedly realized that the self-study was serving as care for ourselves. Because Buddhist compassion extends to both self and other in interdependent ways, we realized that it is also important to take care of ourselves as we strive to care for our students.

As Melissa noted,

> Well, it might be silly, but writing this all out feels good, just because I am writing what I want to write without thinking about producing something for an assignment. It feels like I have a sympathetic listener. (March 30, 2021)

Later, Nozomi wrote,

> I know Melissa wrote that writing these out was comforting, and I realized that reading through Melissa's reflections and thoughts were also very comforting. Because there was so much that I related to, it really made me feel that I am not alone. (April 12, 2021)

In this way, we found that the self-study process allowed us to support each other in our efforts to enact care for our students during a difficult time, demonstrating the interdependent nature of an educational community.

A Caring Relationship Starts with Inner Change

The second theme is that a caring relationship starts with our own inner change. Although care involves both the *carer* and the *cared-for* (Noddings, 2013), care is not something we do to or for students but something we do with students. Therefore, it is certainly more difficult to generate care for students when they do not engage with the course responsibly by accepting responsibility for their own errors or reaching out and being honest when they are struggling. On the other hand, when students reach out or show interest in developing a genuine relationship with us, it is much easier to create a caring relationship. As Nozomi shared,

There was one student I had a difficult time connecting with. She didn't smile, her introduction was very factual, and her responses to my questions were minimal. We ended the call in 5 minutes. The rest of my students were surprisingly engaging, and many asked me personal questions such as how I got into teaching at DePaul and what kind of research I do. When we get to know their history, personality, and interests, that person becomes an actual three-dimensional human being, not a two-dimensional figure on a screen. I noticed that establishing these relationships is truly a mutual process. It is much easier when students are open and willing to connect. (April 1, 2021)

Still, regardless of their response, we felt called to bring out our caring selves, do our best to continue to express care, and not take rejection personally, knowing that there might be other things going on in our students' lives that we do not know about. Further, because it is difficult, these are precisely the opportunities for us to grow in our capacity of compassion. The following journal entry by Nozomi illustrates such an effort to suspend judgment and respond with compassion.

I had one student who needed my permission to be late to class in order to enroll in her physics class that had a 20-minute overlap with my class. Due to her wording in the email, I was a little upset that she took for granted that I would give permission, but I read the following passage from Daisaku Ikeda.

"To only speak of benefiting others leads to arrogance. It conveys a sense of self-righteousness, as if we are somehow doing others a favor by 'saving' them. Only when we recognize that our efforts on others' behalf are also for our own sake will we be filled with humble appreciation for being able to develop our lives." (Ikeda, 2015, pp. 104–105)

After reading this, I literally swallowed all the words I wanted to say, and responded with compassion to her email. I also took the initiative to reach out to the registration office if they needed anything else from me. In the end, everything worked out. When I met again with this student, I could tell that she was deeply suffering, or at least not satisfied with her current life, and she herself said "I'm struggling" multiple times regarding her career circumstances. To be honest, she seemed to be looking down on K-12 teaching, but I tried my best to suspend any judgment, and just listened. (April 1, 2021)

By using the model of Bodhisattva Never Disparaging as inspiration, Nozomi was able to maintain a caring relationship with her student regardless of the student's disposition. Later in the quarter, the student expressed her appreciation, saying that Nozomi was the only professor who took the time to meet one-on-one and provide support to complete assignments.

Practical Expressions of Care

The third theme is the practical expressions of care in our respective courses. We identified two interrelated expressions of care: emotional and pedagogical/ instructional. The emotional expression involved proactively reaching out to students, meeting with them one-on-one and having the curiosity to get to know them at a personal level, empathizing with students' struggles, and sometimes providing encouragement. As Melissa wrote in her journal to Nozomi,

> I implemented your practice of 15-minute meetings with my Stakeholder Relationships students. It is helpful because it gives me an idea of what the students think would be useful for them to learn. … Another benefit is the emotional connection with the students. It's less scary to face that first class because I have already met three of the students via the 15-minute meetings. I learned a lot about them that I would not have otherwise. (March 30, 2021)

In fact, Melissa took her efforts to provide emotional support further by implementing mindfulness practices during her synchronous class meetings. As she explained during one of our video conferences, Melissa attempted different ways of "being embodied, being connected; paying attention to our emotional selves and our spiritual selves, just as teachers and educational leaders are called to do in K-12 settings" (February 28, 2021). She facilitated short guided meditations, art activities, a get-to-know-you exercise for breakout sessions designed to establish a safe space to share vulnerabilities, and a listening session that consisted of an inspirational musical performance by a former student, followed by reflective journaling. She explained, "I've been trying to open each class with something [that addresses] the emotional needs students might have and make the online class more of an intimate setting" (February 28, 2021). She had to challenge her fear of doing something unorthodox and worried students might feel she was transgressing conventional classroom boundaries between the cognitive and the emotional but student reactions were appreciative.

While these emotional connections are important and are often considered as the crux of care, we realized that caring for our students, especially in a virtual setting, also involves thoughtful and intentional planning at the pedagogical or instructional level. Using imaginative empathy, we recognized the need to be explicit in our directions, in how we frame the courses, and in explaining our purposes behind our assignments. This reduced student anxiety and prevented cognitive overload. For example, Nozomi started each class with critical self-reflection, writing along with introductory activities that engaged all students in low-demand tasks. In addition, we both strove to reduce the workload and be flexible with deadlines. We also recorded videos explaining the assignments so that students could go back and re-listen after class. Both of us received positive feedback from our students about these efforts.

Implications

We conclude with the implications of this study for our fellow teacher educators but also with the hope that our own growth serves as a model for our students, who are teacher and leader candidates.

The first theme of self-study as self-care, which was unexpected, made it apparent that we need a community that supports caring engagement with our colleagues. We faculty are also affected by COVID and other struggles just as our students are. While working remotely, we did not have as many opportunities to talk with our colleagues about our struggles and ideas. Even with different experiences and positionalities, we had similar struggles, and it felt good to be able to share and be validated. Further, we learned from each other and were inspired to try many new ideas.

The implication of the second theme—a caring relationship starts with our own inner change—is that by critically examining our attitude toward students who challenge us, we can respond with compassion even though it is not our natural reaction in the moment. Although on the surface it seems like caring relationships require the response of the cared-for, if we think of it strictly from a Buddhist perspective, their external response should not dictate how we behave or even feel. Just like Bodhisattva Never Disparaging, we should believe in the dignity of our students' lives and expand our own capacity of compassion regardless of how they respond. Through such efforts, we allow our students to help us grow.

With regard to the third theme of the practical manifestations of care, although we identified a common thread of emotional and pedagogical aspects, the specific manifestations looked different for each of us. Thus, the practical actions to embody care are context-dependent and require the creativity of teachers to find what is best for them and their students. Just as we found new, creative ideas and inspiration from each other through this collaborative self-study, teachers need opportunities to engage in dialogue about their teaching and learn from fellow educators.

Finally, based on the recognition that the need to embody compassion for students will never go away, we identified a number of strategies we will continue post-COVID. We plan to continue our practice of meeting with each student for 15 minutes at the beginning of a quarter. We will continue to use tools, like recorded lectures and screencast explanations of assignments, to give our students more flexible learning options and reduce their stress. We will employ more activities that address social-emotional learning. In addition, we will make efforts to regularly check in with our colleagues, especially those we might not see in person. Most of all, even though the memories of the intense struggles we faced during COVID might fade, we will continue to bring to our interactions the awareness that our students are going through struggles that will not be apparent on the surface. By keeping in mind our profound interconnectedness, we will cultivate relationships of mutual growth in order to enrich all of our lives.

Throughout this self-study, we noted that our efforts to enact Buddhist compassion in our classrooms were met with positive feedback from our students. Many of our students, especially those who were already in some teaching capacity, identified specific strategies we used in our classrooms that they were eager to implement with their students. Further, some of our students were interested in conducting self-study as a way to improve their teaching. In these ways, we believe that we were able to model how to pursue self-improvement toward caring relationships. At a time when teacher education is often focused on the teaching of knowledge and skills (Schubert & He, 2020), our efforts in this study brought care and compassion to the center of our teacher education curriculum. We hope that our efforts as teacher educators will foster teachers and educational leaders who can enact care and compassion with their students.

References

Braun, V., & Clarke, V. (2006). Using thematic analysis in psychology. *Qualitative Research in Psychology, 3*(2), 77–101.

Goulah, J. (2012). Realizing Daisaku Ikeda's educational philosophy through language learning and study abroad: A critical instrumental case study. *Critical Inquiry in Language Studies, 9*(1–2), 60–89.

Goulah, J. (2018). The presence and role of dialogue in Soka education. In P. Stearns (Ed.), *Peacebuilding through dialogue: Education, human transformation, and conflict resolution* (pp. 55–70). George Mason University Press.

Goulah, J. (2021). Introduction: Daisaku Ikeda, and hope and joy in education. In I. Nuñez & J. Goulah (Eds.), *Hope and joy in education: Engaging Daisaku Ikeda across curriculum and contexts* (pp. xiii–xxxiv). Teachers College Press.

Gu, M., & Ikeda, D. (2012). *Heiwa no kakehashi: Ningen kyōiku wo kataru* [A bridge of peace: Discussion on human education]. The Institute for Oriental Philosophy Press.

Ikeda, D. (2010). *A New Humanism: The university addresses of Daisaku Ikeda.* I. B. Tauris.

Ikeda, D. (2012). *My dear friends in America: Collected addresses to the SGI-USA since 1990* (3rd ed.). World Tribune Press.

Ikeda, D. (2015). *The wisdom for creating happiness and peace: Selections from the works of Daisaku Ikeda, Part 1: Happiness.* World Tribune Press.

Ikeda, D. (2017). *The new human revolution* (Vol. 1). World Tribune Press.

Ikeda, D., Saito, K., Endo, T., & Suda, H. (2000). *The wisdom of the Lotus Sutra* (Vol. 1). World Tribune Press.

Ikeda, D. (2021). *The light of learning: Selected writings on education.* Middleway Press

Inukai, N. (2021). Ikeda/Soka studies in education: A review of the anglophone literature. *Sōka Kyōiku [Value-Creating Education] 14*, 25–38.

LaBoskey, V. K. (2004). The methodology of self-study and its theoretical underpinnings. In J. J. Loughran, M. L. Hamilton, V. K. LaBoskey, & T. Russell (Eds.), *International handbook of self-study of teaching and teacher education practices* (Vol. 2, pp. 817–869). Kluwer Academic Publishers.

Noddings, N. (2013). *Caring: A relational approach to ethics and moral education* (2nd ed.). University of California Press.

Samaras, A. (2011). *Self-study teacher research: Improving your practice through collaborative inquiry.* Sage Publications.

Schubert, W. H., & He, M. F. (2020). Practicing care and compassion. *Oxford Encyclopedia of Education.*https://doi.org/10.1093/acrefore/9780190264093.013.619

Thayer-Bacon, B. J. (2003). *Relational "(e)pistemologies".* Peter Lang.

Unger, F., & Ikeda, D. (2016). *The humanist principle: On compassion and tolerance.* I. B. Tauris.

12

LESSONS LEARNED

Approaching Care for Preservice and Novice Teachers after COVID-19

Jennifer Baumgartner and Angela W. Webb

As the COVID-19 pandemic roiled teaching and learning around the world in Spring 2020, teachers were initially hailed as heroes for their quick pivots to virtual/remote learning, their responsiveness to students' needs, and the care they showed for students during this abnormal and tumultuous time—and teachers met these new and increased professional expectations while also juggling novel demands in their personal lives. Yet, as teachers in the classroom showed care for their students, how was care shown to them and to those studying to become teachers? In this chapter, we reflect on our evolving understandings of care in response to pandemic teaching and learning. As we work to make sense of preservice and novice teachers' experiences, we also consider our roles and obligations in supporting them during this demanding time.

Caring For Preservice and Novice Teachers

Originally conceptualized as something that occurs in familial relationships, the concept of care is now accepted and discussed by professions and institutions. While definitions differ, most include the same key elements: those who care, those who are cared for, and a belief in the importance of care. Care in teacher education and teacher induction involves listening, taking meaningful action, and creating and sustaining a culture of care for preservice and novice teachers, as well as the profession (Noddings, 2012). Ingrained within this is the need to care both *for* and *about* preservice and novice teachers. As described by Noddings (1984, 2015), caring for happens in direct person-to-person interactions; it "requires attention and response cultivated in relation" (Noddings, 2015, p. 74). Caring about, on the other hand, can be more nebulous, "involv[ing] a certain benign neglect," (p. 112) as Noddings (1984) initially described it. Even so, caring about

DOI: 10.4324/9781003244875-16

could be foundational to justice inasmuch as "it is instrumental in establishing the conditions under which 'caring for' can flourish" (Noddings, 1999, p. 36). Specifically, "we can and should care about everyone and work from that basic attitude to establish policies that will facilitate the caring-for that must occur on-site. Both forms of caring are essential" (Noddings, 2015, p. 75).

Caring takes many different forms, both in and out of the classroom (Noddings, 1992), and is complicated further by perceptions and expectations of care. To this end, we cannot know what caring is without listening to someone and understanding their needs (Noddings, 2012). As teacher educators, our experiences tell us only about our own needs, drawn from how we experienced our teacher education programs and initial years in the classroom. Thus, those of us who work with and support preservice and novice teachers have a limited basis upon which to presume or assume their needs during this unprecedented pandemic teaching. Instead, we must listen and respond to the stated needs of those we purport to care about since care should "[emphasize] receptivity, relatedness, and responsiveness rather than rights and rules" (Isenbarger & Zembylas, 2006, p. 122). As we—preservice teachers, novice teachers, and teacher educators—navigate responses to and consequences of the pandemic together, rights and rules mean little when teaching and learning have altered in ways few of us imagined or prepared for.

Teacher education is a time when preservice teachers analyze their beliefs about, form new visions of, and develop subject matter knowledge for teaching; their understandings of learning and learners grow as they begin to cultivate a repertoire of practices and tools for teaching (Feiman-Nemser, 2001). When novice teachers transition from teacher education into the induction phase of their careers, their learning continues as they gain local knowledge of students, curriculum, and school contexts; design responsive curriculum and instruction; enact a beginning repertoire of practice in purposeful ways; create a classroom learning community; develop a professional identity; and learn in and from practice (Feiman-Nemser, 2001). Unavoidably, the induction phase of a teacher's career is marked by continuous and tremendous learning of and socialization into the profession (Feiman-Nemser, 2003).

School divisions increasingly offer structured, formalized induction and mentoring programs to shepherd novice teachers through this career phase (Strong, 2009). Yet, because induction can also be conceptualized as a period of learning and a process of socialization, novice teachers are inducted into the profession even in the absence of formalized supports and systems (Feiman-Nemser, 2010)—and, as we have seen during the COVID-19 pandemic, even when not in the physical school building. Thus, the support novice teachers receive warrants responsiveness to their needs and experiences in order to champion better beginnings in the classroom, especially during times of upheaval. Certainly, schools and school divisions, as well as university-based teacher education programs, share responsibility in providing such care.

Our Collaboration

Although we have different contexts as teacher educators, we both believe in the importance of care in our work with preservice and novice teachers. Jennifer is an early childhood teacher educator who works with preservice teachers seeking pre-kindergarten through grade 3 certification at a large, research-intensive university in the southern United States. Angela is a secondary science teacher educator at a large public university with high research activity in the southeastern United States. Though in different areas and now at different universities, talking with one another about how to best educate and serve teachers is not new to us. Our collaboration and conversations started in 2017 when, while working at the same university, we collaborated to pilot an online induction group offering emotional and instructional support for recent graduates of the secondary Master of Arts in Teaching and undergraduate early childhood education programs (see Gamborg et al., 2018).

It seemed natural, then, to restart our conversations on teacher education, induction, support, and care when the pandemic began. We shared our concerns, approaches, and thoughts on providing care to preservice and novice teachers; these conversations have continued almost two years into the pandemic. This time of worry, struggle, and discomfort led us to explore not only the literature associated with care but also to reflect on our own experiences to better understand preservice and novice teachers' experiences of care during COVID-19.

Caring for Preservice Teachers during COVID

As we talked with each other about caring for and about (Noddings, 1984, 1999, 2012, 2015) preservice and novice teachers during COVID, three main threads emerged in our conversations: (1) the importance; (2) the complexity; and (3)the cost of caring. In the sections that follow, we first introduce these themes and then offer our personal reflections on each before connecting our experiences and reflections.

The Importance of Caring

The ethic of care tells us that the cared-for and the carer have a shared interest in each other's well-being (Held, 2006; Mor, 2018). During the pandemic, the work of teacher educators in providing care to preservice teachers was made visible in new ways. The stress and strain of completing a teacher education program, while engaged in remote teaching and learning, came with the added pressures of the unknown surrounding the pandemic. Preservice teachers and teacher educators had to work together to navigate rapid changes. In our conversations, we took the need for care as a given but struggled to understand what it meant in this new context.

Jennifer: It isn't hard for me to see the connection between teaching and caring. It always seemed obvious that, in order to intentionally instruct, I must care about the experiences, motivations, comfort, and learning of my students. But how I should provide care was less clear. I suppose I simply "felt" my way through it, striving to give my students support and feedback as they did the work to become teachers. I never received any direct training on how to provide care nor was it clearly stated in the professional code of ethics (National Association for the Education of Young Children, 2004).

During the earliest days of the COVID-19 pandemic, I experienced this need for care in new ways. In the abrupt change to remote learning, the most pressing needs consuming my thoughts were how to teach my classes and finish the semester. In the chaos of those early days, there were so many decisions to make, often without much information. I worried that the decisions I was making might not address students' real needs, but rather only those I imagined. I felt like a new teacher again as my classes changed from in-person to remote, from active learning classrooms to stilted conversations over Zoom, from discussions and observations in real time to asynchronous feedback. It seemed that the tools I had developed to communicate and provide care for students were gone and I needed to develop new ones that would be helpful to each student.

Like many of my colleagues, I was helping my own children with their schoolwork at home, so I was stretched in many ways. It was important to be efficient, but the stress of the pandemic made me very aware of what work "counted." Time on Zoom meetings was work, time preparing for classes was work—but what about the emails to students to check on them? What about the social connection time added to the Zoom class? Did this "count" as work? It seemed important but perhaps I should have just plowed through the content. The uncertainty about my role as a caring teacher educator was neither new nor changed: The crisis merely made it visible.

Angela: Pre-pandemic, I took care for granted as an explicit construct in the context of teacher education, believing that "good teachers care, and good teaching is inextricably linked to specific acts of caring" (Rogers & Webb, 1991, p. 174). On course evaluations, the preservice teachers I worked with reported feeling cared for and appreciative of the community I built and nurtured in my teacher education courses. However, if you had asked me pre-pandemic whether establishing and fostering community was *care*, per se, I likely would have said no. After all, it's just something that good teachers—and teacher educators—do. The COVID-19 pandemic and the concurrent racial, political, and social unrest in the United States, however, served to both clarify and complicate for me the role and practice of care in teacher education.

I realize now that how care is shown, perceived, received, and discussed is far more nuanced than I once believed. Pre-pandemic, I somehow took for granted the key role of relationships in care: Care was something I showed toward preservice teachers, not necessarily something we co-constructed through relationships. Yet the community I worked to foster among preservice teachers during our online classes and maintain via connections in group messaging applications served as a lifeline for current and former preservice teachers as they navigated coursework, student teaching, and their initial years in the classroom during the pandemic.

In addition, the conversations I had with each class about the importance of caring for themselves became even more important, as their students, administrators, and school communities were asking them to take care of others in more and different ways than ever before. "You can't pour from an empty cup"; "you can't give what you don't have"—phrases I've said time and again when working with preservice and novice teachers took on bigger, inescapable meanings in these unprecedented and unpredictable contexts. Further, as care-related demands on teachers and teacher educators crescendoed over the duration of the pandemic, the non-neutral quality of care became palpable. We cannot afford to continue talking about the ways in which teachers and teacher educators can and should care for themselves and their students without attending concomitantly to the systems, practices, and policies they work within and against.

During the pandemic, we were forced to re-evaluate what was *essential*. Caring for preservice teachers was critical as we all faced new challenges and shifting boundaries (Bartolic et al., 2021), but how this care should be provided or received became more pressing questions. While we all experienced the pandemic, our personal experiences and how we, individually, felt and dealt with its effects varied. As a result, meaningful care for preservice and novice teachers became more individualized and responsive to their specific pandemic experiences.

The Complexity of Caring

Providing care to others is complex, even in the best of times, and the complexity inherent to caring relationships was only exacerbated during the COVID-19 pandemic. In our conversations, we discussed the challenges we faced in how to best support preservice teachers during virtual/remote learning including whether, and in what ways, to privilege emotional support, academic support, or both. Somewhat unexpectedly, our care—as demonstrated by frequent check-ins, adapted assignments, and flexible due dates—presented new challenges to our preservice teachers as we learned together how to navigate this broader, more malleable learning space.

Jennifer: Initially, I focused on providing emotional support: checking in with students, asking about their wellness, providing opportunities for connection with others in the class. But as time went on, other approaches emerged, especially increased flexibility in learning opportunities and assessments, such as offering extended time and different options for completing assignments. The challenge was that what one student needed was in conflict with what another needed. One needed more flexibility; another needed more structure. Some were lost in the sea of offerings. It wasn't clear to me what each student really needed, and it wasn't clear to many of them, either.

In any crisis—and especially during the pandemic—the person in the midst of crisis is often unable to assess their needs or stress level and this was true of my preservice teachers. In offering these opportunities, sometimes they couldn't make decisions that were in their own best interests. For example, offering Zoom gave flexibility, reducing time spent in traffic, allowing time to attend to sick family members, and address other tasks. At the same time, learning on Zoom was often compromised by distractions and missed learning opportunities present in the classroom setting. In conversations with colleagues, I heard worry about losing "rigor" or "setting a precedent" or even concern that preservice teachers would "take advantage." The benefit of a reflecting space with a colleague like Angela is that I continued to return to the preservice teachers' viewpoint. I was coming to think more about how my care might involve helping these preservice teachers think critically about what they needed.

Angela: It is difficult for preservice and novice teachers to truly care for their students if they are not authentically cared for and about themselves (see Noddings, 1984, 2015). Yet, how do you care for preservice teachers that you do not get to see and interact with in person? How do you care for novice teachers who are transitioning into teaching during a global pandemic without adding an undue burden or expectation to their already intense and demanding jobs? Additionally, and perhaps independent of the pandemic, balancing care for self with care for others in authentic ways—within institutions and systems that do not seem to value either—further adds to this complexity.

Much of how preservice and novice teachers are supported in their education and development is grounded in scholarship (e.g., Feiman-Nemser, 2001, 2003; Moir, 1999) and enacted by those who purport to care: university-based teacher educators like myself and Jennifer, mentors, administrators, instructional coaches, and professional developers. Regardless of how well-intentioned and research-based, however, how I worked in the past to support preservice and novice teachers was based, in part, on assumptions of needs as opposed to specific, expressed needs (Noddings, 1984).

Yet, none of us who support preservice and novice teachers have learned to teach or been inducted into the teaching profession during a global pandemic. We simply lack any previous context or experience for making sense of the lived experiences of current preservice and novice teachers during these times. How, then, are we to know how to best support and care for them without asking and listening? And how can we do this in ways that do not increase the burdens preservice and novice teachers now carry? Therein lies the sticky wicket of caring for and about preservice and novice teachers: So much of what they were prepared for in their teacher education programs is now upended.

As we considered how we to care for preservice and novice teachers during the pandemic, it became evident not only that we could not necessarily assume what they needed during this time but also, as is true during crisis, that they might not always be able to assess and name their needs. Careful and intentional listening was needed as preservice and novice teachers described their experiences, challenges, worries, and fears (see Webb et al., 2020). Yet, to listen meant taking time to engage—a resource that was a luxury for many of us. And so, we are still left considering how to best know what preservice and novice teachers need during a time when they, themselves, might not be able to identify and communicate those specific needs—and when our asking likely places an additional burden on their already constrained and precious time, as well as their cognitive and emotional resources.

The Cost of Caring

Since the onset of the pandemic, outlets such as *Inside Higher Education, The Chronicle of Higher Education,* and *EdSurge* have been rife with articles and blogs about faculty experiences during the pandemic, articulating that we were not, in fact, okay (e.g., Flaherty, 2020) and drawing attention to increased levels of burnout (e.g., McClure, 2021; Tugend, 2020). Though some teacher educators thrived during the pandemic, many of us suffered as demands increased and supports were stagnant, at best, or diminished, at worst. We were not exempt from the costs of caring for others during the pandemic.

> **Jennifer**: During the pandemic, we teacher educators experienced some shifts ourselves. We did not receive care from administrators as we were asked to work all hours, respond to all needs, learn dozens of new technological applications, all as we cared for our own family members, schooled our children at home, and worried about finances and world peace. Caring for others took time, energy, focus, emotional, and physical strength at a time when these resources were precious. More was increasingly required of us and teacher educators had to make hard choices.
>
> In making these choices, I found myself pondering what really mattered. I know what matters to my university: what is measured in faculty evaluations and weighed in promotion and tenure decisions. Time spent on caring for students is time that couldn't be used for things that "count." While I was well aware of this chronic issue in higher education, the demands of the pandemic seemed to both

bring it more sharply into focus and make it fuzzy at the same time. In order to do the teaching and scholarship that counted, I had to do a lot of work that didn't: learning new programs, altering lesson plans, recording and re-recording lectures. Each choice to spend resources in one area meant I had fewer to use in another place. These choices were hard. And stressful.

Angela: The cost of doing care work can never be the exact same for every carer. We each bring varied and intersecting identities, lived experiences, and outside expectations and responsibilities to our care for preservice and novice teachers and our fellow teacher educators. Like others, I often found myself expected to care in more and different ways for the preservice and novice teachers I work with. Yes, some of these expectations were self-imposed—things I thought I needed or ought to do to help them through the pandemic—but others were external and expected with little additional care extended to me and my colleagues. Expectations placed on us to care increased yet our internal and external resources for being able to show that care did not.

I, for one, pushed forward in trying to give what I simply didn't have the reserves to give, finally hitting a breaking point of compassion fatigue and burnout a year into the pandemic. This caused a jolt to how I saw myself as a teacher educator, a threat to my identity that I'm still working to overcome. Some students undoubtedly noticed; likely others did not, as some comments on course evaluations still spoke of the class community I fostered and the care I showed. Yet, during this time, any remaining shreds of care I could muster were at a cost to my own wellbeing.

As my and my colleagues' expressed needs (see Noddings, 1984) were overlooked at an institutional level, I was left thinking about the nuanced distinctions between caring for and caring about (Noddings, 1984, 2015). Unfortunately, but perhaps all too commonly, I struggled to care for the preservice and novice teachers I worked with during the pandemic, all the while wondering who was there to care for or about me as a teacher educator. Yes, upper administration at my university talked of caring about students, faculty, and staff, yet, in the midst of the unfolding pandemic, it seems to me that their caring about translated into few actions to actually care for.

Caring is work and it takes resources of time, tools, and energy. During the pandemic, nearly all of us experienced either a strain on resources or fear of losing resources (see Hobfoll, 1989). Each decision we made to expend our resources meant fewer resources to invest in other relationships, activities, or situations. This was consequential to the work of many academics, especially women (e.g., Kramer, 2020; Schieber, 2020). In some cases, privileging care for students and providing high-quality learning experiences meant choosing to put a career on hold (i.e., stopping the tenure clock) or derailing it entirely (i.e., leaving faculty positions due to burnout, loss of productivity.).

The pandemic necessarily drew attention to the invisible work of care that happens at colleges and universities around the world. Cracks in expectations of care were exposed, however, along with this newfound attention. Put simply, faculty, including teacher educators, cannot show authentic care for their students without being cared for and about by their institution. Regardless of recent neoliberal moves to commodify higher education, we cannot escape the reality that teaching and learning—like care—are relational. Thus, we learned a two-fold truth from our pandemic experiences: There is a concurrent need for colleges and universities to recognize and reward the care work that faculty do *and* translate their talk of caring about faculty into action. Otherwise, our current morale problem in higher education will persist (McClure, 2021) to the detriment of our caring relationships with students.

Moving Onward

We are all looking for the lessons learned from the pandemic. In truth, this time has offered us an opportunity to really reflect on care for preservice and novice teachers. Our experiences reinforced the need to listen and respond to their needs. Caring for preservice and novice teachers with what makes sense to us or in the ways we think we would want can miss the mark. Instead, it is critical to listen to the perspectives and needs of preservice and novice teachers. This act of authentic listening is itself a form of care.

   We would be remiss to conclude our discussion of caring during the upheaval of the COVID-19 pandemic and current racial, social, and political injustice without acknowledging that "care is not a neutral notion" (de la Bellacasa, 2017, location 763). In fact, "academic, civic, social, personal, cultural, political, moral, and transformative learning goals and behavioral dimensions" (Gay, 2018, p. 62) are implicated in caring-based education, be it K-12 education or teacher education. With listening an integral part of caring, it is critical to keep in mind that

> listening, like speaking, is not neutral. Listening with care is an active process of intervening in the count of whom and what is ratified as concerned… Calls for a more radically democratic way to listening…could reconnect the politics of care to more than thirty years of discussion in feminist science studies, crystallizing in the argument associated with 'standpoint theory' that thinking from marginalized experiences as political (i.e., as problematic) has a potential to transform knowledge (Harding, 1991). (de la Bellacasa, 2017, location 1033)

From our pandemic experiences, we also learned more about the importance of helping preservice and novice teachers build skills in caring for themselves as well as skills to advocate for what they need. This is critical work—as critical as teaching instructional techniques and curriculum approaches. This is the work that will more extensively prepare preservice teachers and allow novice teachers to remain in the classrooms for years to come, to be fully present, to care for their students. Through this work, teacher educators play a significant role in developing a culture of care for preservice and novice teachers.

Amid calls to return to 'normal' post-pandemic, we recognize that our pre-pandemic versions of care will be insufficient as we take stock of what care can and should entail in our work to educate and support preservice and novice teachers amid yet-to-be-seen pandemic-related challenges and outcomes. In this chapter, we have offered reflections on our caring work with preservice and novice teachers during the pandemic as well as our vision for care as we continue to navigate the still-unfolding phases of the COVID-19 pandemic. As we move onward, one thing is clear: We cannot go back.

References

Bartolic, S. K. Boud, D., Agapito, J., Verpoorten, D., Williams, S., Lutze-Mann, L., Matzat, U., Moreno, M.M., Polly, P., Tai, J., Marsh, H.L., Lin, L., Burgess, J., Habtu, S., Rodrigo, M.M., Roth, M., Heap, T., & Guppy, N. (2021). A multi-institutional assessment of changes in higher education teaching and learning in the face of COVID-19. *Educational Review*, 1–17.

de la Bellacasa, M. P. (2017). *Matters of care: Speculative ethics in more than human worlds* [eBook edition]. University of Minnesota Press.

Feiman-Nemser, S. (2001). From preparation to practice: Designing a continuum to strengthen and sustain teaching. *Teachers College Record*, *103*(6), 1013–1055.

Feiman-Nemser, S. (2003). What new teachers need to learn. *Educational Leadership*, *60*, 25–29.

Feiman-Nemser, S. (2010). Multiple meanings of new teacher induction. In J. Wang, S. J. Odell, & R. T. Clift (Eds.), *Past, present, and future research on teacher induction: An anthology for researchers, policy makers, and practitioners* (pp. 15–30). Rowman & Littlefield Publishers.

Flaherty, C. (2020, November 19). Faculty pandemic stress is now chronic. *Inside Higher Ed*. www.insidehighered.com/news/2020/11/19/faculty-pandemic-stress-now-chronic.

Gamborg, L., Webb, A. W., Smith, A., & Baumgartner, J. I. (2018). Understanding self-efficacy of newly hired teachers during induction. *Research in Contemporary Education*, *3*(2), 16–26.

Gay, G. (2018). *Culturally responsive teaching: Theory, research, and practice* (3rd ed.). Teachers College Press.

Held, V. (2006). *The ethics of care: Personal, political, and global*. Oxford University Press.

Hobfoll, S. E. (1989). Conservation of resources: A new attempt at conceptualizing stress. *American Psychologist*, *44*(3), 513–524.

Isenbarger, L., & Zembylas, M. (2006). The emotional labour of caring in teaching. *Teaching and Teacher Education*, *22*(1), 120–134.

Kramer, J. (2020, October 6). The virus moved female faculty to the brink. Will universities Help? *The New York Times*. https://www.nytimes.com/2020/10/06/science/covid-universities-women.html?smid=em-share.

McClure, K. R. (2021, September 27). Higher ed, we've got a morale problem—and a free t-shirt won't fix it. *EdSurge*. www.edsurge.com/news/2021-09-27-higher-ed-we-ve-got-a-morale-problem-and-a-free-t-shirt-won-t-fix-it.

Mor, N. B. (2018). Teacher education in a post-modern liberal democratic society. *Research in Education, 100*(1), 10–31.

Moir, E. (1999). The stages of a teacher's first year. In M. Scherer (Ed.) *A better beginning: Supporting and mentoring new teachers* (pp. 19–23). Association for Supervision and Curriculum Development.

National Association for the Education of Young Children. (2004). *Code of ethical conduct: Supplement for early childhood adult educators.* www.naeyc.org/sites/default/files/globally-sha red/downloads/PDFs/resources/position-statements/ethics04_09202013update.pdf.

Noddings, N. (1984). *Caring: A feminine approach to ethics and moral education.* University of California Press.

Noddings, N. (1992). *The challenge to care in schools: An alternative approach to education.* Teachers College Press.

Noddings, N. (1999). Response: Two concepts of caring. *Philosophy of Education Archive,* 36–39.

Noddings, N. (2012). The caring relation in teaching. *Oxford Review of Education, 38*(6), 771–781.

Noddings, N. (2015). Care ethics and "caring" organizations. In D. Engster & M. Hamington (Eds.), *Care ethics and political theory* (pp. 72–84). Oxford University Press.

Rogers, D., & Webb, J. (1991). The ethics of caring in teacher education. *Journal of Teacher Education, 42,* 173–181.

Schieber, N. (2020, September 29). Pandemic imperils promotion for women in academia. *The New York Times.* www.nytimes.com/2020/09/29/business/economy/pandemic-women-tenure.html.

Strong, M. (2009). *Effective teacher induction and mentoring: Assessing the evidence.* Teachers College Press.

Tugend, A. (2020). "On the verge of burnout": COVID-19's impact on faculty well-being and career plans. *The Chronicle of Higher Education.* https://connect.chronicle.com/rs/931-EKA-218/images/Covid%26FacultyCareerPaths_Fidelity_ResearchBrief_v3% 20%281%29.pdf.

Webb, A. W., Higdon, R., & Pyle, E. J. (2020). Induction into the great unknown: Supporting newly hired science and math teachers during the COVID-19 pandemic. *VASCD Journal.* http://vascd.org/uploads/fall-2020.pdf.

13

CARING FOR PRESERVICE TEACHERS' PROFESSIONAL AND PERSONAL GROWTH DURING AND AFTER COVID

Rosalyn Hyde and James de Winter

The pastoral aspects of teachers' role are well-established, as are their relationships with students (O'Connor, 2008). The role extends beyond the cognitive aspects of learning to the affective domain and the impact this has upon student learning and wellbeing more generally. In addition, an increasing body of literature addresses the health and wellbeing of preservice teachers (see, for example, Manning et al., 2019; Philpott, 2015). The COVID-19 pandemic has made us pay more attention to, and try to more deeply understand, care for preservice teachers. The dual academic and professional nature of teacher education programs put a great deal of demand on students, many of whom are still in their early 20s. For many, there are both job stresses from placements alongside academic stresses from coursework, an extremely demanding combination. How to care for our preservice teachers as we navigate the COVID-19 pandemic is the focus of this chapter.

Context

In England, a significant amount of teacher preparation for the secondary school level is through short, intensive Post Graduate Certificate in Education (PGCE) programs. These typically last nine months and two-thirds of that time must be spent in a school teaching placement. Though there are many different types of programs in England and a very large number of providers, programs are highly regulated through a set of competency standards called the Teachers' Standards (Department for Education, 2011), a centrally set and recently introduced Initial Teacher Training Core Content Framework (Department for Education, 2019) and programmatic inspections by the Office for Standards in Education, Children's Services and Skills (Ofsted). Successful completion of a program leads to the PGCE (in most cases) and Qualified Teacher Status.

DOI: 10.4324/9781003244875-17

Following the rapid early spread of COVID-19, England entered a national lockdown mid-March 2020. Schools and universities closed; all but those in essential services were required to work from home; all but essential shops closed; and many of the working population found themselves on furlough. As teacher educators, we found ourselves suddenly plunged into online teaching, for which many of us were under-skilled and ill-prepared. The vast majority of preservice teachers were unable to continue with their school teaching placement. England came out of this first lockdown in July 2020 but with social distancing requirements remaining and, over the autumn period, additional regional restrictions were in place. A second shorter national lockdown followed in November and then a longer third national lockdown from January to March 2021, from which the return to normality has been very gradual.

In September 2020, schools returned to fully open, subject to social distancing restrictions, with intermittent short-term closures due to local outbreaks of COVID; however, the third national lockdown brought online schooling for most pupils. University restrictions meant that teaching for the academic year 2020–21 was either done online or using a blended model with some socially distanced in-person teaching. Unlike the period of the first national lockdown, preservice teachers were not withdrawn from school teaching placements but continued to learn to teach under supervision, either in classrooms with social distancing or through teaching online.

We are both highly experienced teacher educators, working in different universities, in different secondary school curriculum subjects (Ros in mathematics, James in physics) and on programs with both similarities and differences. We met for the first time when we both attended an online seminar about support for preservice teachers in response to COVID. Although the seminar focused on technology, James contributed that this was a secondary concern for him, as he was spending large amounts of time addressing the personal wellbeing of the beginning teachers with whom he was working. This view connected strongly with Ros's own experience, and she contacted him afterwards, suggesting the collaboration that forms this chapter.

Understandings of Care

Our use of the word *care* in this chapter is grounded in the work of Noddings (1992) regarding care in schools. Noddings' (1992) definition of care is that "when I care, I really hear, see or feel what the other tries to convey" (p.16); when we are cared for, we are "understood, received, respected, recognised" (p. xi). Noddings' (1992) central argument is that we cannot separate education from our humanity. This forms the basis of her claim that schools must rethink their curriculum in order to take care into account properly. Hackenberg (2005) views learning and caring as a single system and conceives caring as "work towards balancing the ongoing depletion and stimulation" (p. 45). While her work specifically focuses on mathematics teaching, these notions are helpful more widely in considering the connectedness of, and relationship between, learning and care. As O'Connor (2008) explains, caring is "primarily defined as those emotions, actions and reflections that result from a teacher's desire to motivate, help or inspire their students" (p. 117).

Noddings' (2005) work also develops the notion of inferred and expressed needs, where expressed needs come from the person being cared for and inferred needs from the person trying to care. She proposes that failing to recognise the latter can lead to children missing out on opportunities to "develop individual talents, intrinsic motivation, and the joys of learning" (p. 147). Isenbarger and Zembylas (2006) consider this work emotional labour: "When emotions are underplayed, overplayed, neutralised or changed according to specific emotional rules...in order to advance educational goals, teachers perform 'emotional labour'" (p. 122). This is also worthy of consideration, particularly given the demands programs make on the emotional resources of preservice teachers.

The role of the teacher educator is multi-faceted (Grant-Smith et al., 2018) and complex, given we hold the roles of teacher and assessor while maintaining a pastoral role. We see care as teacher educators in the context of more than, and not limited to, wellbeing and mental health. Our focus is not on making preservice teachers feel better in the short term, although that would be of benefit. Rather, we see care as a process of trying to move preservice teachers into developing professional wellbeing, whereby they are equipped to deal with uncertainty as practicing teachers.

Methodology and Research Design

Once we established that the concept of care as a teacher educator was a shared concern, highlighted by our experiences during COVID, we wanted to explore this in a more formal, structured way. Our aim was to better understand our experiences, learn from each other, and help identify how this might inform future practice. We quickly established a personal rapport that built shared values and trust. This led us to the methodology of Self-Study of Teacher Education Practices (S-STEP) because of the study's "emphasis on practice and its improvement" (Craig & Curtis, 2020, p. 83). It allows for developing "deep understandings of our practice and thinking about it by creating particular, compelling accounts of our practice and our personal practical, embodied, and tacit knowledge as we act in our practice" (Pinnegar et al., 2020, p. 111) and for the development of "a deeper understanding of teacher education practices" (p. 116). Teacher knowledge is seen as enacted with knowledge revealed through practical action, judgement, and deliberation (Vanassche & Berry, 2020). The process described below was of the reframing and redefining type described by Loughran and Northfield (1998) as we repeatedly reflected on our experiences, both separately and together.

Our research drew on our individual reflective writing over the two academic years in which the COVID-19 pandemic caused much interruption to preservice teacher education programs. We each had already been keeping personal notes about our responses to the COVID situation in the 2019–20 academic year, recording things we had implemented, adapted, or developed and how these had gone. Once we met and decided to research this process more formally, we collated and expanded these notes, continuing this process over the rest of the 2020–21 academic year. This chapter draws from our writings over this period. We wrote as we wished in the early stage of data collection: writing stories, writing about individuals and events, writing about our own developing understandings of caring for preservice teachers. Although care was a focus of the project, we did not initially have a fixed or constrained definition of what that might include, so we did not place any restrictions on what we recorded or talked about. We wrote individually and shared our writing, reflecting on one another's experiences asynchronously, and drew on the literature that we were individually reading to make connections and to explore our understandings. We also met virtually to consider our written reflections and to challenge and interrogate each other.

Using Noddings' (2005) work led to us form the following questions, which we used to frame our discussions and to see what emerged:

- How can we identify the expressed needs of preservice teachers?
- How can we identify the inferred needs of preservice teachers?
- What can and should we do in response to these needs?
- How do we manage competing/contradictory needs?
- How do we negotiate and balance needs?
- What growth might be possible when we meet these needs?

We used these questions as a basis for our online meetings. We further considered our responsibilities as teacher educators and the aims and purposes of our caring activities towards preservice teachers. We read one another's writing and talked until we agreed that we had nothing more to say and had identified the elements that summarized our discussion. These then formed the basis of further asynchronous writing, where we wrote reflections and responses to reflections for each of these elements, excerpts of which are drawn on in the next section. While the quotes are attributed to specific authors, they followed multiple interactions between us both and are a product of joint thinking.

Reflecting on the S-STEP Process

Using the S-STEP methodology was new to us and, in addition to identifying our understandings of care, working together gave both of us a different language with which to reflect on our work through an explicit focus on an under-explored aspect of our practice:

It has given words to an idea that was part of my role but ill-defined. I had taken the pastoral role of my job seriously, invested in it and found it really rewarding…I had not really given it much direct thought in terms of what it meant and how I thought about it and working together and talking about 'care' has really helped me look at this part of my practice. (James)

For both of us, the experience has been one of professional learning and development. This has been a rich opportunity to share practice and expertise meaningfully, to interrogate one another's understandings, have our own understandings challenged, and to reflect on our practice using critical friendship and collaboration (Bullock, 2020) which was both cross-disciplinary and cross-institutional (Lighthall, 2004 as cited in Bullock, 2020). We see our experiences playing a part in "developing an understanding of practice within its context that ultimately helps to inform the improvement" (Vanassche & Berry, 2020, p. 192) of teacher education. Our understanding of care has been enriched through working together as critical friends since "colleagues are likely to frame an experience in ways not thought of by the person carrying out the self-study" (Loughran & Northfield, 1998, p. 13). We found the experience has developed our knowledge and understanding as teacher educators and impacted our practice as a professional development.

Professional and Personal Growth as Care

The first element emerging from our reflections was that care by teacher educators is both personal and professional and leads to preservice teachers' professional growth as teachers. Because of this outcome, we understand care as being different from simply caring for the inferred and expressed needs of preservice teachers.

As we collaborated, we realized that we needed to explore what we meant by care for preservice teachers:

> I have never considered myself as particularly pastoral…the care I offer tends to be less focused on supporting their emotional needs and is usually of a practical nature. Programs often make demands on preservice teachers that they had not anticipated or that they feel unprepared for; in my experience, many are unprepared for the emotional rollercoaster that is often their experience on a PGCE. (Ros)

> I am not sure I ever really considered care as a thing previously. I was aware that there was a pastoral role in my teacher educator job and valued that, but I had not given it much direct thought…I realized that while the pastoral side was part of it, things are more complex than I had considered. (James)

Using Noddings' (2005) terms, we saw immediate or personal needs as expressed needs and professional growth as an inferred need. Our experiences during the pandemic clarified that sometimes we needed to offer care for immediate or personal needs before we could offer care for professional growth. However, recent work with science teachers notes that "people's wellbeing suffers when they cannot realise [sic] values that are important to them" (Manning et al., 2019, p. 40). Therefore, teacher educators' caring towards preservice teachers is also about working with that missing realization.

It was very evident during lockdown that how preservice teachers felt could impact how they functioned; sometimes their personal needs were great. Our previous experiences indicated that not attending to preservice teachers' personal needs could have a negative impact upon their professional development as a teacher. Our conceptualization of care is therefore rooted in attending to the professional development of preservice teachers through helping them become as good a teacher as they can be. Care is a professional responsibility in the role of a teacher educator and we have learnt that, sometimes, this means we need to go further than providing emotional support and reassurance to challenging preservice teachers' behaviours and providing stimulus for appropriate personal growth. We see this type of care as paying attention to the human factors and mediating what we do in light of that, but with teacher development as the objective.

This understanding encouraged us to use our COVID experiences to consider whether there was a distinction between personal and professional care:

> I have found this distinction very helpful in my thinking…I want to pick "they become a great teacher/slightly tense relationship with me" over "they become ok teacher/good mates" and this seems a simplistic but helpful way to keep this in mind. I am reminded of the times when I have had to have a difficult conversation with a trainee where I need to identify problems, sometimes that they are not aware of, or at least how serious they are. I'll do it with humanity, but I need to make sure that they know the seriousness of the challenges that they face otherwise I am not doing my job as a teacher educator. (James)

Our dilemma was that our experience suggested growth and development as a teacher is influenced by personal wellbeing, and so the distinction is a blurred one. It was more evident during COVID that we needed to attend to the personal to help create space for the professional. However, we learnt that we need to do this consciously. Our affective responses to preservice teachers' wellbeing needs can be used to help them move into a space where they are able to return to a focus on what they need to do to develop as a teacher. Personal and professional both matter and need attention but the priority, or ultimate goal, has to be the professional ones.

Explicit Provisions of Care

In considering the individual and nuanced nature of the care we gave our preservice teachers during COVID, we also reflected on the situations we encountered where we did not have prior experience to inform our judgements. As experienced teacher educators, we recognize that we rely on a considerable degree of tacit knowledge about what we do, why, and when. Part of our learning going forward, then, is to recognize the importance of this tacit knowledge when navigating and balancing professional and personal aspects of care appropriately:

> Reflecting on our conversations, I have noted that there was a whole level of tacit knowledge and experiences that we have both accumulated over the years that enabled us to talk and engage really well and for each of our stories to have meaning and resonances without lots of extra detail needed. I also realised how comparatively easy it was to know what I might have done in a similar situation or agree with an approach you took. (James)

> The personal care and the professional care can be of very different types. They are separate but there is a dynamic relationship between them. We have to make choices about when and how to intervene—both intentional and incidental interventions. The judgements we make are often based on our tacit knowledge and prior experience as teacher educators as we work out 'what they need'. We need to acknowledge that the care we offer is differential and person-specific. It is variable and context-specific. (Ros)

Periods of teaching solely online and not seeing our preservice teachers in person caused us to consider how we had previously identified opportunities to enact care and how this had changed by necessity:

> This is a big one for me going forward, post COVID. Previously I'd relied on incidental opportunities to spot when a trainee might need some support…COVID has meant that relationships were not built in quite the same way and the nature (online) and regularity…of opportunities to be reactive and say "let's have a chat" were significantly diminished…As I see my provision of care more clearly, I also feel that I need to look for ways that this can be provided and to all equitably. (James)

> Previous to COVID I taught my preservice teachers in a classroom with them working round tables in groups. I am currently teaching them either online or with them spread out (socially distanced) in a large lecture theatre. It had been my practice to look for indications of need to have a quiet word and to sidle up to groups of preservice teachers while they were working to observe and listen. Neither of these strategies are possible currently. I have found this frustrating as well as worrying in that I feel that I have less of a sense of their wellbeing. (Ros)

We are both proactive and reactive in caring for preservice teachers. Working online meant that the mechanisms we used to care changed, as did the ways in which we identified those that we thought were in need of some kind of care. We found our-selves challenged by our recognition of the extent to which we had previously relied on our own tacit abilities to spot cues that a preservice teacher was in difficulty. We might have missed signals from preservice teachers that we were not tuned into so, going forward, we will both consider how we can plan more structured ways of identifying those who might be in need of care. While we have always sought to encourage pre-service teachers to approach us when they are in difficulty, we will now be thinking about how we can make our caring role more explicit to preservice teachers.

Caring as Teacher Educators

Our experiences as teacher educators during COVID-19 caused us to consider our motives in caring for preservice teachers while deepening our recognition that we needed to take into account our own needs, energy, and ability to care:

> A particularly interesting personal and professional lesson I have learned as a combination of COVID and talking to you is to think about when I should choose to not do things. Giving a definition to care as a thing, but a professional thing, has perhaps made it easier for me to say no to doing things that I might have thought were part of my job and would have done. Now I wonder if I did these things partly as a result of me perhaps focussing too much on the personal or seeing it above/before the professional...An example might be that a few weeks ago I was shattered, drained and exhausted. There was an evening 'catch up meeting' for the physics group...I cancelled, something that I would not normally do...I knew that they would be fine and thinking that I was not depriving them of care that mattered made it easier to cancel. (James)

Going forwards, we recognize that we have limited capacity; we need to make decisions about where to best place our efforts in order to be impactful in our caring. In our experience, preservice teachers benefit from understanding why their teacher does specific things. Making decisions explicit might be a way to ensure that care—of which we all have a limited capacity—is most impactful:

> Not all care is necessary and possibly not all of it is needed. (Ros)

> Crikey, there is so much to agree with in this sentence. The lines are blurred and it is not always clear but being stress tested in COVID both in terms of what might be needed (or seen to be needed) and what was possible has made it easier to see that the provision of care has edges. (James)

James also reflected that he spent much of the COVID period supporting preservice teachers in the personal probably more than was necessary. He realized that he does not need to do all the things he might be inclined to do, and that experience has helped develop internal checks and limits that he might not have done otherwise. Ros now finds herself considering the purpose of the care she is offering and the way in which it contributes to professional growth as well as personal. We are both better able to ask, "Do I really need to do this?" because our understanding has developed as to how personal and professional care helps us to make choices.

Final Remarks

Our work develops Noddings' (1992) definition of care by applying it to the work of teacher educators with preservice teachers. In this context, it further develops Noddings' (2005) notions of inferred and expressed needs, identifies that these apply in our teacher education contexts, and reiterates the essential role of care in learning. For both of us, the COVID period has been significant in furthering our thinking about care in that it has made us more concerned about the wellbeing of our preservice teachers. Our COVID experiences helped us to recognize the extent to which care is part of teacher educators' roles as well as the importance of embedding care in our programs.

We now view our care for preservice teachers through the lens of both personal and professional care, with a focus on care that leads to professional growth. This allows us to work more impactfully as teacher educators while still recognizing that there is a need for the personal aspects of care. Our work together allowed us to recognize and value our tacit knowledge about caring for preservice teachers but also to recognize that this is not always sufficient, particularly in times of unusual crisis. For newer teacher educators, building up tacit knowledge takes time and the support of more experienced colleagues, which needs to be recognized by all concerned.

For all teacher educators, we recommend building opportunities into programs to explain and explore the personal and professional needs of preservice teachers deliberately and explicitly. Part of our experience as teacher educators caring for preservice teachers during the uncertainty of lockdowns has been having to admit to professional uncertainty. The professional uncertainty of COVID's disruption to normal practice, while not always welcomed, facilitated and promoted our professional growth. Within these challenges and in the context of this research, we have a better idea of the provision of care as part of our roles. We are clearer about the difference between but also the connections between personal and professional care. We are better able to see what provision of this care might look like, how to facilitate it, and also to realize what falls outside this remit, enabling us to pay better attention to our own needs. The hope is that this will yield benefit for our preservice teachers and us as teacher educators.

References

Bullock, S. (2020). Navigating the pressures of self-study methodology. In J. Kitchen, A. Berry, S. Bullock, A. Crowe, M. Taylor, H. Gudjonsdottir, & L. Thomas (Eds.), *International handbook of self-study of teacher education practices* (2nd ed., pp. 245–268). Springer.

Craig, C., & Curtis, G. (2020). Theoretical roots of self-study research. In J. Kitchen, A. Berry, S. Bullock, A. Crowe, M. Taylor, H. Gudjonsdottir, & L. Thomas (Eds.), *International handbook of self-study of teacher education practices* (2nd ed., pp. 57–96). Springer.

Department for Education. (2011). *Teachers' standards*. Crown Copyright.

Department for Education. (2019). *ITT core content framework*. Crown Copyright.

Grant-Smith, D., de Zwann, L., Chapman, R., & Gillett-Swan, J. (2018). "It's the worst, but real experience is invaluable": Pre-service teacher perspectives of the costs and benefits of professional experience. In D. Heck & A. Ambrosetti (Eds.), *Teacher education in and for uncertain times* (pp. 15–33). Springer.

Hackenberg, A. (2005). A model of mathematical learning as caring relations. *For the Learning of Mathematics, 25*(1), 45–51.

Isenbarger, L., & Zembylas, M. (2006). The emotional labour of caring in teaching. *Teaching and Teacher Education, 22*(1), 120–134.

Loughran, J., & Northfield, J. (1998). A framework for the development of self-study practice. In M. Hamilton (Ed.), *Reconceptualising teaching practice: Self-study in teacher education* (pp. 7–18). Falmer Press.

Manning, A., Towers, E., Brock, R., & Damon, H. (2019). Supporting the wellbeing of science teachers: Developing a well being session for trainee science teachers, and an interview study of teachers' views of wellbeing support. *ASE International, 8,* 40–43.

Noddings, N. (1992). *The challenge to care in schools: An alternative approach to education.* Teachers College Press.

Noddings, N. (2005). Identifying and responding to needs in education. *Cambridge Journal of Education, 35*(2), 147–159.

O'Connor, K. E. (2008). "You choose to care": Teachers, emotions and professional identity. *Teaching and Teacher Education, 24*(1), 117–126.

Philpott, C. (2015). Creating an in-school pastoral system for student teachers in school-based initial teacher education. *Pastoral Care in Education, 33*(1), 8–19.

Pinnegar, S., Hutchinson, D., & Hamilton, M. (2020). Role of positioning, identity, and stance in becoming S-STEP researchers. In J. Kitchen, A. Berry, S. Bullock, A. Crowe, M. Taylor, H. Gujonsdottir, & L. Thomas (Eds.), *International handbook of self-study of teacher education practices* (2nd ed., pp. 97–134.). Springer.

Vanassche, E., & Berry, A. (2020). Teacher educator knowledge, practice, and S-STEP research. In J. Kitchen, A. Berry, S. Bullock, A. Crowe, M. Taylor, H. Gudjonsdottir, & L. Thomas (Eds.), *International handbook of self-study of teacher education practices* (2nd ed., pp. 177–214). Springer.

14

CARE BEYOND COVID AS A TEACHER AND TEACHER EDUCATOR

Crystal L. Beach

Care. A four-letter word that is easier to say than understand, especially in the challenging times that all educators have faced during the COVID-19 pandemic. In the teaching profession—at all levels—we have been applauded and celebrated for our hard work, and then just as quickly criticized and chastised for questioning our safety and our students' well-being. Yet, we continue to rise above the challenges COVID-19 presents, from facilitating our face-to-face, hybrid, and virtual learning classrooms to navigating the personal challenges faced on journeys that many walked alone.

Before COVID-19, I can honestly say that I never thought about what care meant to me. I also never thought of myself as an emotional person. Perhaps this is because I viewed needing care or showing emotion as weakness on my part. Perhaps this is because I was so busy that I thought I would fall behind and not accomplish my goals if I took time to focus on personal and professional care. Perhaps this is because "if we [women] show emotion, we're dramatic...if we stand for something, we're unhinged" (Campaigns of the world, 2020).

Whatever the case for my lack of focus—or what I now see as my lack of understanding—on care before COVID-19, I will be the first person to admit that I am terrible with embracing care and making emotion visible. In fact, when I stop to think about my journey as a Division 1 college athlete and dual-degree undergraduate and graduate student to full-time teacher and (practically full-time) PhD student, I find moments where I had to intentionally stop and do something "different" to ensure I was giving myself the care I needed in those busy moments. For me, this meant walking around my university's Drillfield, snapping pictures with my boxer, Dane, or attending training lessons with my bulldog, Briggs. The long hours and dedication to achieve my professional goals are some of the moments I am most proud of, moments that I share with current teacher

DOI: 10.4324/9781003244875-18

education students who also want to pursue their PhD. Those moments also made me realize the importance of prioritizing care. However, since COVID-19, I now understand that prioritizing care requires intentional work on my part and attention to where and how I spend my emotional energy.

I share this reflection from a myriad of roles working in and across teacher education. I teach preservice and inservice teachers; I am a student teacher mentor and supervising teacher; and, at the time of the pandemic, I was a high school English language arts (ELA) classroom teacher (I am now an Academic Specialist working with teaching and learning at the secondary level). In addition, my perspective has been shaped by the unfortunate reality of becoming very ill with COVID-19 in January 2021. I am what doctors call a COVID-19 long hauler, medically known as PASC or post-acute sequelae of SARS-CoV-2 (Chung et al., 2021). I still suffer the effects of this terrible virus almost a year after contracting it.

Wearing many educational hats and surviving COVID-19 have helped me reflect on care both personally and professionally. I'm not sure I have taken my own advice or done well in caring for myself—and I know I am not alone in this, as I talk to teacher education colleagues all over the country. For this reason, this reflective piece starts by discussing how I understand care as a teacher educator and then moves to what I have learned about care since the start of the pandemic. Specifically, I am sharing the lessons I've learned and how I have worked to redefine care since COVID-19 arrived, why intentionality matters, why we must be honest with our students (and ourselves), why learning environments matter, and why we should not forget all we have learned through this pandemic, including our understanding of care, as we look to the future of teacher education.

Redefining Care

In March 2020, educators rushed to reconsider what teaching and learning would look like as universities and public schools made the switch overnight to virtual learning. Teacher educators not only had to consider how student teachers' placements would continue but also how their own classes would be modified to meet the demands of our reality. Suddenly, a surge of "how-to's" erupted in our field: how to help teachers avoid burnout (Fleming, 2020), how to apply helpful strategies to virtual teaching (Snelling & Fingal, 2020). Yet, teacher educators know that the field we build each year already faces tough issues of burnout (Walker, 2018) and decline (Owens, 2015; Will, 2019) and our student teachers have received best research-based teaching strategies from our courses.

I share this reminder to say that, while those instances of how-to—or what I call quick care—resources might have been helpful in the moment, they are not expressly intentional actions nor did they show an understanding of care during a time in which K-12 students, student teachers, mentor teachers, and those of us in teacher education scrambled to understand the mass trauma we were facing with COVID-19 (Prideaux, 2021). Yes, *trauma* is what we experienced and continue to experience, and it will look differently for each of us. Yet, thinking about trauma and calling it what it is makes people emotionally uncomfortable. Therefore, care has not been intentional, prioritized, and focused on sustainability or emotional energy; it is cobbled together to quickly suppress uncomfortable emotions. And to understand this, then, we must remember in our redefinition of care to consider more than quick-fix options. Band-aids only last so long, after all. Our redefinition needs to recognize trauma and consider how empathy can help us connect with others around us, too.

For example, we know that there is a great deal of information emerging about trauma-informed teaching practices (Roberts, 2020). How does it connect to the personal/professional trauma teachers have experienced during this time? How does prioritized and intentional care help with the emotional energy spent in understanding the trauma affecting teaching practices? How does empathy help us support our student teachers so that they can best support and empower their students in K-12 classrooms?

These questions require us to take a step back and acknowledge the immense trauma school communities experienced, and continue to experience, because of the pandemic (Jones, 2021; Willetts, 2021). It is important for us to remind our student teachers that, without this consideration, not even the best lesson plans and research-based strategies will positively influence student learning. These considerations help us learn from each other and the students in our classrooms to create communities of light even in dark times, where lesson plans change to do what those students need (Beach, 2019). Care, then, becomes not a quick fix option but an intentional practice of understanding the contexts in which we teach, calling trauma out for what it is and what it is doing to our communities, and making space for the emotional undertaking of teaching and learning within times of trauma.

We also cannot ignore our pre/inservice teachers' lived experiences and the emotional trauma they might be carrying themselves. As Dunn (2021) discussed,

> My goal in centering emotion work in my preservice teacher praxis is to make emotion work visible and assign value to it. Doing so attends to teacher well-being by recognizing teachers are people who care for other people while also trying to care for themselves. (p. 150)

Here, emotion work means considering how teachers hide or change their emotions to make others feel more comfortable (Dunn, 2021). Yet, Dunn (2021) notes that too much suppression can make teachers feel unwell and not provide a space where teachers consider how emotion affects their relationships with students. When we make emotion work visible by giving value to it and acknowledging "teachers as human beings who do emotion work, we name the experience [or trauma], make space for it, and possibly reduce the isolation teachers might feel when they find themselves teaching in the midst of difficult experiences" (Dunn, 2021, p. 150). This visibility can create bridges that help us embrace our personal and professional care, which is why redefining care and calling trauma what it is, is imperative in teacher education.

The importance of (re)defining what care was and now is has become increasingly important. From my experience, care was something I personally thought of as a much-needed break to clear one's head before getting back to work. It lacked empathy; it lacked any intentional action. Now, care means doing whatever is needed for mental, emotional, and physical well-being. It means it's okay to say, "No." It means it's okay to shut the computer off and read a book, or yes, even sleep—and sleep a lot. It means that empathy is an intentional part of the caring process as we work with colleagues and student teachers who have experienced trauma related to COVID-19.

The Importance of Being Intentional

As I consider what embracing care might look like now, there are important lessons about intentionality that I have learned during the pandemic. When I lost two of the most important people in my life in the early months of the pandemic, I struggled with whether I should let my student teachers or colleagues know; I did not want to appear weak or unprepared. However, I knew I had to step away for a few days to take care of myself, and with an asynchronous course, my student teachers needed to know why I would not be responding right away. What I found was support from colleagues who offered to help as needed and understanding, patience, and concern from my student teachers during a time of immense struggle made visible by intentionally self-advocating for my need for a few days away.

These are the moments we must continue to model for our student teachers so they bring to their classrooms the same intentional practices of care to be the best teachers they can be for their K-12 students. Being intentional means that we must create spaces for stories and experiences of loss and trauma within our classrooms (Dunn & Johnson, 2020; Dutro & Bein, 2014). Without intentional care, we risk losing learning spaces that invite all student teachers (and their K-12 students) to be a part of the classroom community—a community impacted by the trauma of the pandemic.

We must normalize the process of dedicating intentional practices of care for ourselves and being honest about our emotions if we are to be our best selves for the students in our teacher education programs. We must intentionally avoid the "emotional management" engaged in by the teachers in Dunn and Johnson's (2020) study on loss in the ELA classroom because "they seemed to identify their roles as teachers to be about staying in control of their emotions and the curriculum. Their descriptions of teaching suggested that students' comfort and learning were prioritized over teacher's emotion" (p. 17). Emotional management suggests that we keep emotions out of the classroom to focus on our professional responsibilities of curriculum and instruction. Too many times our emotional management pushes aside the care that we might need, yet I believe that if we do not create space for intentional, visible care, our professional responsibilities suffer. After all, what our student teachers learn from us in these tough moments is how to continue the cycle of emotional management that they will then carry into their own classrooms.

Modeling Honesty for Student Teachers

As previously mentioned, embracing care personally and professionally are ongoing learning experiences for me. When working as a supervising teacher with two student teachers during the 2020–21 school year, I told them both from the start I was not sure how to teach during COVID-19. Looking back, I realize that care during those early pandemic days meant letting them know it was okay to not have all of the answers or the perfect lesson plans (always but especially then).

So, when modeling instructional planning for my student teachers, I invited them to join the process and outline a full semester for their secondary ELA classes, making sure they understood that this living, breathing document could, should, and would change over the course of the semester based on our needs and those of our students. We needed to be honest with ourselves and acknowledge that the pandemic could and would change things over night, just as it did for me.

Enter January 2021—I test positive after being as careful and safe as I could. I remember crying when I received the news as I feared the unknown, worried about my classes and supervising responsibilities, and felt the worst I have ever felt in my life. I shared this reality with one of my student teachers during a Zoom meeting as we looked ahead to her work in the classroom with my indefinite return. I had to be honest with her that it might not be as simple as a 14-day quarantine (and it was not, unfortunately). My student teacher and I would later joke about how our shared trait of tenacity and a dedication to planning kept her classroom running as smoothly as it could during that time. She mentioned that the time I spent to show the planning process was one of the most beneficial parts of our time together and she now understood that the planning process is one that cannot be glossed over.

Ultimately, the best I could do while teaching during COVID-19 (and with it) was to be as honest as I could with my student teacher about every aspect of the job because she needed to know the intricate and often unknown parts of what teaching brings. She deserved to know how we—the "experts"—wobbled through our own new understandings of what teaching and learning looked like and continues to look like, lest we forget that the pandemic is not over (as of winter 2021).

In addition, I worked hard to model to my student teachers what "logging off" means and to tell them why this is important. Let's be honest with ourselves— there are so many times we feel we have to answer emails immediately or else. In reality: or else, what? Our understanding of time and caring about how we spend that time is something we can also share with our student teachers. In fact, I told them I removed my work email long ago from my cell phone. I learned as an early-career teacher that it was not healthy or feasible for me to incessantly check my email and respond at all hours of the day or night.

COVID-19 reminded me of this important lesson, one I felt the need to share with my student teachers. It is fine to log off and put ourselves first, especially when our health needs to take top priority (as it always should). Even today, though there are times I need to make a grading or teaching deadline, I now do not feel bad when I must turn the screen off because of lingering COVID-19 symptoms that affect my work; I'm also not ashamed to ask for an extension should I need one. Honesty, then, is an integral part of the caring process as we envision the teaching and learning environments that we hope to create within our teacher education programs.

Fostering a Caring Teaching and Learning Environment

As K-12 schools and universities here in Georgia looked to reopen in August 2020, there was an increased focus on safety and wellness. The experts, including the Georgia Department of Health, weighed in and announced they would "continue to provide guidance and recommendations to districts and schools on navigating the academic, social, and emotional effects of the COVID-19 pandemic on [K-12] students and employees" (Georgia Department of Education, 2020, p.1). Moving forward, teachers tried to navigate the need for an increased focus on social and emotional learning in response to the pandemic while community members voiced outrage that teachers would focus their attention there (Downey, 2021). And teacher educators had to prepare student teachers to work within these K-12 classrooms and communities to best support their students' social and emotional learning needs. First and foremost, then, we must foster those environments in our own courses, too.

When we model best practices of intentional care, we naturally (and intentionally) foster caring teaching and learning environments. For example, we know that deadlines are a part of life. Our syllabi and course schedules clearly outline expectations for our student teachers. Yet, we also know life happens (as evidenced by many of the examples I have previously shared from my own life in the past year of the pandemic), so we must keep in mind the social and emotional components of our students' learning needs within our teacher education courses. Honest conversations with our student teachers about their safety and well-being are something we must build into our courses as well as our relationships.

So, when a student in my teacher education course alerted me to the difficulties she was currently facing, I revised the course expectation without hesitation—because life happens and our care in those moments matters. Later in my course evaluations, I read,

Dr. Beach was very understanding and supportive in a time that has been truly awful for me. I learned a lot, too, not only about digital literacies and how to apply them, but about the kind of supportive teacher I want to be in the future. Had I not had this experience, I may have quit and given up. Thank you so much. You'll never know how much it meant to me.

This example is a simple moment where I tried to foster a caring teaching and learning environment through empathy but also created a lesson learned by student *and* professor.

Another way in which we help foster a caring teaching and learning environment is to help our student teachers remember what matters most when they enter their future classrooms: their students—not test scores, not perfect lesson plans, not new strategies, but the students entering their classroom every day. Doing what's right in that specific moment is what students need. In Georgia, State Superintendent Woods (2020) reminded all of us in education of his expectations:

Testing is a federal requirement, and we will follow the law, but we will also continue to pursue a path of common sense and compassion. We cannot control the federal testing requirement, but we can control its high-stakes components. It is time to be bold. To our districts, families, educators, and students: don't worry about the tests. Given the unique environment we are in, they are neither valid nor reliable measures of academic progress or achievement. I repeat: do not worry about the tests. Worry about meeting the students and teachers where they are. Worry about a safe and supportive restart. Worry about the well-being of your students and teachers. Worry about doing what's right.

Worry about the well-being of your students and teachers: doing what's *right*. This is what we need to emphasize to our student teachers even after the pandemic ends to help them recognize when to be bold and do what's right, whether that means making a curricular choice or advocating for all of the unique learners in their classrooms. This is the notion behind intentional, honest, caring teaching and learning spaces. The necessity of bold choices that result in doing the right thing for all is an important lesson we should not forget from our lessons learned during the pandemic.

Embracing Care

Our actions must support what we believe about care in education in ways that have not necessarily been discussed or enacted previously. Is a return to "normal" really what's best for us and our profession? I would argue, from my experiences, that the pandemic has taught us nothing is normal, and our notion of normalcy should never be what it was pre-COVID-19. As the saying goes, when you know better, you do better, and we must do better for ourselves and our student teachers.

For me, every choice I make as a teacher educator, supervising/mentor teacher, and secondary instructional coach now focuses explicitly on cultivating an awareness of care so that empathy is intentionally and automatically embedded in my courses and interactions. As I've discussed in this chapter, that means redefining what care means today, being intentional with our actions to create spaces for care, modeling honesty for student teachers, and fostering a caring, empathetic teaching and learning environment that helps us remember what education should be as we strive to do what's right for our students. As Bouton (2016) notes,

> The path [of understanding empathy and including it in teacher preparation] is not a simple path, but vital to meeting students' needs in the preK-12 classrooms throughout our nation. With more research and attention paid to the socio-emotional trait of empathy we will continue to push forward to achieve classrooms where all children can thrive. (p. 22–23)

As we look ahead, then, empathy is a large part of the equation needed to prepare our student teachers for their future classrooms and something that should be a part of the foundation in our teacher education programs. Our intentional choices as teacher educators can empower student teachers as they head into their own classrooms.

Ultimately, we are living in extremely challenging times that affect everything we do. It did not have to be this way but it is, because a malignant, dangerously transmissible virus became politicized and wrapped up in vitriolic ignorance that brought out the worst in many people. If there's one lesson that I learned from surviving COVID-19, it's that work will always be there, so we must value ourselves (and others) and know when we need to show ourselves (and others) the care we need. We must *embrace* care, not make it an afterthought because we are afraid others will view us as weak.

Embracing care ensures that the support student teachers receive is what they need. Embracing care also reminds us that, as teacher educators, we influence the direction of our field by our care of it. Our jobs as teacher educators have never been more important than now, as we work to teach, encourage, and inspire the next generation of post-COVID-19 teachers. If we do not take the time now to consider the importance of care and learn from our experiences during this pandemic, how can we continue to grow, ourselves and as a profession, as we look to the future?

References

Beach, C. L. (2019, February 5). Turning darkness into light: Opportunities to build community and learn from our students. *The Teacher Casebook*. www.teachercasebook. com/casebook/turning-darkness-into-light-opportunities-to-build-community-and-learn-from-our-students.

Bouton, B. (2016). Empathy research and teacher preparation: Benefits and obstacles. *SRATE Journal 25*(2), 16–25.

Campaigns of the world. (2020, January 11). Nike – Dream crazier. *YouTube*. www.youtube. com/watch?v=zWfX5jeF6k4.

Chung, T., Morrow, A. K., Brigham, E. P., Mastalerz, M. H., & Venkatesan, A. (2021, April 1). COVID 'Long Haulers': Long-term effects of COVID-19. *Johns Hopkins Medicine*. www.hopkinsmedicine.org/health/conditions-and-diseases/coronavirus/covi d-long-haulers-long-term-effects-of-covid19.

Downey, M. (2021, May 27). OPINION: Are parents missing lesson in social and emotional learning? *Get Schooled Blog*. www.ajc.com/education/get-schooled-blog/opinion-are-parents-missing-lesson-in-social-and-emotional learning/ GV6NUUM7Z5GJTJFXZ SRKIYLP7E.

Dunn, M. B. (2021). When teachers hurt: Supporting preservice teacher well-being. *English Education, 53*(2), 145–151.

Dunn, M. B., & Johnson, R. A. (2020). Loss in the English classroom: A study of English teachers' emotion management during literature instruction. *Journal of Language and Literacy Education, 16*(2), 1–21.

Dutro, E., & Bien, A. C. (2014). Listening to the speaking wound: A trauma studies perspective on student positioning in schools. *American Educational Research Journal, 51*(1), 7–35.

Fleming, N. (2020, May 8). Curbing teacher burnout during the pandemic. *Edutopia*. www.edutopia.org/article/curbing-teacher-burnout-during-pandemic.

Georgia Department of Education. (2020). Georgia's path to recovery for K-12 schools. *Georgia Department of Education and Georgia Department of Public Health*. www.gadoe.org/ wholechild/Documents/Georgia%27s%20K-12%20Recovery%20Plan.pdf.

Jones, T. (2021, February. 11). Beloved teacher, coach dies of COVID-19 after coaching in person. *WSB-TV*. www.wsbtv.com/news/local/clayton-county/beloved-teacher-coach-dies-covid-19-after-coaching-in-person/J5O3IEQPHNG6PGCIRLRQO2LXF4.

Prideaux, E. (2021, February 3). How to heal the 'mass trauma' of Covid-19. *BBC*. www. bbc.com/future/article/20210203-after-the-covid-19-pandemic-how-will-we-heal.

Owens, S. J. (2015, December). Georgia's teacher dropout crisis: A look at why nearly half of Georgia public school teachers are leaving the profession. *Georgia Department of Education*. www.gadoe.org/External-Affairs-and-Policy/communications/Documents/Tea cher % 20Survey%20Results.pdf

Roberts, L. M. (2020, July 28). Trauma-informed teaching during COVID-19. *Vanderbilt Center for Teaching*. https://cft.vanderbilt.edu/2020/07/trauma-informed-teaching-during-covid-19.

Snelling, J., & Fingal, D. (2020, March 16). 10 strategies for online learning during a coronavirus outbreak. *ISTE*. www.iste.org/explore/learning-during-covid-19/10-strategies-online-learning-during-coronavirus-outbreak.

Walker, T. (2018, January 1). Teacher burnout or demoralization? What's the difference and why it matters. *National Education Association*. www.nea.org/advocating-for-change/ new-from-nea/teacher-burnout-or-demoralization-whats-difference-and-why-it.

Will, M. (2019, December 3). Enrollment in teacher-preparation program is declining fast. Here's what the data show. *Education Week*. www.edweek.org/teaching-learning/ enrollment-in-teacher-preparation-programs-is-declining-fast-heres-what-the-data-show/ 2019/12.

Willetts, M. (2021, January 21). 2 teachers due of COVID within 24 hours in same Georgia school district, officials say. *The Macon Telegraph.* www.macon.com/news/state/georgia/article248682435.html.
Woods, R. (2020, September 3). Superintendent Woods on U.S. Department of Education's lack of support for common-sense testing waivers. *Georgia Department of Education.* www.gadoe.org/External-Affairs-and-Policy/communications/Pages/PressReleaseDetails.aspx?PressView=default&pid=800.

15

ATTENDING TO THE EXPRESSED NEEDS OF PRESERVICE AND NOVICE TEACHERS POST-COVID

Kara DeCoursey

At the outset of the COVID-19 pandemic with the accompanying educational changes and school closures, teacher educators and their preservice teachers (PSTs) faced significant challenges as instruction was forced online and in-person practica and classes were interrupted (Konig et al., 2020). Educators had to quickly adapt to unfamiliar conditions and reevaluate their understanding of how teacher education processes work (Thompson et al., 2020). Under these circumstances, PSTs were particularly affected just as they were beginning their educational journeys and developing their professional identities (Ruohotie-Lyhty, 2013). As Delamarter and Ewart (2020) note, PSTs often struggled with feelings of fear, panic, and overwhelming stress at times while navigating their changing environment.

Supportive learning environments, strong collaboration (Cullen et al., 2013), trusting human relationships (Li, 2011), and emotional support and social connections (Jones & Ryan, 2014) have been important aspects of PSTs' educational experiences in the past. Traditionally, teacher education programs have relied on face-to-face learning and interactions, practica, and field experiences, as well as mentor-mentee relationships between PSTs and instructors, experienced teachers, and supervisors (Gilles & Britton, 2020). In these relationships, PSTs have ordinarily filled the role of the "cared-for," and mentors, more experienced teammates, administrators, course instructors, and program supervisors filled the roles of "carers" for the PSTs or novice teachers (Noddings, 2012).

The COVID-19 pandemic thrust everyone into cared-for positions—but who was to provide the care? How were those in traditional carer roles to help and support PSTs when they themselves required similar support? In this chapter, I examine the experiences of three novice teachers during the pandemic and consider implications regarding care in teacher education moving forward.

DOI: 10.4324/9781003244875-19

Needs and the Caring Relation

Nel Noddings (2005) described care in education as teachers giving concerted attention to the needs of students, developing trusting relationships with them, and helping them learn skills to satisfy their own needs. This ethic of care also includes the caring relation, i.e., the interactions between individuals when one is the carer and one is the cared-for. Individuals in a caring relationship are often unequal, and the carer is responsible for things the cared-for is not able or expected to do; however, both parties must contribute to the relationship for it to be established and maintained (Noddings, 2012).

Both inferred needs and expressed needs exist within the caring relationship. The cared-for individual produces the expressed needs, and the carer determines the inferred needs. Inferred needs are inherent in these relationships as a carer interprets the needs of the cared-for but it is important that carers deliberately focus on the particular expressed needs of the cared-for individual and genuinely attempt to understand and respond appropriately to those needs (Noddings, 2005). A carer asks, "What are you going through?" and attentively and respectfully listens to understand (Weil, 1977).

The uniqueness of my three participants' concerns and experiences caused me to wonder about the importance of meeting PSTs' expressed needs, as communicated from the perspective of the PSTs (i.e., cared-for), and not the needs assumed by the mentor, school, or institution/program (i.e., carer; Noddings, 2012). The recognition that each PST experiences the stresses of becoming a teacher in different ways, and that they are situated differently within social, cultural, and political contexts, is crucial to avoid assumptions about their needs and to avoid providing only generalized forms of support and guidance. Using Noddings' work on care in education as a framework, I consider the difficulties in this process as well as the ways in which teacher education might improve and implement a caring relation in teacher education.

Inquiry about Care through Narrative

As a research assistant in August 2020, I worked with Dr. Kortney Sherbine on a narrative inquiry study of three elementary education students who were finishing their last semester of undergraduate coursework at a public university in the northeastern United States (Sherbine & DeCoursey, 2021). They had been in the midst of student teaching when the COVID-19 pandemic forced instruction online in the spring of 2020; in the fall of 2020, they began teaching elementary school fully online. As part of this study, we collected written narratives from each participant in response to provided prompts and conducted unstructured interviews with each of them.

Narrative inquiry is the exploration of individuals' experience as story, experience that is honored, composed, and lived over time (Clandinin, 2013). In this study, we attended to the lived stories of our three participants by exploring their experiences with the understanding that "the narratives someone tells about herself or himself are never complete; they form an ongoing process of co-construction and re-construction" (Sermijn et al., 2008, p. 644). As tellers, researchers, participants, and educators, we then collaborated to compose co-constructed contextual, dynamic summaries of the novice teachers' experiences (Sherbine & DeCoursey, 2021). In line with narrative inquiry methodology, we demonstrated the wholeness and ongoing nature of their experiences and avoided reducing their experiences to themes and conclusions (Clandinin, 2013).

In this chapter, however, I draw on participants' narratives to present their experiences as whole stories in their own words before using the framework of care to determine common themes. I engaged in a process of data analysis that focused on the shared experiences of the three participants (Clandinin, 2013), reading and analyzing the personal narratives the PSTs wrote and shared with us. With my experiences as a former elementary teacher and my current role as a teacher educator in mind, I identified resonant patterns and themes that were reflected across these written accounts (Clandinin, 2013). Noddings' perspectives on care offered a lens by which to finalize my analysis by viewing their narratives in terms of caring relationships and by turning the identified themes into ways care in teacher education can develop in meaningful ways.

As our participants moved from cared-for roles during their coursework and student teaching to carer roles in their elementary classrooms, their experiences during COVID-19 begged the question of how teacher educators can navigate care with/for PSTs as they transition into teaching. I consider this question by first presenting portions of the three novice teachers' narratives, collected in Fall 2020 for the narrative inquiry study. I then highlight the complexity of their transitions into teaching during the pandemic and describe common themes identified in the narratives before considering potential avenues for enacting care in teacher education going forward.

Kelly's Narrative

Kelly was placed in a small public elementary school's first grade classroom to student teach. She had taken a significant amount of responsibility in her mentor teacher's classroom and building relationships with students when the COVID-19 pandemic caused school closures. The school shifted to online instruction, but attendance was not mandatory, and Kelly had few teaching opportunities outside of several small group lessons. At the end of the school year, Kelly struggled through the interviewing process: She did not feel prepared to interview and sensed that school administrators were looking for someone with more experience. She ended up taking a job as a long-term substitute at a virtual academy in a large, affluent, suburban school district, teaching a fourth grade class online, both synchronously and asynchronously:

Luckily, my school was very proactive and thought of great ways to keep in contact with the students to continue learning [during my student teaching]. I quickly learned how to use platforms such as Zoom, Seesaw, and FlipGrid. I was able to continue teaching but not in the way I wanted to. It was very difficult, especially since some students did not show up. I created activities on Seesaw and we had synchronous Zoom sessions. These were not mandatory. Most of my kids showed up and I was able to do some small group learning in breakout rooms. I felt that my student teaching experience was cut short because I did not get to teach 100% of the time. I only made it up to 75% of teaching the class. I felt very unprepared going into interviews and applying for jobs. It was scary to think I didn't technically complete my student teaching.

My first week of teaching consisted of "getting to know you" activities and learning the virtual world. It was very fun and uplifting. But once we got into the upcoming weeks, that's where my stress began. I still have no idea what I am teaching and I tend to write lesson plans the night before. I have to ask a million questions to my team members since I am not familiar with the curriculum. I had no materials in the beginning. I am starting to become adjusted now, but the negative emails started to roll in. "My child is failing." "I am devastated with what is happening to my child." "My child cries every night and isn't understanding the material." "My child feels sick each morning because they don't want to go to school." Of course, me being my sensitive self, I took this personally. I had to remind myself that I was doing everything I could for these kids. I created extra worksheets, stayed after school on TEAMS to call students separately and work with them, emailed parents constantly, called parents, and spent entire weekends creating material that I did not need to create.

It is hard to hear from parents that the students are struggling, but I have to remember that they are not used to learning virtually. There are so many factors at home that can cause stress and distractions. I have told myself to keep it light and fun again. I want the kids to enjoy school and not be scared of it. It is so hard not teaching them in person. I care so much. And I don't want to be the reason they struggle in fifth grade…I don't want them falling behind. So I put a lot of pressure on myself. (October 2020)

The prominent issues in Kelly's narrative were her fears about her student teaching being cut short, her difficulties with unknown curriculum materials, and her personal psychological and emotional concerns as she dealt with struggling students. Kelly felt the weight of her students' current learning and future success but did not always feel equipped to meet their needs. She worked to overcome these problems by asking her team many questions, creating materials and assignments, and spending her time outside of work hours communicating with parents. In these ways, she took on the role of carer without feeling supported or prepared to do so.

Sabrina's Narrative

Sabrina completed her student teaching in a third grade classroom at a public elementary school in the rural northeastern United States. The school was brand new, and she had access to new Chromebooks, printers, books, and other resources. The COVID-19 pandemic caused school closures the week of spring break and her school remained closed for an additional week before continuing in an online format. Sabrina attended the online school sessions but did not have many opportunities to teach because her mentor teacher, uncomfortable and inexperienced with online learning, wanted to stay in control of the class. After attending a virtual job fair, Sabrina was hired as a third grade teacher in the southwestern region of the United States and began teaching fully online in August 2020:

> Coronavirus happened during spring break [of student teaching]. We had the week off, then were told school was cancelled until they could devise a plan. School remained closed for another week or two until we came together as a district to create an online learning plan. I continued attending online school sessions but rarely taught online. I didn't experience much in terms of teaching. My mentor teacher was uncomfortable in the online setting and wanted to remain completely in control of the situation. However, I had the chance to observe the use of choice menus for students' weekly work and (at the beginning) online meetings were twice a week for SEL [social emotional learning] check-ins. Eventually, they moved from optional work to one to three direct instruction lessons a week with little required work from the students.
>
> In all honesty, I was slightly relieved when the coronavirus shut the schools down. My mentor teacher was incredibly knowledgeable and there is a lot I was able to learn from her but I feel our teaching styles didn't mesh. I often felt out of the loop and not yet ready to take on 100% of the teaching on top of turning in assignments, working two jobs outside of school, and living at home where I was expected to contribute and participate, not to mention [that] my husband was living with my family and me while we waited for his visa to come through so he could work.
>
> I absolutely did not feel prepared for this school year in the slightest. This is unrelated to being online and more related to the requirements of my school and district. I didn't know how to plan for them, what was expected of me, how to utilize their curriculum or preferred apps, who I needed to contact for IT help, how to fill out my tax forms, the difference between a time card and a clock hour, how to find my benefits. I have one mentor. They are supposed to help me with planning. They also observe me and give me feedback. Most of my questions go unanswered because my mentor does not know my school well. We also have instructional coaches. Each week

we have a PLC meeting with our teams as well. Again, just all around feeling unsupported despite the requirements put into place. I teach in my 600 square foot apartment with all white walls and poor lighting trying to be quiet so my husband's class doesn't hear me. Not at all what I originally had in mind for a classroom. (October 2020)

Sabrina's narrative focuses on personal and professional stresses, such as not understanding the logistical aspects of teaching and feeling as if there was no place to have her questions answered. She struggled with day-to-day teaching concerns and general life stresses as well as the difficulty of accepting that her situation was not at all what she had anticipated. Despite having a strong desire to question, learn, and connect, Sabrina lacked the support, answers, and communication that exists in caring relationships.

Jill's Narrative

Jill was placed in a first grade classroom at an elementary school in the northeastern United States for student teaching. Rather than teaching online when schools were closed, her school prepared packets for students to complete at home. Thankfully, Jill's mentor teacher gave her ample opportunities to teach before the school was shut down and her experience was cut short. She began interviewing for teaching positions but quickly ended up discouraged and exhausted when she did not get called back or receive job offers. She was eventually hired for a first grade teaching position at a charter school in a suburban area in the northeastern United States and began teaching fully online in Fall 2020:

When schools were shut down [during student teaching], I felt a sense of relief at first. I thought it would just be two weeks. I thought this would be a well-deserved break (The week we found out, the university was on spring break, but my school was not). However, as time proceeded, I missed my kids, I missed teaching, and I realized that I was missing a lot of opportunities. From student teaching to finding a job was mentally exhausting. Every morning I was hunting for new job openings. However, due to COVID, I feel a lot of jobs did not open up. I had a few interviews but not many call backs. It was extremely stressful. Thankfully, my mentor during student teaching allowed me to take over the majority of the class. I was basically teaching the entire day except for one subject. She felt confident that I was ready, and this helped me become more confident in myself. So, I did feel prepared going into my own classroom.

I have a mentor that I have to meet with once a week (state required). We discuss ways to analyze data, complete tasks, and [manage] different procedures that the school takes for students if we need to recommend them for special education, counseling, or behavior management. My mentor makes sure I understand our school's foundation and helps me in any way I need.

Honestly, virtual teaching is mentally and physically exhausting. I have to entertain my students from 7:45am-1:35pm. They cannot interact with one another on their own. They cannot have centers and just enjoy each other's company. I have to be the one in charge at all times. I love having a student lead the classroom but I cannot do this virtually. I can't because I have to physically unmute each student, there are constant internet and computer issues, and half of the students cannot stay focused on the computer. So, I stay in charge. Of course, my students lead classroom discussions with help from me but they cannot have small groups and discuss on their own because we are not allowed to have breakout rooms without an adult in each room. Virtual learning has a lot more difficult tasks for the teacher. (October 2020)

Jill also missed out on teaching opportunities during her student teaching experience. An extremely stressful job-hunting experience and concerns about the quality of her students' learning experiences in the virtual environment contributed to the frustrations she felt as a novice teacher. As a new teacher, Jill lamented the limited interaction her students had with each other and struggled to facilitate student-led teaching and learning. She felt pressure to care for her students in meaningful ways but helpless in doing so within the online classroom setting.

Resonant Themes

From Kelly's, Sabrina's, and Jill's narratives, I identified and framed three themes through notions of care (Noddings, 2012): expressed needs, psychological distress, and logistical concerns. The personal narratives show that PSTs' and novice teachers' *expressed needs* vary widely and depend on many personal and professional factors. The PSTs desperately wanted to meet their students' individual needs, understand curricular materials, and communicate effectively with colleagues and parents. While commonalities existed throughout the three participants' stories, the particularities between their situations were clear.

The participants' *psychological distress* was communicated repeatedly in the narratives through the stress, confusion, and exhaustion they experienced during the transition from student teaching to classroom teaching. The participants dealt with pressures from home, among coworkers, and with their mentors/administrators and felt ill-prepared to face the amount of responsibility they were given. Becoming a teacher in the best of times is a challenge. The participants' narratives demonstrate that, under continually unpredictable, changing circumstances, psychological distress can be significantly heightened for PSTs and novice teachers.

The participants also expressed concern with *logistical concerns*. They experienced varying degrees of responsibility with teaching and leadership during their student teaching; once in the classroom, they were given different levels of support by the schools and districts in which they taught. Lesson planning, professional development, and curricular program requirements varied widely, and the participants generally felt unsure of the demands placed upon them or where to turn for help when necessary.

Discussion

These themes reveal the gaps in knowledge, preparation, and psychological resiliency the participants had during the COVID-19 pandemic, as well as the need for more intentional, explicit care as we move beyond it. The way forward is to "confront the challenge…of finding new means of conceiving, engaging, and expressing the felt impasses of the present…a time to test, engage, and experiment with new ways of being in the world and with the world" (Howe & Pandian, 2016, para. 4–7 as cited in Bozalek et al., 2020, p. 15). To do so, teacher education can implement concepts of care (Noddings, 2012) by drawing on the presented themes.

A first step is identifying the expressed needs of PSTs and novice teachers by creating a space for them to talk. The participants' transitions from official cared-for roles as PSTs and student teachers to carer roles as teachers were noticeably difficult. Undoubtedly, the COVID-19 pandemic added unusual challenges to the process of becoming a teacher. However, many of the concerns experienced and expressed by our participants exist for PSTs outside the pandemic, since beginning teaching experiences are in formal undergraduate and graduate courses, in professional development sessions, and with their mentor teachers.

The participants' narratives demonstrate an insufficient support system of intentional safe spaces for PSTs and novice teacher to share their true feelings and needs. Conversations should be frequent and flexible, taking place between students, instructors, and/or supervisors and mentors and occurring in virtual or in-person spaces, such as video calls, one-on-one meetings, small groups, dialogue journals, and emails. This could sound overwhelming and impractical on top of everything else but establishing a climate of care "is not 'on top' of other things, it is *underneath* all we do as teachers. When that climate is established and maintained, everything else goes better" (Noddings, 2012, p. 777).

A second step to building caring relationships is listening with intention, described by Noddings (2012) as a process that involves the carer and cared-for engaged in meaningful conversations. Once intentional spaces are created for meaningful conversations to happen, the carer must listen and reflect before responding. The response can vary depending on the understanding and resources of the carer but should be positive if possible. The cared-for fulfills their role by telling the carer what they need and feel (Noddings, 2012). Implementing this type of engaged listening throughout coursework in teacher education, student teaching, and the first year(s) of teaching is a necessary, powerful way to support future teachers and set them and their students up for success.

A third step is teaching connection. Teacher educators can demonstrate how to think aloud and encourage PSTs to do so as a way to connect through meaningful dialogue, especially since they might not realize that their thoughts and emotional needs should be taken into account by their own teachers and mentors (Bracho, 2020). Bracho (2020) shifted his teacher educator practice during the pandemic by integrating *cariño*, "a core aspect of border pedagogy that emphasizes critical thinking, culturally sustaining curriculum, intersectional identities, liminality, and strong bonds between student and teacher" (p. 16). He implemented mindfulness practices, conducted personal check-ins with his students, engaged in discussions about their inner and outer lived realities and experiences, and provided informal settings for PSTs to connect with each other and with him, albeit virtually.

Conclusion

It is unclear whether the COVID-19 pandemic caused or created these issues or if it merely exacerbated and revealed weaknesses of support, care, and mental health resources in existing teacher education programs. Whatever the root cause, current and future obstacles that PSTs and novice teachers will face necessitate the formation of spaces for learning their true needs and taking steps to meet those needs. More regular, systematic forms of reaching out and providing support for the social, cultural, and emotional needs of PSTs and novice teachers can help them develop into capable, caring teachers for their future students. Our preservice-turned-novice teachers, Noddings' (2005, 2012) thoughts on care, and our current social and educational climate provide important insights into how teacher education can better navigate care. Listening, connecting, and coming together in intentional spaces to build caring relations are ways that teacher educators can support their PSTs now and moving forward.

References

Bozalek, V., Zembylas, M., & Tronto, J. C. (Eds.). (2020). *Posthuman and political care ethics for reconfiguring higher education pedagogies.* Routledge.

Bracho, C. A. (2020). Reclaiming uplift: Caring for teacher candidates during the COVID-19 crisis. *Issues in Teacher Education, 29*(1/2), 12–22.

Clandinin, D. J. (2013). *Engaging in narrative inquiry.* Routledge.

Cullen, R., Kullman, J., & Wild, C. (2013). Online collaborative learning on an ESL teacher education programme. *ELT Journal, 67*(4), 425–434.

Delamarter, J., & Ewart, M. (2020). Responding to student teachers' fears: How we're adjusting during the COVID-19 shutdowns. *Northwest Journal of Teacher Education, 15*(1), Article 3.

Gilles, B., & Britton, S. (2020). Moving online: Creating a relevant learning experience for preservice teachers in the time of COVID-19. *Electronic Journal of Science Education,* 19–28.

Jones, M., & Ryan, J. (2014). Learning in the practicum: Engaging pre-service teachers in reflective practice in the online space. *Asia-Pacific Journal of Teacher Education, 42*(2), 132–146.

König, J., Jäger-Biela, D. J., & Glutsch, N. (2020). Adapting to online teaching during COVID-19 school closure: Teacher education and teacher competence effects among early career teachers in Germany. *European Journal of Teacher Education*, *43*(4), 608–622.

Li, Z. (2011). Learners' reflexivity and the development of an e-learning community among students in China. *Research in Learning Technology*, *19*(1), 5–17.

Noddings, N. (2005). Identifying and responding to needs in education. *Cambridge Journal of Education*, *35*(2), 147–159.

Noddings, N. (2012). The caring relation in teaching. *Oxford Review of Education*, *38*(6), 771–781.

Ruohotie-Lyhty, M. (2013). Struggling for a professional identity: Two newly qualified language teachers' identity narratives during the first year at work. *Teaching and Teacher Education*, *30*, 120–129.

Sermijn, J., Devlieger, P., & Loots, G. (2008). The narrative construction of the self: Selfhood as a rhizomatic story. *Qualitative Inquiry*, *14*(4), 632-650.

Sherbine, K., & DeCoursey, K. (2021). A narrative inquiry of three novice teachers' experiences during the coronavirus pandemic. [Manuscript submitted for publication].

Thompson, A., Darwich, L., & Bartlett, L. (2020). Not remotely familiar: How COVID-19 is reshaping teachers' work and the implications for teacher education. *Northwest Journal of Teacher Education*, *15*(2), Article 2.

Weil, S. (1977). In G. A. Panichas (Ed.), *Simone Weil reader*. David McKay Company, Inc.

16

CREATING CARE-FULL COMMUNITIES AFTER COVID

Supporting Care as a Strategy for Wellbeing in Teacher Education

Sharon McDonough and Narelle Lemon

The advent of the COVID-19 pandemic has altered the ways we live and work for millions around the globe. As we write this chapter, in the state of Victoria, Australia, we have been through multiple lockdowns and periods of remote learning, moving towards what is described as COVID-normal life. In the Australian context, we write from a relatively privileged position, with the ability to work safely from home, and with areas of our country relatively free of the virus. We are conscious, however, that this pandemic is far from over for many. Also far from over are the ripple effects of the pandemic on our lives, on our wellbeing, and on our education systems.

In this chapter, we focus on care framed within the realm of wellbeing. Wellbeing is a slippery term to define, often associated with the gross domestic product of a nation, but with an elusiveness that sees various different definitions available for those who work in this space (Dodge et al., 2012; Ereaut & Whiting, 2008; Higgins & Goodall, 2021; Pollard & Lee, 2003). Some consider wellbeing as involving "family, community and society as a whole" (La Placa et al., 2013, p. 116). Dodge et al. (2012) argue that wellbeing is frequently referred to by description of the dimensions it includes, rather than by clear definitions of what it is.

From a positive psychology perspective, wellbeing is the scientific study of the strengths that enable individuals and communities to thrive and flourish (Lottman et al., 2017). From this perspective, flourishing means "to live within an optimal range of human functioning, one that connotes goodness, generativity, growth, and resilience" (Fredrickson & Losada, 2005, p. 678). While definitions of wellbeing might be contested, researchers do agree that wellbeing is complex, intersects with a number of concepts, can be developed, and is based on "good" (Lyubomirsky, 2010; Seligman, 2011). Based on these critical aspects of wellbeing, we draw on the

DOI: 10.4324/9781003244875-20

following definition of wellbeing for this chapter to underpin and frame the discussion of care during the pandemic:

> Wellbeing is diverse and fluid respecting individual, family and community beliefs, values, experiences, culture, opportunities and contexts across time and change. It is something we all aim for, underpinned by positive notions, yet is unique to each of us and provides us with a sense of who we are which needs to be respected. (McCallum & Price, 2016, p. 17)

We argue that we need to pay explicit attention to the concepts of care and wellbeing at all levels of education, and that we can learn from the experiences of inservice teachers to identify opportunities for enacting a focus on care and wellbeing in preservice teacher education. In doing so, we argue that we have the opportunity to create "care-full" education communities, which are those that focus on supporting care and wellbeing for all members. As we interrogate notions of care and consider these in light of both individual and system actions, we identify some proactive actions that support wellbeing.

Why We Need a Focus on Wellbeing and Care

Across the globe, the pandemic has caused periods of lockdown, the cessation of face-to-face teaching, and a shift to flexible and remote learning in both university and schooling contexts. These shifts have resulted in an intensification of work practices for teachers and university faculty (Darling-Hammond & Hyler, 2020; Kim & Asbury, 2020; Lemon & McDonough, 2021; Trust & Whalen, 2020; van der Spoel et al., 2020) as they moved to deliver education programs virtually, with Czerniewicz et al. (2020) arguing that how "we in education have attempted to ameliorate the challenges we and our students have encountered have taken the form of acts of care" (p. 948). They note, however, that these challenges and acts of care occur within broader social, cultural, and political contexts, writing that "there is an expressed hope that, somehow, this 'wake-up' call will result, post-pandemic, in reshaping the intersections of equity, inequality and teaching online for the better" (Czerniewicz et al., 2020, p. 947).

Despite this hope, the pandemic has highlighted—and for some, intensified—existing inequities in the education system, with preservice teacher candidates reflecting on their experiences, arguing "It's like the veil has been lifted. The students who are failing right now are the students who were failing before. They are now further disenfranchised because of this pandemic" (Glenn et al., 2020, p. 6). In the face of the continuing pandemic, these inequities, and the impacts on wellbeing for students and teachers, it is time to consider processes for enacting systematic approaches for wellbeing and care in education contexts. We draw from our own research with inservice teachers to argue that systematic approaches to care and wellbeing must start with preservice teachers and teacher education programs.

Care: Concepts and Contestation

In higher education, care has not been a central focus of research (Anderson et al., 2020; Mariskind, 2014). The pandemic provides a timely catalyst to reconsider what care might look like at individual, institutional, and systemic levels. In their work, Shoffner and Webb (2020) argue that the COVID-19 pandemic has altered our understanding and "enactments" (p. 2) of care. They acknowledge the complexity of care as a concept and practice but contend that "care for students is essential to the mission and vision of higher education" (p. 3).

Historically, care is a contested concept, with Mariskind (2014) arguing that there is "no agreement on what the term means or how it should be put into practice" (p. 307) and contending that care can be viewed as a "disposition, an ethic, or a practice" (p. 308). Tronto (1993) positions care as an ethical stance, conceptualizing the stances of caring about, taking care of, care giving, and care receiving. Noddings (2012) argues an approach to care ethics extends beyond the familial to wider community and global relationships and recognizes that "the caring relation is ethically (morally) basic" (p. 771). She suggests elements of caring such as attentiveness, responsiveness, listening, and thinking, to highlight the cognitive and affective dimensions of care.

Care has been recognized as problematic and contested, however, due to associations as an individualized, familial, and gendered concept. As a site of contestation, the association of care with gender and with concepts such as "vulnerability, emotion and the private sphere further genres and thus devalues care" (Mariskind, 2014, p. 308). Mariskind (2014) posits that care needs to move from familial and gendered notions to "a daily human activity undertaken in both private and public domains that supports human flourishing" (p. 308). Such a shift would also enable the reconstruction of white, Western conceptions of care that align care as an individualized and feminized practice towards conceptualizations that acknowledge the communal nature of care (Mariskind, 2014).

Communal notions of care enable and facilitate conceptions of "caring-as-activism" (Mariskind, 2014, p. 309). Anderson et al. (2020) examine Tronto's (1993) work and argue that conceptualizing care as an ethical, activist stance "enables responsiveness to unequal relations of power, connoting a level of engagement that reaches beyond self-interest, takes action and accepts a burden of some kind" (Anderson et al., 2020, p. 2). In moving beyond the self, care can be "an organizational concept that requires action beyond acknowledgement" (Shoffner & Webb, 2020, p. 5) and "attention to, not avoidance of, troublesome knowledge" (Anderson et al., 2020, p. 13). A communal and activist approach to care necessitates that we do not shy away from difficult conversations and situations, but that we seek solutions to the problematic challenges of our time. Such a communal and activist approach to care necessitates that we enact conversations, actions, and systems for care at all levels of education, including preservice teacher education.

Adopting a communal, activist approach to care can support the wellbeing of both students and staff in higher education contexts. Keeling (2014) argues that, when we think of higher education only as an institution, we remove the humanity of those involved. The institution needs to respond to, support, and acknowledge barriers to students' wellbeing; put simply, "the institution as an institution must notice and act" (Keeling, 2014, p. 146). Previous studies in higher education (Anderson et al., 2020; Mariskind, 2014; Walker & Gleaves, 2014) highlight the ways that individual teachers demonstrate "attentiveness, openness, awareness of students' lives and other commitments, responsiveness to students' learning needs and investment in students' well-being *and* learning" (Anderson et al., 2020, p. 11; emphasis in original). An individual, rather than an institutional and systemic focus on care, "marginalises [sic] caring practices" (Mariskind, 2014, p. 316) and leaves caring responses as ad hoc and unsustainable, as they are reliant on individual capacities rather than institutionalized approaches. In advocating for a communal, institutional ethic of care that supports wellbeing, we are not advocating for yet another accountability metric to tick off but, rather, a meaningful and authentic orientation towards care of self, others, and community.

Teachers and Teaching: Care and Wellbeing During a Pandemic

This chapter is informed by research conducted in Australia during the period of June–July 2020 to examine the impact of the shift to remote teaching on teachers' work lives and wellbeing. Using an ecological framework based on the work of Bronfenbrenner (1979) to guide the study, we collected data from 137 Australian teachers via an online questionnaire. The ecological model consists of a series of systems that individuals interact with which mediate development, such as the microsystem which is closest to the individual (Bronfenbrenner, 1979) and comprised of interactions with those in their immediate environment (e.g., family, students, colleagues). The survey had ten questions: four to elicit demographic information and six inviting participants to share their experience of remote teaching, the impact of this on their work and workload, and the strategies and resources they used to cope during this shift.

The findings of our research revealed the multiple challenges inservice teachers faced as they sought to implement quality teaching and learning for their students: an intensification of work; managing caregiving responsibilities while teaching remotely; being the subject of media debate; and learning new technologies and ways of working. We argue that these challenges and their impacts provide "us with an opportunity to consider *what matters most* as we move forward" (Lemon & McDonough, 2021, p. 1; emphasis in original). As we found, the pandemic prompted teachers to not only care for their students in different ways but also for each other and themselves.

Teachers revealed care of self and others as they described how letting go of notions of perfectionism and acknowledging everyone was doing their best supported wellbeing during the pandemic. They described finding new ways to work, learn, and connect that supported care and relationships as a central focus, such as modifying existing tasks and curriculum to place relationships and the wellbeing of their students as a central goal during the periods of remote learning (Lemon & McDonough, 2021). With the intensification of online working practices, teachers identified the need to switch off as a way to position self-care as worthy of attention and protect wellbeing. Teachers also described finding new ways to communicate with parents/carers that gave a sense of a combined, shared purpose, something which is also identified in other research conducted during periods of remote learning (e.g., Kim & Asbury, 2020). Working collaboratively with colleagues to support, rather than to compete, was identified as central to promoting care for self and others and for providing care to students during such uncertainty. Teachers described enacting strategies and opportunities for calm and stillness as a means of dealing with the challenges, the stress, and the uncertainty of living through lockdowns, remote learning, and a global pandemic (Lemon & McDonough, 2021).

While teachers were able to identify the actions that they, their colleagues, and in some instances, their schools, implemented to support wellbeing, our research highlighted inequities in workloads, resources, access to technology, and support (Lemon & McDonough, 2021). The focus on the individualized nature of care actions enacted by teachers for their students, their colleagues, and themselves highlights the need for attention and strategies for care as activism and communal care to support wellbeing. Using our research with inservice teachers, we have identified opportunities to develop processes, strategies, and systems for an explicit focus on, and attention to, care and wellbeing in teacher education.

The Role of Care and Wellbeing in Teacher Education

In the Australian context, like other international contexts, there is a need to reframe discussion, development, and enactments of care and self-care in the discipline of education at all levels. In initial teacher education itself, wellbeing and care for self and others are not always honored; there are complexities also present with the crowded nature of the initial teacher education curriculum and the intersection of both external accreditation requirements and university requirements. In Australia, the Australian Professional Standards for Teaching (Australian Institute for Teaching and School Leadership, 2017) clearly outline the capacities and skills required by teachers, with university initial teacher education programs needing to identify how their programs assist preservice teachers in developing the skills and knowledge associated with the standards. While there is a focus on identifying and supporting student wellbeing needs (Lemon, 2021), such as in Standard 4.4: Maintain student safety (Australian Institute for Teaching and School Leadership, 2017), explicit attention to issues of teacher wellbeing is absent. At the graduate teacher level, for example, Standard 4.4 includes that teachers can "describe strategies that support students' wellbeing" (Australian

Institute for Teaching and School Leadership, 2017). Similarly, concepts of care are largely confined to regulatory and legal requirements of teachers pertaining to duty of care.

We know that there are systemic problems with teacher attrition, mental health, high expectations, over testing, crowded curriculum, societal ideals of a teacher, and lack of resources (Betoret & Artiga, 2010; Madaliyeva et al., 2015; Qiu, 2018; Schnaider-Levi et al., 2017; Skaalvik & Skaalvik, 2017). Conversations, systems, and processes around care and wellbeing are required for teachers in the profession but also for those who are becoming teachers—so in both initial preservice teacher education and in ongoing teacher education and professional learning for teachers. When working with preservice teachers, this becomes visible in the negotiation between their professional and personal identity (Lemon, 2021; Lemon & McDonough, 2020). In the journey of becoming a teacher, initial teacher education is a fundamental stage of training whereby wellbeing can be introduced and positioned as both an individual and collective action.

For preservice teachers undertaking initial teacher education studies and entering the profession of teaching, there are many layers of political and systemic influences that can be rather confronting. These can impact wellbeing, while also raising the need of being able to care for self both hedonically and eudemonically (Lemon, 2021). Often the focus can be on aspects of the profession that are connected to a deficit way of thinking of wrongs, negatives, and issues. But what happens when we focus on flourishing and what is good? What happens when we value conversations about care, self-care, and wellbeing with preservice teachers? What can happen when we embed approaches to care and wellbeing as central elements of both policy and practice?

Embedding Care in Teacher Education to Support Wellbeing

Keeling (2014) argues that to make learning, wellbeing, and the success of learners a priority requires an institutional ethic of care rather than actions from individual academics. He posits that a shift to this focus would require "significant, nonincremental, changes in policies and practices throughout the academy, with fundamental changes in our academic, social, and campus cultures" (pp. 147–148). We draw from his framing of institutional ethic of care guidelines to structure a series of principles for teacher education.

Using the insights generated from our research into the experiences of inservice teachers, we propose a series of principles of care in teacher education that support both individual and communal wellbeing among preservice teachers. This explicit attention to care and wellbeing at the preservice level is a lever for creating ongoing change across education systems. In doing so, we make use of the insights generated during the global pandemic to reconsider processes and practices to create education systems that focus on care as a supportive mechanism for wellbeing. Through making use of these principles, we can work towards creating education systems that are more 'care-full' as we move beyond COVID. In this context, care-full systems are those that pay attention to the individual and system level actions we can take to support care and wellbeing for all.

Challenge Deficit Views of Teaching

Our research with teachers highlighted the detrimental impact that negative media representations of teachers and teaching can have on their wellbeing (Lemon & McDonough, 2021). Contested discourses and views of teaching dominate the news cycle, while policy reforms come from deficit views that demand unrealistic perfection from teachers. Sharing experiences of failure and imperfection are ways to disrupt metanarratives of perfection that function as acts of care for self and for others (Brown, 2010). Through challenging deficit views, we can continue to advocate for the teaching profession and for teachers as a form of care as activism. As noted above, too frequently discourses around teaching can focus on deficit images or views.

Create Care-Full Communities of Practice

Our research with inservice teachers highlighted the benefits that came when colleagues and leaders shared practices and strategies for supporting care and wellbeing. As a principle for embedding care as a supportive mechanism for wellbeing, we advocate for communities of practice where we talk about care, self-care, and wellbeing. These communities of practice can occur between faculty and between faculty and preservice teachers. The concepts should not be hidden or glossed over but placed as central to our shared dialogue. Only through creating space and time for these conversations can we begin to create opportunities for the sharing of views, perspectives, strategies, and approaches for ways to make care and wellbeing a central focus in our work.

Embed Care and Wellbeing Perspectives at the Course and Program Level

In our research with inservice teachers, we identified when teachers adapted their curriculum to focus on the wellbeing of their students as a primary focus. While inclusion of the concepts of care and wellbeing at the policy level are important in enacting system level change, it is at the individual course and program level that we can embed strategic approaches to wellbeing and care. By mapping strategies, concepts, and approaches towards care and wellbeing as throughlines in courses, we can build the skills, capacities, and content knowledge of preservice teachers. This knowledge can be about individual strategies but also about ways that they might work with others in their educational community to proactively develop care-full approaches as a supportive mechanism for collective wellbeing.

Enact Policy Level Change

Through our research with inservice teachers, we have identified that in order to operationalize concepts of care and wellbeing, they have to be enacted at the policy level. Without this enactment, the shared conversations and communities of practice can only go so far, since policy level change is the way that we can move from individual to collective action and work. Through including explicit reference to care and wellbeing (for self, others, and community) in our policies, our teacher professional standards, and the vision and mission of our teacher education faculties, we can begin to take concrete steps towards creating care-full communities. As part of a collective, community action for care, we can advocate for the teaching profession with government, media, and the broader community. In these interactions, we need to advocate for care and wellbeing as central pillars of our education communities, including both students and teachers. Without explicit attention to care for all in our education communities, we will not be able to create supportive, care-full communities that support wellbeing in our schools.

Conclusion

If the pandemic has taught us one thing, it is that we are connected in ways that we had never considered or acknowledged. We have all experienced the pandemic but for each of us the experience has been different. Yet, when we think of ourselves from the perspective of common humanity, a focus and enactment of care in the everyday practice of our lives and work has become essential. Given the dynamic nature of the COVID-19 pandemic and the skills developed by teachers, opportunities exist to enact change in teacher education to support more equitable practices and foster teacher wellbeing. As our research with inservice teachers highlights, embodying care with preservice teachers is important for both individual and communal wellbeing. By doing so, we have the opportunity to create care-full education communities that pay attention to the individual and system level actions we can take to support care and wellbeing for all.

If we educators, future educators, and students cannot support one another now, when will this be? If now is not a time for collective action to position care as central to what we do, how we are, and how we collectively process, suffer and heal, then what has the pandemic taught us? There has been a collective shift in the ways we need to learn and live throughout the pandemic, and the lessons that we have learnt highlight the need for us to take action collectively and systematically to embed care into the everyday practice of our lives and work. As teachers and teacher educators, we have a unique opportunity to spark a collective movement for change in education and community.

References

Anderson, V., Rabello, R., Wass, R., Golding, C., Rangi, A., Eteuati, E., Bristowe, Z., & Walker, A. (2020). Good teaching as care in higher education. *Higher Education, 79*, 1–19.

Australian Institute for Teaching and School Leadership. (2017). *Australian Professional Standards for Teachers*. www.aitsl.edu.au/teach/standards.

Betoret, F. D., & Artiga, A. G. (2010). Barriers perceived by teachers at work, coping strategies, self-efficacy and burnout. *The Spanish Journal of Psychology, 13*(2), 637–654.

Bronfenbrenner, U. (1979). *The ecology of human development: Experiments by nature and design.* Harvard University Press.

Brown, B. (2010). *The gifts of imperfection.* Hazelden Publishing.

Czerniewicz, L., Agherdien, N., Badenhorst, J., Belluigi, D., Chambers, T., Chili, M., de Villiers, M., Felix, A., Gachago, D., Gokhale, C., Ivala, E., Kramm, N., Madiba, M., Misiri, C., Mgqwashu, E., Pallitt, N., Prinsloo, P., Solomon, K., Strydom, S., ... Wissing, G. (2020). A wake-up call: Equity, inequality and COVID-19 emergency remote teaching and learning. *Postdigital Science and Education, 2*, 946–967.

Darling-Hammond, L., & Hyler, M. E. (2020). Preparing educators for the time of COVID ...and beyond. *European Journal of Teacher Education, 43*(4), 457–465.

Dodge, R., Daly, A., Huyton, J., & Sanders, L. (2012). The challenge of defining wellbeing. *International Journal of Wellbeing, 2*(3), 222–235.

Ereaut, G., & Whiting, R. (2008). What do we mean by 'wellbeing'? And why might it matter?. Research Report No DCSF-RW073, Department for Children, Schools and Families. Linguistic Landscapes. http://dera.ioe.ac.uk/8572/1/dcsf-rw073%20v2.pdf.

Fredrickson, B. L., & Losada, M. F. (2005). Positive affect and the complex dynamics of human flourishing. *American Psychologist, 60*(7), 678–686.

Glenn, S., Kall, K., & Ruebenson, K. (2020). COVID-19, equity and the future of education: A conversation between teacher candidates. *Northwest Journal of Teacher Education, 15*(1), 1–8.

Higgins, J., & Goodall, S. (2021.) Transforming the wellbeing focus in education: A document analysis of policy in Aotearoa New Zealand. *International Journal of Qualitative Studies on Health and Wellbeing, 16*(1). www.tandfonline.com/doi/full/10.1080/17482631.2021.1879370.

Keeling, R. P. (2014). An ethic of care in higher education: Well-being and learning. *Journal of College and Character, 15*(3), 141–148.

Kim, L.E., & Asbury, K. (2020). 'Like a rug had been pulled from under you': The impact of COVID-19 on teachers in England during the first six weeks of the UK lockdown. *British Journal of Educational Psychology, 90*(4), 1–22.

La Placa, V., McNaught, A., & Knight, A. (2013). *Discourse on wellbeing in research and practice. International Journal of Wellbeing, 3*(1), 116–125.

Lottman, T. J., Zawaly, S., & Niemiec, R. (2017). Well-being and well-doing: Bringing mindfulness and character strengths to the early childhood classroom and home. In C. Proctor (Ed.), *Positive Psychology Interventions in Practice* (pp. 83–105). Springer International Publishing.

Lemon, N. (2021). Wellbeing in initial teacher education: Using poetic representation to examine pre-service teachers' understanding of their self-care needs. *Cultural Studies of Science Education, 16*(3), 931-950.

Lemon, N., & McDonough, S. (2021). If not now, then when? Wellbeing and wholeheartedness in education. *Educational Forum, 85*(3), 317–335.

Lemon, N., & McDonough, S. (2020). *Building and sustaining a teaching career: Strategies for professional experience, wellbeing and mindful practice.* Cambridge University Press.

Lyubomirsky, S. (2010). *The how of happiness: A practical guide to getting the life you want.* Piatkus.

Madaliyeva, Z., Mynbayeva, A., Sadvakassova, Z., & Zholdassova, M. (2015). Correction of burnout in teachers. *Procedia – Social and Behavioral Sciences, 171,* 1345–1352.

Mariskind, C. (2014). Teachers' care in higher education: Contesting gendered constructions. *Gender and Education, 26*(3), 306–320.

McCallum, F., & Price, D. (2016). *Nurturing wellbeing development in education.* Routledge.

Noddings, N. (2012). The caring relation in teaching. *Oxford Review of Education, 38*(6), 771–777.

Pollard, E. L., & Lee, P. D. (2003). Child well-being: A systematic review of the literature. *Social Indicators Research, 61*(1), 59–78.

Qiu, H. (2018). Research on the burnout of high school teachers based on teacher professional development. *Open Journal of Social Sciences, 6*(12), 219–229.

Schnaider-Levi, L., Mitnik, I., Zafrani, K., Goldman, Z., & Lev-Ari, S. (2017). Inquiry-based stress reduction meditation technique for teacher burnout: A qualitative study. *Mind, Brain, and Education, 11*(2), 75–84.

Seligman, M. E. P. (2011). *Flourish.* Random House Australia.

Shoffner, M., & Webb, A. W. (2020, November 19). Questioning care in the academic world. *Teachers College Record.*

Skaalvik, E. M., & Skaalvik, S. (2017). Dimensions of teacher burnout: relations with potential stressors at school. *Social Psychology of Education, 20*(4), 775–790.

Tronto, J. (1993). *Moral boundaries: A political argument for an ethic of care.* Routledge.

Trust, T., & Whalen, J. (2020). Should teachers be trained in emergency remote teaching? Lessons learned from the COVID-19 pandemic? *Journal of Technology and Teacher Education, 28*(2), 198–199.

van der Spoel, I., Noroozi, O., Schuurink, E., & van Ginkel, S. (2020). Teachers' online teaching expectations and experiences during the Covid19 pandemic in the Netherlands. *European Journal of Teacher Education, 43*(4), 623–638.

Walker, C., & Gleaves, A. (2016). Constructing the caring higher education teacher: A theoretical framework. *Teaching and Teacher Education, 54,* 65–76.

PART IV

(Re)Framing Care

17

CULTURALLY RESPONSIVE CARING FOR ASIAN AMERICAN PRESERVICE TEACHERS

During and After COVID

Lin Wu

> Historically, pandemics have forced humans to break with the past and imagine their world anew. This one is no different. It is a portal, a gateway between one world and the next. We can choose to walk through it, dragging the carcasses of our prejudice and hatred, our avarice, our data banks and dead ideas, our dead rivers and smoky skies behind us. Or we can walk through lightly, with little luggage, ready to imagine another world. And ready to fight for it. Arundhati Roy (2020)

When I returned to the United States after visiting my family in China in late 2019, news of a deadly virus in Wuhan started to circulate on Chinese social media. Shortly after, China's government implemented a national lockdown to contain the virus (later named COVID-19), while the US federal government downplayed its severity. As I read reports of decreasing revenues for Asian-owned businesses and increasing anti-Asian attacks in the United States, I pondered how to discuss these phenomena with preservice teachers as a Chinese male immigrant teacher educator. When the 45th US president called COVID-19 the "Chinese virus" in March 2020, I was even more concerned for the Asian American preservice teachers in my class, who had to cope with the reignited yellow peril trope that pathologizes Asian people as causes and carriers of contagious diseases (Tchen & Yeats, 2014).

Before the COVID-19 pandemic, many US teacher education programs lacked culturally responsive curricular and faculty representation for Asian American preservice teachers (Han, 2019). During the COVID-19 pandemic, escalating anti-Asian xenophobia further marginalized Asian Americans in educational institutions and the larger US society (Tessler et al., 2020). Many educators in the United States, including Asian Americans, have also experienced increasing burnout during the COVID-19 pandemic (Stafford-Brizard, 2021). Thus, caring for Asian American

DOI: 10.4324/9781003244875-22

preservice teachers post-COVID-19 requires some new approaches, one of which involves a moral commitment and justice-oriented actions to heal the psycho-emotional wounds inflicted by anti-Asian rhetoric and hate crimes related to COVID-19 while helping Asian American preservice teachers reimagine the pandemic as a portal to a new world.

The Essence and Importance of Caring in Education

Noddings (2005) defined caring in education as an act of responsiveness that addresses students' multidimensional needs. She recommended that teachers guide students in "caring for self, intimate others, global others, plants, animals, and the environment, the human-made world, and ideas" (p. 173). A caring-centered education emphasizes students' intellectual development and psycho-emotional well-being and is even more vital to the success of students of color. For example, Valenzuela (1999) observed that many Mexican American students demand authentic caring from their teachers to create trusting and respectful relationships that engage them with meaningful learning. Native Alaskan students meet high academic expectations better when teachers filter instruction through emotional warmth and interpersonal relationships (Kleinfeld, 1975). Similarly, African American students tend to respond well to "warm demanders," or teachers who demand academic rigor and provide emotional support for success (Ware, 2006).

Gay (2018) explained the connection between culture and caring and defined culturally responsive caring as honoring the cultural heritages of ethnically diverse students and caring *for and about* their "competence, agency, autonomy, efficacy, and empowerment" (p. 58). The three tenets anchoring culturally responsive caring are: (1) holding high expectations for students and helping them actualize their potential; (2) building a culturally congruent learning community and attending to students' psycho-emotional well-being; and (3) cultivating an academic, ethical, and emotional partnership with students to equip them with the knowledge and skills to address injustices (Gay, 2018). Considering the rupture caused by the COVID-19 pandemic, culturally responsive caring for Asian American preservice teachers post-pandemic entails holding high expectations for them to become culturally competent, creating a culturally affirming learning environment to nurture their holistic development, and sustaining genuine connections to expand their pedagogical repertoires to tackle anti-Asian racism and other racial inequities.

Contexts of My Reflections and Recommendations

After working as a teacher and principal in a public charter school in Southern Arizona for seven years, I relocated to Washington State to pursue a doctoral degree in multicultural education at a predominantly white institution (PWI) in 2015. Subsequently, my academic training and working experiences helped me obtain a full-time instructor position in a teacher education program at another local PWI in 2019. I worked with two cohorts of mostly white, middle-class, female preservice teachers and taught graduate courses on instructional planning and multicultural education. When the Washington State governor issued a statewide stay-at-home order to slow the spread of COVID-19 in March 2020, all my courses transitioned to online delivery. Afterward, I continued to teach online until my contract ended in December 2020. The ensuring sections are based on my teaching of the multicultural education course that prepares *all* preservice teachers among the two cohorts to promote racial justice in US K-12 schools. Specifically, I described how I differentiated culturally responsive caring for the seven Asian American preservice teachers given the suffering inflicted on Asian Americans during the COVID-19 pandemic.

Holding High Expectations to Develop Cultural Competence

Ladson-Billings (2009) defined cultural competence as becoming knowledgeable of one's own cultural heritage while improving the ability to navigate other cultures. As anti-Asian xenophobia intensified during the COVID-19 pandemic, I knew it was crucial to include caring as a critical feature of developing the cultural competence of the Asian American preservice teachers. I began the course by asking them to read *Claiming the Oriental Gateway* (Lee, 2011) to examine how Asian American students were treated in K-12 public schools in Washington State before and during World War II. I then paired the study with Au (2020), who traced the "Chinese virus" pathology to historical anti-Chinese movements, and Vossoughi et al. (2020), who explained the connections between US imperialistic invasions of Asian countries and recurring anti-Asian racism. I also encouraged the Asian American preservice teachers to read *Strangers From a Different Shore* (Takaki, 1998), listen to *Home: Word* (Magnetic North & Taiyo Na, 2011), and watch *Asian Americans* (Tsien, 2020) to acquire more knowledge about Asian American history and culture.

I also helped all the preservice teachers, especially Asian Americans, improve their knowledge about the educational experiences of other groups of color. This was done by studying how Black, Indigenous, and Latinx children faced systemic racism in US K-12 schools and how their parents and other community members mobilized resources to seek justice (García et al., 2012; Lipsitz, 2011; McCarty, 2018). I then asked the preservice teachers to reflect in writing to connect anti-Asian racism during the COVID-19 pandemic with the experiences of students of color in the case studies described in the written resources. I also recommended books on Latinx, Indigenous, and Black histories (Acuña, 2019; Dunbar-Ortiz, 2015; Wilkerson, 2011). These instructional materials conveyed my expectations for the Asian American preservice teachers: to see the shared struggles and resilience between themselves and other people of color in becoming culturally competent teachers.

When a Vietnamese American preservice teacher did not turn in his journal reflections on the due date, I asked via e-mail if he was doing well. He informed me that he was late with his assignments because he had been helping his mother as she dealt with some health issues. I encouraged him to take more time to complete his work and take good care of his mother and himself. When he turned in his reflections, I provided timely feedback, asked for a revision, and extended the deadline again. After three rounds of revisions, his work met the "exceed" level on the grading rubric. Later, he told me via Zoom, "My parents are first-generation immigrants. They don't speak much English and work all the time. I rarely had teachers who understood our family and pushed me to do better. So, thank you!" I smiled and said, "You're welcome! I know you don't often get teachers who look like you, so I do my best to make sure you are challenged and prepared to become a successful teacher." This scenario suggests that culturally responsive caring for Asian American preservice teachers should contextualize high academic expectations with sensitivity to their struggles and assist them in developing cultural competence with personal warmth.

Building a Culturally Affirming Environment to Nurture Holistic Development

Many of the Asian American preservice teachers attended predominantly white K-12 schools in Washington State that mainly focused on achieving desirable standardized test scores. This schooling method and the model minority stereotype that renders all Asian Americans academically oriented cause many Asian American students to develop communication and achievement anxiety (Pang, 1998). Thus, I often included cooperative learning activities to create an environment that affirms Asian American communal cultural norms (Au, 2009). For example, when analyzing the case studies mentioned earlier, I instructed everyone to collaborate on group presentations. During preparation, I moved among breakout rooms to assist Asian American preservice teachers as needed. Afterward, I started with small breakout room presentations and gradually transitioned to whole-class presentations. This pedagogical approach helped many Asian American preservice teachers become more comfortable and confident in sharing their knowledge in public as the course progressed.

Hall and Yee (2012) stated that the false belief that all Asian Americans are academically and economically successful has "contributed to the general neglect of the mental health needs of Asian Americans" (p. 185). Such neglect during COVID-19, when Asian Americans were targets of racial hatred, further compromised their sense of belonging in mainstream society. Hence, I often used emotional check-ins to monitor the Asian American preservice teachers' well-being. For example, I would ask, "Who are you bringing into our class today and why?" and instruct everyone to complete a five-minute free write. Once everyone returned to the main room after sharing in small breakout rooms, I asked a few volunteers to speak and then shared my story:

> My grandmothers left this world in early 2020. Due to the travel ban between the United States and China, I could not fly home to attend their funerals. They had gone through many wars, so I bring them to class today to honor their lives and my ancestral lineage. And if any of you has been grieving this year, know that you're not alone.

A gender-queer Vietnamese American preservice teacher messaged me on Zoom and stated, "I've been struggling with mental health issues because my family went through much war-related trauma. Thank you for making a beautiful space in our class to share your struggles and make me feel seen." A biracial (Japanese and British) female preservice teacher emailed me later and said, "Lin, it is powerful that you acknowledge your grief to break down the racialized mental health stigma impacting our community. May your grandmothers' spirits be at peace. I will keep them in my thoughts."

According to Lee (2009), the model minority stereotype also leads many Asian American youths to develop negative self-concepts when they underperform in school. As I conveyed high expectations for the Asian American preservice teachers, I used creative activities to nurture their ethnic identity. For example, I asked everyone to assemble an identity bag with five items illustrating their ethnic heritage, cultural communication style, and family. One preservice teacher included an Irish hat to depict his paternal ancestors' immigration story and a "Live with Aloha" stone to portray his maternal ancestors' journey from Japan to Hawai'i. As the course progressed, I shared my identity development stories with him and recommended books such as *We Gon' Be Alright* (Chang, 2016) to nurture his biracial identity. When the course concluded, this preservice teacher officially hyphenated his Irish last name with his mother's Japanese surname. These pedagogical techniques indicate that culturally responsive caring can create a learning environment that affirms Asian American preservice teachers' ethnic identity and prepares them to become well-rounded teachers.

Sustaining Genuine Connections to Expand Pedagogical Repertoires

My high expectations and emphasis on holistic development helped me introduce asset-based pedagogies to counter the culturally deficit paradigms plaguing children of color in US K-12 schools. For example, I assigned everyone to read two chapters of *Struggling to Be Heard* (Pang & Cheng, 1998) and *Culturally Responsive Teaching* (Gay, 2018), then used jigsaw methods to examine case studies of how teachers in different content areas can implement asset-based pedagogies for Asian American students (Chang & Rosiek, 2003; Pham & Lee, 2014; Rodríguez,

2018). Moreover, I helped all the preservice teachers understand funds of knowledge (Moll et al., 1992), culturally relevant pedagogy (Ladson-Billings, 2009), culturally sustaining/ revitalizing pedagogy (McCarty & Lee, 2014), and hip-hop pedagogy (Adjapong & Emdin, 2015) and their potential for promoting racial justice for Latinx, African American, Indigenous, and Asian American students.

I also modeled how to use asset-based pedagogies in teaching. For example, one tenet of culturally relevant pedagogy is developing students' sociopolitical consciousness. After reading this theory, I provided statements, such as "The United States is a melting pot of immigrants." and "It is a Chinese virus because it started in China." I asked everyone to probe each statement collaboratively and use the course materials to propose a counter-narrative if they agreed that the statement served the dominant group. One team that included two Asian American preservice teachers stated, "Based on Sensoy and DiAngelo (2017), the melting pot is a master narrative since it perpetuates American exceptionalism. Our counter-narrative is that the United States is still racially segregated in schools, neighborhoods, and the larger society." Another Asian American preservice teacher stated for his group, "Au (2020) suggests that the 'Chinese virus' is a master narrative because it downplays the US disastrous response to the virus by blaming China. Here is our counter-narrative: It's called COVID-19. Ethnicity is not a virus."

In further developing the curriculum and instruction of the course, I used various projects to expand all the preservice teachers' pedagogical repertoires. One project was integrating *Since Time Immemorial* (Office of Superintendent of Public Instruction, 2015), a curriculum endorsed by all 29 federally recognized tribes in Washington State, in different content areas to promote tribal sovereignty. A Chinese American male preservice teacher explained the constraints and possibilities of using this curriculum and culturally responsive teaching to promote the learning and well-being for Indigenous students in US K-12 schools:

> It is unlikely that I can teach an entire unit on Indigenous history as a future math teacher. However, I can collaborate with social studies teachers to develop lessons in culturally responsive ways. By using math and social studies as self-expression outlets, we can study colonization without sacrificing the well-being of Indigenous students.

Another project asked everyone to conduct critical family history research (Sleeter, 2016). Each preservice teacher interviewed a family member over 21 years of age and analyzed the interviewee's experiences of white supremacy and perceptions of race relations in US society through the lens of critical race theory (Ladson-Billings & Tate IV, 1995). The following excerpt from a biracial (British and Korean) preservice teacher showed how this project expanded his pedagogical repertoires for addressing racial injustices:

Whiteness as property seemed implausible when I first read critical race theory, but it kept showing up in my family's history. My grandfather was denied medical school due to his race, but I had not connected it with the rights of exclusion and disposition. My grandmother changed her first name to sound more 'American,' but I had not connected it with the rights of reputation and status. This project showed that Asian Americans have been treated as inferior to whites in the US. When adapting this project in my class, I would have the students fill out a chart and complete a multiple choice quiz to ensure that they know how to use whiteness as property as a framework to analyze structural racism.

These learning materials and activities communicated my concern for helping Asian American preservice teachers learn to center racial justice in their professional trajectories and personal lives. My pedagogical approaches also sustained a genuine connection between myself and the Asian American preservice teachers beyond the multicultural education course. When the gender-queer Vietnamese American preservice teacher struggled to complete their practicum at a predominantly white, middle-class school, they reached out to me and said, "I'm exhausted helping white students understand how systemic racism works when many resist examining their white identity. Why do you put yourself through some white students' racial gaslighting and abuse?" I replied,

I do it because some white people have told me that I am not smart enough to get a doctoral degree. I do it so that teachers like you will not feel isolated when you get into teacher education programs. I do it for my kid to have a better future. And I do it to honor my ancestors. So, when you teach, you teach for our people, with struggle and dignity and with love and hope.

I delivered a similar message to the biracial (Japanese and British) female preservice teacher at her cohort's graduation ceremony on Zoom in June 2020:

What an honor to have worked with you! I appreciate your dedication to our class discussions and assignments. Your criticality toward education for justice will be an asset to any school. Remember, when you get into 'good trouble,' you've got family here lifting you. And remember, I'm counting on you to become a teacher educator one day!

Having read the institution's statements on the commitment to racial justice amidst growing anti-Asian hatred and after the murder of George Floyd, this preservice teacher was frustrated to learn that the institution did not offer me a tenure-track position despite my extensive academic training and teaching experiences. Hence, she reciprocated my caring during her valedictorian speech. In part, she said,

> The pandemic has shown us that this is the best time to go into teaching because the boundary of possibility is in flux, and we have the opportunity to shape change. On this note, what is shaping change in our program? How are faculty members learning from the Black Lives Matter movement and supporting students of color in tangible ways so that they are here for graduation? How does the university support faculties of color, especially those well-trained in multicultural education, by offering them tenure-track positions? So, here we are. We cannot go back to the old normal. Let's shape change!

Culturally Responsive Caring as a Portal to Justice

When the murder of six working-class East Asian women by a young white man took place in Georgia in March 2021, many educational institutions and organizations issued solidarity statements supporting Asian Americans. Scholars such as Au and Yonamine (2021) also called for educators to honor the grief of and fight for Asian America. Unfortunately, my conversations with many preservice and in-service Asian American teachers suggested that few colleagues had reached out to them as white supremacy terrorized our existence, and rarely did those solidarity statements materialize in actions that made them feel cared for. Thus, caring for Asian American preservice teachers post-pandemic must address their psycho-emotional well-being, resist the model minority stereotype, prepare them with pedagogical tools to counter the yellow peril trope, and align their quest for justice with other communities of color.

Duncan-Andrade (2009) observed that "effective teaching depends most heavily on one thing: deep and caring relationships" (p. 191). I hope my chapter imparts some useful strategies that teacher educators can adapt in their curriculum, pedagogy, and assessment to build deep and caring relationships with Asian American preservice teachers and engage them in meaningful learning. By contextualizing culturally responsive caring with COVID-19, teacher educators can model shedding "the carcasses of our prejudice and hatred" and help Asian American preservice teachers imagine the pandemic as "a gateway between one world and the next" (Roy, 2020). In so doing, Asian American preservice teachers will be well prepared to reclaim their humanity and fight for a more racially just world post-pandemic.

Acknowledgments

I am grateful to Drs. Angela Webb, Melanie Shoffner, and Geneva Gay for their generous feedback on earlier drafts of this chapter. Any remaining shortcomings are my own.

References

Acuña, R. F. (2019). *Occupied America: A history of Chicanos* (9th ed.). Pearson.

Adjapong, E. S., & Emdin, C. (2015). Rethinking pedagogy in urban spaces: Implementing hip-hop pedagogy in the urban science classroom. *Journal of Urban Learning Teaching and Research, 11*, 66–77.

Au, K. (2009). Isn't culturally responsive instruction just good teaching? *Social Education, 73* (4), 179–183.

Au, W. (2020). "I don't like China or Chinese people because they started this quarantine:" The history of anti-Chinese racism and disease in the United States. *Rethinking Schools, 34*(4), 56–63.

Au, W., & Yonamine, M. (2021). Dear educators, it is time to fight for Asian America. *Rethinking Schools, 35*(3), 9–11.

Chang, J. (2016). *We gon' be alright: Notes on race and resegregation.* Picador.

Chang, P. J., & Rosiek, J. (2003). Anti-colonialist antinomies in a biology lesson! A sonata form case study of cultural conflict in a science classroom. *Curriculum Inquiry, 33*(3), 251–290.

Dunbar-Ortiz, R. (2015). *An Indigenous people's history of the United States.* Beacon Press.

Duncan-Andrade, J. M. R. (2009). Note to educators: Hope required when growing roses in concrete. *Harvard Educational Review, 79*(2), 181–194.

García, D. G., Yosso, T. J., & Barajas, F. P. (2012). "A few of the brightest, cleanest Mexican children": School segregation as a form of mundane racism in Oxnard, California, 1900–1940. *Harvard Educational Review, 82*(1), 1–25.

Gay, G. (2018). *Culturally responsive teaching: Theory, research, and practice* (3rd ed.). Teachers College Press.

Hall, G. C. N., & Yee, A. (2012). U.S. mental health policy: Addressing the neglect of Asian Americans. *Asian American Journal of Psychology, 3*(3), 181–193.

Han, K. T. (2019). Exploring Asian American invisibility in teacher education: The AsianCrit account. In K. T. Han & J. Laughter (Eds.), *Critical race theory in teacher education: Informing classroom culture and practice* (pp. 71–81). Teachers College Press.

Kleinfeld, J. (1975). Effective teachers of Eskimo and Indian students. *The School Review, 83* (2), 301–344.

Ladson-Billings, G. (2009). *The dreamkeepers: Successful teachers of African American children* (2nd ed.). Jossey-Bass.

Ladson-Billings, G., & Tate IV., W. F. (1995). Toward a critical race theory of education. *Teachers College Record, 97*(1), 47–68.

Lee, S. J. (2009). *Unraveling the "model minority" stereotype: Listening to Asian American youth* (2nd ed.). Teachers College Press.

Lee, S. S. (2011). *Claiming the Oriental gateway: Prewar Seattle and Japanese America.* Temple University Press.

Lipsitz, G. (2011). *How racism takes place.* Temple University Press.

Magnetic North & Taiyo Na. (2011). *Home: Word* (deluxe ed.) [Album]. Media Factory.

McCarty, T. L. (2018). So that any child may succeed: Indigenous pathways toward justice and the promise of Brown. *Educational Researcher, 47*(5), 271–283.

McCarty, T. L., & Lee, T. S. (2014). Critical culturally sustaining/revitalizing pedagogy and Indigenous education sovereignty. *Harvard Education Review, 84*(1), 101–124.

Moll, L. C., Amanti, C., Neff, D., & Gonzalez, N. (1992). Funds of knowledge for teaching: Using a qualitative approach to connect homes and classrooms. *Theory Into Practice, 31*(2), 132–141.

Noddings, N. (2005). *The challenge to care in schools: An alternative approach to education*. (2nd ed.). Teachers College Press.

Office of Superintendent of Public Instruction. (2015). *Since time immemorial: tribal sovereignty in washington state*. www.k12.wa.us/student-success/resources-subject-area/time-immemorial-tribal-sovereignty-washington-state.

Pang, V. O. (1998). Educating the whole child: Implications for teachers. In V. O. Pang & L. L. Cheng (Eds.), *Struggling to be heard: The unmet needs of Asian Pacific American children* (pp. 265–301). State University of New York Press.

Pang, V. O., & Cheng, L. L. (Eds.). (1998). *Struggling to be heard: The unmet needs of Asian Pacific American children*. State University of New York Press.

Pham, M. T., & Lee, J. H. X. (2014). Poetic justice: Cambodian American literary visions. In J. H. X. Lee (Ed.), *Southeast Asian diaspora in the United States: Memories and visions, yesterday, today, and tomorrow* (pp. 178–207). Cambridge Scholars Publishing.

Rodríguez, N. N. (2018). From margins to center: Developing cultural citizenship education through the teaching of Asian American history. *Theory & Research in Social Education, 46*(4), 528–573.

Roy, A. (2020, April 3). The pandemic is a portal. *Financial Times*. www.ft.com/content/10d8f5e8-74eb-11ea-95fe-fcd274e920ca.

Sensoy, Ö., & DiAngelo, R. (2017). *Is everyone really equal? An introduction to key concepts in social justice education* (2nd ed.). Teachers College Press.

Sleeter, C. E. (2016). Critical family history: Situating family within contexts of power relationships. *Journal of Multidisciplinary Research, 8*(1), 11–23.

Stafford-Brizard, B. (2021). Supporting teacher well-being in a time of crisis. *Educational Leadership, 78*(8), 84–86.

Takaki, R. (1998). *Strangers from a different shore: A history of Asian Americans* (rev. ed.). Little, Brown and Company.

Tchen, J. K. W., & Yeats, D. (Eds). (2014). *Yellow peril!: An archive of anti-Asian fear*. Verso.

Tessler, H., Choi, M., & Kao, G. (2020). The anxiety of being Asian American: Hate crimes and negative biases during the COVID-19 pandemic. *American Journal of Criminal Justice, 45*(4), 636–646.

Tsien, J. (Executive Producer). (2020). *Asian Americans* [TV series]. PBS.

Valenzuela, A. (1999). *Subtractive schooling: U.S.-Mexican youth and the politics of caring*. State University of New York Press.

Vossoughi, S., Shirazi, R., & Vakil, S. (2020). As tensions with Iran escalate, it is time to challenge empire in the classroom. *Rethinking Schools, 34*(3), 12–15.

Ware, F. (2006). Warm demander pedagogy: Culturally responsive teaching that supports a culture of achievement for African American students. *Urban Education, 41*(4), 427–456.

Wilkerson, I. (2011). *The warmth of other suns: The epic story of America's great migration*. Vintage Books.

18

DEVELOPING CRITICAL CARING PEDAGOGY

Teacher Education in Service of Students in Black Rural Spaces after COVID

Tonya B. Perry, Martez Files, Samantha Elliott Briggs, Hannah Jurkiewicz, Ashton Ray, and Larrell Wilkinson

Octavia, a Black rural high school student, was sent home in March 2020 and told that all her high school courses would be moved online. She was expected to shift immediately and continue her studies without any hiccups. Once home, she learned her grandmother was sick; as her grandmother struggled to breathe, she was rushed to the hospital and diagnosed with COVID-19. About two weeks later, her grandmother passed away. Octavia and her mom both contracted COVID-19, experiencing mild symptoms while losing their taste and smell. As Octavia recovered, her mother was laid off from her job, which further destabilized her home. Her teachers constantly emailed her because her grades were suffering: She had all Fs in her courses, a far cry from the straight-As she maintained before the pandemic. She and her three siblings in rural Alabama were without adequate internet access, with only school-issued Chromebooks to complete their online assignments, yet she was still expected to maintain her same academic performance. Her grandmother's death, mother's lay-off, sluggish internet, and limited electronic devices were never considered. Although she eventually graduated and went on to attend a prominent university, Octavia suffered through her senior year. She is not the same student that she was before COVID-19.

Unfortunately, Octavia's experience is not unique. COVID-19 has disproportionally impacted people of color in America, particularly Black and Latinx peoples. Black rural spaces are particularly affected by COVID-19 because of the disproportionate impact of social determinants (Centers for Disease Control and Prevention, 2020), like the lack of qualified and high-quality doctors and healthcare providers, as well as employment opportunities, in these regions. These inequities also impact schooling. Teachers are tasked with thinking about how they might respond to students like Octavia who live and exist on the margins, contending with the ways in which social determinants, including discrimination,

DOI: 10.4324/9781003244875-23

healthcare access and utilization, and educational income, impact communities of color at high levels. This is why we believe there must be a transformation in teacher education.

Transformation of the teaching profession begins with teacher educators. Creating a *careforce* of teachers, as opposed to a workforce, who show up for every student, support families, and care for communities is a tall task. However, the pandemic has taught us valuable lessons about the need to adapt to change as a process, not the micro-tasks that temporarily cause us to rethink an activity or strategy. Critical caring pedagogy is a systemic, long-lasting approach to inclusive change that impacts generations. Teacher education courses that center care, innovative change practices, and opportunities to collaboratively tackle challenges with Black rural students, families, and communities should be the norm for future teachers, not the exception.

In this chapter, we, as teacher educators, explore care in Black rural education through the lens of critical caring pedagogy. Our explorations encourage us to consider the impact of COVID-19 on Black rural education and, consequently, the need for teacher education post-COVID to better prepare teacher candidates to meet the needs of their Black rural students.

Contextualizing Care in Teacher Education

Our education systems are failing students from our most vulnerable communities (Love, 2019). Some teachers are not trained to implement pedagogical approaches that center equity and justice and are grounded in academic rigor and high expectations (Darling-Hammond, 2000). Social justice, community activism, and civic engagement are central tenets of socially just societies (Freire, 1972). It makes sense, then, that teachers should be educated to create more livable and loving communities in the classroom. Indeed, teaching should be understood as a humanizing process. Creating sustained relationships allows teachers to build bridges, offer support to colleagues, mentor young people, establish networks with young professionals, and learn daily (Milner, 2010). Teaching during the pandemic has taught us that liberatory, freeing practices should be included in teacher education. The next generation of teachers must be able to adjust to change, know our students, and alter our practices.

As we prepare a new generation of teachers who have witnessed, lived through, and will teach in the aftermath and long-standing effects of COVID-19, we must face the truth about gaps in teacher education. Research suggests that a majority of the teaching workforce is not prepared for the critical cultural teaching required to instruct diverse students (Darling-Hammond, 2016; Krummel, 2013; Milner, 2007), even before COVID-19. Developing teacher candidates now as caring, conscious, critical educators will require these prospective teachers to remain even more open to understanding students' lives and experiences (Morrell, 2009; Nieto & Bode, 2008; Steinberg & Garret, 2016).

Teacher educators, then, must provide intensive, authentic instruction and support to teacher candidates to reach this high-achieving stage of development. This work requires a type of care ethic that grapples with the moral obligation of caring as a relational approach (Noddings, 1984). Noddings (1984) contends that

> [If I act, or do not act on something] without reflection [around] the cared-for, then I do not care. Caring requires me to respond [with] an act of commitment: I commit myself either to overt action on behalf of the cared-for…or I commit myself to thinking about what I might do. But the test of my caring is not wholly in how things turn out; the primary test lies in [examining] what I considered, how fully I received [this person or community], and whether [they are made better as] a result of the completion of my caring. (p. 81)

By Noddings' (1984) logic, caring involves advocacy and introspection. We argue that caring—specifically critical caring pedagogy—could have a more material effect than laws and policies in addressing oppressive, abusive, and destructive forces. As Noddings (1984) described, caring reminds us to act and reflect on our actions and potential actions. When we prioritize care, we can honestly think about how our pedagogical approaches and curricular choices impact our students, their families, and their communities. Care, as an ethical and moral obligation, is critical to our collective survival (Love, 2019).

Critical Caring Pedagogy

However, when referring to teaching, care is not enough. We must add criticality to our practice in order to prepare teachers more completely, wholly, and intentionally. Criticality allows us to deliberately examine our practices, particularly our caring practices. Muhammad (2020) defines criticality as understanding power structures and equity. When applying criticality to caring pedagogy, we then have a new way to think about critical caring pedagogy as the art of teaching that centers and cares for students while, at the same time, understanding the complexities of history and examining biases about families and communities that can impact care and equity (Kinloch, 2018; Mirra, 2018; Watson et al., 2016). Critical caring pedagogy asks us to examine ourselves more deeply, reflect more often, prepare to find openings in our own thinking, fill them with life-giving, nurturing practices, innovate more imaginatively, and fight more fiercely for equity for our Black rural students. Only then can we say we have worked to be a responsive, critical, post-COVID educator.

Black Rurality

As we have worked and created community in Black rural spaces in Alabama for almost a decade, Alabama provides some context for understanding Black rurality.

Many rural Alabama communities have not been granted access to modern housing, quality health care, quality food sources, profitable careers, and rigorous education. According to the Rural Health Information Hub (n.d.), the average per capita income for Alabama residents in 2019 was $44,145, with the rural capita income at $37,095; the poverty rate in rural Alabama is 18.5 percent, contrasted to 14.8 percent in urban areas of the state. Furthermore, 18.8 percent of the rural population has not completed high school, while 12.3 percent lack a high school diploma. In 2018, the unemployment rate in rural Alabama was 3.3 percent, comparatively higher than urban areas at 2.9 percent. When layers of race—and racism—are added, the differences morph into grave disparities.

Impact of COVID-19 on Black Rural Education

In 2020, all high school seniors should have been focused on college applications, financial aid, job shadowing, and internships. Unfortunately, their experience was surviving a global pandemic with insufficient direct instruction, loss of routine and structure, loss of motivation for school, social isolation, mental health challenges, personal and familial health decline, and deaths (Centers for Disease Control and Prevention, 2020).

Those factors were doubly compounded for rural students already subjected to social and political neglect and demonized or erased in academic literature. Black rural youth are landlocked into areas in which others refuse to live, build hospitals, and create businesses, adding to the stresses of poverty and food insecurity. COVID-19 only exacerbated these gaps between Black rural America and other groups and geographic landscapes (Goldhill, 2021). Mueller et al. (2021) found that the COVID-19 pandemic had wide-reaching impacts on rural wellness, citing from their research that half of the rural participants believed the pandemic has negatively impacted their overall lives directly.

Rural education expert Mara Tieken notes the unique challenges rural schools, and the 15 percent of US students attending them, faced amid the pandemic (Anderson, 2020). Reiterating much of what we understand about rural education, Internet access and limited broadband internet, Tieken addressed the digital divide, which creates insufficient access to technology. During the pandemic, about 27 percent of rural school districts required direct instruction through recorded lessons, real-time teaching, or similar methods, yet "only 63 percent of rural adults say they have access to the internet at home" (Ratledge et al., 2020, p. 1). In Alabama's Perry County, for example, only half of the 600 students at Francis Marion School had reliable internet access, with one in five students having no connection at all, and the school district could not afford to provide access (Peyton, 2020). As Tieken (Anderson, 2020) expressed, adequate internet access should be considered as necessary as access to clean water in today's age; without it, students face severe challenges and disparities: "We need to think about not merely equality, but equity. Some places will need more money, perhaps because of generations of underfunding their schools or higher costs around transportation or other things."

One family's story in Washington County, Mississippi relates the experiences of many rural Black families during the pandemic (Harris, 2020). Without a computer or broadband internet at home, a single mother of four used her phone so her children could access the internet to complete school assignments. Her oldest daughter needed better access when the phone's hotspot was not enough to do research and write papers, so she took them to a McDonald's parking lot in order to access wi-fi. The family sat cramped together in the car so the eldest could write her paper, under pressure to get things done quickly so they could go home and spread out. Rather than rely on her eldest daughter to watch the younger ones while she worked, the mother was at home so she could watch over her children and support their learning. Although her food stamps were doubled, she often needed to take advantage of the free lunches and snacks provided by the school to have enough to eat. Unfortunately, this, too, is consistent in Black rural areas. About 78 percent of counties with high rates of food insecurity are rural, requiring children to depend on schools for their meals (Harris, 2020).

Building a Critical Caring Pedagogy in Teacher Education

Critical caring pedagogy affirms the importance of cultural awareness and deliberate actions. These life-giving, family-oriented practices support contextualized learning, problem-based learning in schools for out-of-school problems, and strength-based critical instruction for diverse students using authentic practices (Falk-Rafael, 2005; Falk-Rafael & Betker, 2012). One way to reframe teacher education post-COVID is to simultaneously listen to the teachers in Black rural spaces as well as the engaged teacher educators and researchers who inform us about critical caring. This pairing will enhance our understanding of critical caring pedagogy and propel us to embrace the community, parents, and other contextual factors needed to be effective educators in Black rural spaces.

Preparing teacher candidates for post-COVID instruction requires teacher educators to critically analyze their curriculum and infuse critical caring pedagogies into their programs. This involves a substantive connection to understanding the role of technology within homes and with families, a thoughtful review of resources and community supports, and curriculum that is relatable and transformative for students and their families. Through critical caring pedagogy, teacher educators can move teacher candidates away from traditional practices enacted pre-COVID to post-COVID practices that acknowledge and respond to the specific needs of students in Black rural spaces. While we expand on these ideas in the rest of the chapter, we provide a summary below (see Table 18.1).

TABLE 18.1 Critical Caring Pedagogy

Pre-COVID Teaching	Critical Caring Pedagogy in Teacher Education	Post-COVID Teaching
Teachers assume that students will find technology to complete assignments.	Teacher educators actively involve teacher candidates in creating lessons that connect them with the community to address issues of access.	Teachers engage in conversations with students and families to help support technology and connectivity needs.
Teachers leave connectivity concerns to the parents.	Teacher educators connect teacher candidates to families and community to hear their concerns directly and problem-solve solutions.	Teachers problem-solve with the school and community to address the digital divide.
Teachers reject notions of hybridity to address student instructional needs.	Teacher educators integrate technology fully throughout the program across all content areas.	Teachers consider connecting to students as an additional engagement tool for learning.
Teachers talk to the community through traditional notions of parent involvement.	Teacher educators incorporate the voices of parents into the teacher education program.	Teachers create two-way communication with parents with increased parent engagement paradigms.
Teachers assign work to the students that does not lead to a higher-level purpose.	Teacher educators think intentionally about transformational learning and build curriculum for change and problem solving.	Teachers engage students in work through connections and active learning.
Teachers decide curriculum based on standards.	Teacher educators instruct teacher candidates to learn about the community and families first, and then build learning opportunities that meet the learning targets.	Teachers create learning opportunities collaboratively, with input from parents and communities.

Critical Caring Pedagogy and Technology

Virtual learning during COVID-19 exposed gaps for those who have access to technology and those who do not. While many school districts across the country were able to provide computers, tablets, and hotspots for students to access their schooling during the pandemic, rural districts were challenged to provide the necessary resources and connectivity for virtual learning. Broadband internet is not even a viable choice in some rural communities. For example, in Alabama's Black Belt region, broadband availability varies from 44 percent to 0 percent in several counties (Broadbandnow, 2021). The technological divide meant that many teachers in Black rural spaces were forced to provide paper packets and worksheets to support student learning.

Lack of access to technology creates a disproportionately larger divide for already marginalized populations, like those in Black rural spaces. The Coronavirus Aid, Relief, and Economic Security (CARES) Act offers funds to address issues of technological disparity, but it will not fill the holes in the systemic problem. So, with the widespread lack of broadband access complicating learning, schools and teachers across the Black rural areas became partners in problem solving. One solution was to send school buses into the community, carrying hotspots to access the internet. Another was to offer parking lot time for parents to access the school's internet during certain times of the day. Addressing these solutions with teacher candidates encourages them to think creatively to problem solve with communities and to think about families first in order to achieve student success.

Critical Caring Pedagogy and Community

The community aspect of a school is as crucial for the students as it is for the teachers. COVID-19 emphasized the importance of this. For example, only 27 percent of rural school districts expected teachers to provide instruction, while only 43 percent of rural districts expected teachers to take attendance or check-in with their students regularly (Gross & Opalka, 2020). For those teachers able to teach through Zoom or a hybrid model, with some virtual and in-person students, it was not easy to know if students were there, much less engaged and learning. Teachers lacking reliable technology often took materials directly to students (Harris, 2020; Wright, 2021) but, because of pandemic guidelines, could not interact with their students more than waving through their window or speaking to them from a distance. Three rural Black Mississippian students, all from different schools and districts, agreed that they felt disengaged from school, teachers, and classmates (Wright, 2021). As many have noted, the real impact on students will not be lost learning time but the emotional impact of not being with their teachers and classmates.

Schools play a vital role in Black rural communities as a connector, bringing the community together to offer resources for students and their families to use. Teachers have now peered into their students' homes, observing family dynamics and living conditions, and have learned that the relationships between teachers, parents, and students are essential bonds. We cannot—and should not—unlearn this. Instead, we should continue to build on this learning, knowing that the care we share is an integral part of the learning process.

Knowing students—who they are, what they experience, and how they experience it—is an important, but often overlooked, component of teacher development. Teacher educators can model various strategies for teacher candidates that demonstrate critical caring of and for their students, which can permeate through the school walls. By infusing critical caring pedagogy into coursework and field experiences, teacher educators can help teacher candidates understand the students and communities they serve, and thus, create valuable opportunities to connect.

Critical Caring Pedagogy and Curriculum

We teach our teacher candidates to plan for the unexpected—the absent student, the surprise pep rally, the fire drill in the middle of the lesson, the tardy student— but no one was prepared for a pandemic. The pandemic challenged all of us to make difficult decisions based on what we knew about children and families. So, should we teach our teacher candidates to think of change as a process as opposed to teaching them to plan for certain types of change? When we teach teacher candidates to plan for specific incidents, we do not teach them how to innovate, model how to think through change, or model that change for students. So, how do we teach our teacher candidates to see change as an opportunity for growth rather than change as a defeat?

The pandemic has taught us to think differently about teaching and learning— the importance of the standardized tests or maybe the irrelevance of them, the push for engagement in our assignments rather than coverage. Teaching our teacher candidates to embrace change through independence, choice-making, and resourcefulness is not a usual part of the curriculum, but we believe it is a necessary part of growth from this pandemic. We do our teacher candidates a continued disservice when we do not build their criticality, their ability to question the world, and their capability to figure out how to navigate for equity.

Futurist Tools, Tactics, and Strategies

Pre-COVID teacher education should be different from teacher education both during and post-COVID. We cannot go back to educating teacher candidates in ways that are disconnected from families and students, their identities and needs, and opportunities for change. Teacher educators are responsible for enacting critical caring pedagogies to create future teachers who imagine possibilities for their students through deep caring, honor, admiration, and support for the communities they serve.

We offer the following questions for teacher educators to consider as we work to create a post-COVID responsive world for our teacher candidates:

- How am I creating a critical, inviting experience for teacher candidates to learn more about Black rural education and the communities occupied by Black rural students?
- How am I helping teacher candidates think innovatively about teaching in Black rural spaces while honoring their histories?
- How am I developing systems of caring with my teacher candidates?
- What are the ways I am helping teacher candidates think about change as a process for social transformation?

We are called as educators—as members of a *careforce*—to develop frameworks that make this world better for our students. With this in mind, we have articulated critical caring pedagogy as a way to illuminate how teacher education can be reconceptualized and reconfigured with our most vulnerable students—those in Black rural spaces—at the core of this reconfiguration. If we develop teachers who can see themselves as part of their students' families, communities, and lives, they will better understand how their freedom and liberation are tied to their students' freedom and liberation. These teacher candidates will also understand how building a world where their students receive equitable access works to create a better world for them. It allows us to stand in solidarity with our students and their families. In this way, this chapter is a call to action for those hoping to reimagine teacher education, especially regarding the educational practices of teachers hoping to work in Black rural spaces. We must be committed and engaged with the process of recruiting, retaining, and empowering new justice-oriented educators committed to critical caring pedagogy.

References

Alabama Internet Service Providers: Availability & Coverage. (2021, November 1). *Broad-bandNow*. https://broadbandnow.com/Alabama.

Anderson, J. (2020, October 23). Harvard EdCast: Covid-19's impact on rural schools. *Harvard Graduate School of Education*. www.gse.harvard.edu/news/20/10/harvard-edcast-covid-19s-impact-rural-schools.

Centers for Disease Control and Prevention. (2020, July 23). *The role of public health in COVID-19 emergency response efforts from a rural health perspective*. www.cdc.gov/pcd/issues/2020/20_0256.htm.

Darling-Hammond, L. (2000). How teacher education matters. *Journal of Teacher Education*, *51*(3), 166–173.

Darling-Hammond, L. (2016). Research on teaching and teacher education and its influences on policy and practice. *Educational Researcher*, *45*(2), 83–91.

Falk-Rafael, A. R. (2005). Advancing nursing theory through theory-guided practice: The emergence of a critical caring perspective. *Advances in Nursing Science*, *28*(1), 38–49.

Falk-Rafael, A. R., & Betker, C. (2012). The primacy of relationships: A study of public health nursing practice from a critical caring perspective. *Advances in Nursing Science*, *35*(4), 315–332.

Freire, P. (1972). *Pedagogy of the oppressed*. Herder and Herder.

Goldhill, O. (2021, May 26). Shuttered hospitals, soaring COVID-19 deaths: Rural black communities lose a lifeline in the century's worst health crisis. *STAT*. www.statnews.com/2021/05/26/shuttered-hospitals-soaring-covid19-deaths-rural-black-communities-lose-lifeline-in-pandemic.

Gross, B., & Opalka, A. (2020). Too many schools leave learning to chance during the pandemic. *Center on Reinventing Public Education*. www.crpe.org/publications/too-many-schools-leave-learning-chance-during-pandemic.

Harris, B. (2020, November 24). Homework in a McDonald's parking lot: Inside one mother's fight to help her kids get an education during coronavirus. *The Hechinger*

Report. https://hechingerreport.org/homework-in-a-mcdonalds-parking-lot-inside-one-mothers-fight-to-help-her-kids-get-an-education-during-coronavirus.

Kinloch, V. (2018, July). Necessary disruptions: Examining justice, engagement, and humanizing approaches to teaching and teacher education. *Teaching Works*.

Krummel, A. (2013). Multicultural teaching models to educate pre-service teachers: Reflections, service-learning, and mentoring. *Current Issues in Education, 16*(1), 1–7.

Love, B. L. (2019). *We want to do more than survive: Abolitionist teaching and the pursuit of educational freedom*. Beacon Press.

Milner, H. R. (2007). Race, culture, and researcher positionality: Working through dangers seen, unseen, and unforeseen. *Educational Researcher, 36*(7), 388–400.

Milner, H. R. (2010). What does teacher education have to do with teaching? Implications for diversity studies. *Journal of Teacher Education, 61*(1–2),118–131.

Mirra, N. (2018). *Educating for empathy: Literacy learning and civic engagement*. Teachers College Press.

Morrell, E. (2009). Critical research and the future of literacy education. *Journal of Adolescent & Adult Literacy, 53*, 96–104.

Mueller, J. T., McConnell, K., Burow, P. B., Pofahl, K., Merdjanoff, A. A., & Farrell, J. (2021). Impacts of the COVID-19 pandemic on rural America. *Proceedings of the National Academy of Sciences, 118*(1).

Muhammad, G. E. (2020). *Cultivating genius. An equity model for culturally and historically responsive literacy*. Scholastic.

Nieto, S., & Bode, P. (2008). *Affirming diversity: The sociopolitical context of multicultural education* (5th ed.). Pearson.

Noddings, N. (1984). An ethic of caring: From natural to ethical caring. In N. Noddings, *Caring: A feminine approach to ethics & moral education* (pp. 79–103). University of California Press.

Peyton, N. (2020, August 28). 'Who is standing up for us?' – Black, rural students left behind as U.S. schools go online. *Reuters*. www.reuters.com/article/us-health-coronavirus-usa-education-feat-idUSKBN25O1XR

Ratledge, A., Dalporto, H., & Lewy, E. (2020). *COVID-19 and Rural Higher Education: Rapid Innovation and Ideas for the Future*. https://eric.ed.gov/?id=ED608307.

Rural Health Information Hub. (n.d.) *Rural health for Alabama Overview*. www.ruralhealthinfo.org/states/alabama.

Steinberg, M. P., & Garrett, R. (2016). Classroom composition and measured teacher performance: What do teacher observation scores really measure? *Educational Evaluation and Policy Analysis, 38*(2), 293–317.

Watson, W., Sealey-Ruiz, Y., & Jackson, I. (2016). Daring to care: The role of culturally relevant care in mentoring Black and Latino male high school students. *Race Ethnicity and Education, 19*(5), 980–1002.

Wright, A. (2021, March 3). 'It's patchwork': Rural teachers struggle to connect in pandemic. *The Pew Charitable Trusts*. www.pewtrusts.org/en/research-and-analysis/blogs/stateline/2021/03/03/its-patchwork-rural-teachers-struggle-to-connect-in-pandemic.

19

HARBORING TEACHER CANDIDATES

Care During COVID

Elizabeth Laura Yomantas

The COVID-19 pandemic created isolating conditions in teacher education. Teacher candidates completed their clinical experiences in a virtual format, and teacher education courses were held online. Teaching, a profession that has always had physical togetherness as a cornerstone, instantly transitioned into a solo, isolated practice. As a teacher educator, these new challenges left me wondering how I could truly care for teacher candidates (TCs) and create a sense of relational connectedness despite the physical isolation and new stressors of the pandemic.

In response to this pondering, I turned to the concept of harboring. The concept is introduced as a metaphor in Jacqueline Woodson's middle grades novel *Harbor Me* (2018) and was extended to fit the specific needs of the TCs. Harboring's focus on reclaiming humanity and connecting with one another in new ways was utilized to enact care in my courses during the COVID-19 pandemic. This chapter details harboring in connection to care, includes found poems on TCs' experiences of care, and offers suggestions to enact care in teacher education in the post-pandemic classroom based on the TCs' experiences with harboring.

Care in Context

Nel Noddings (1984) stated that "the primary aim of every educational institution and every educational effort must be the maintenance and enhancement of caring" (p. 172). As a teacher educator, my definition of care builds upon Noddings' (1984, 1988) work and extends to include the creation of authentic, humanized learning communities, situated in the context of care, as an ongoing pursuit and area of continual self-study. This definition of care framed my inquiry into how care could manifest in the form of harboring during the COVID-19 pandemic.

DOI: 10.4324/9781003244875-24

The university where I teach is a small, private faith-based institution in southern California. While the university has over 3,000 students, our teacher education program graduates approximately 20 TCs per year. Our small, tight-knit undergraduate program allows TCs to simultaneously earn a bachelor's degree and a single or multiple subject teaching credential. I teach courses at all stages of the program, including educational foundations, intermediate theory and pedagogy, and advanced teaching methods. This chapter is based on the data from a research study conducted with the TCs in EDUC 530: Advanced Teaching Methods and EDUC 531: Clinical Experience 3, co-requisite capstone courses in our teacher education program.

As the instructor of these courses, I am familiar with how demanding this culminating experience is for the TCs each and every semester. Before the pandemic, I taught these courses from a position of care because I was familiar with the demands and ongoing pressures the TCs regularly encounter. However, when our university decided to remain fully online for the fall 2020 semester, I anticipated that pandemic conditions would make it extremely difficult to facilitate care for TCs during this semester of fully online student teaching. I wondered how to build authentic community in these challenging circumstances and considered what curricular and instructional changes I could make in order to care for TCs in new ways.

As I asked these questions, I was reading Jacqueline Woodson's novel *Harbor Me* (2018). The novel modeled the type of community I wished to develop amongst the TCs during the pandemic, so I decided to use this as an anchor text to enact care across various dimensions of the concurrent capstone courses. *Harbor Me* served as an invitation to think about care in new ways during the pandemic.

Harboring

Harbor Me (Woodson, 2018) is a middle grades novel in which a group of students come together regularly during school hours to learn from one another and share in each other's struggles. Harboring is a foundational theme in the novel; together, the teacher and students in the story learn to provide comfort, support, and guidance for one another as they navigate both the regular and unexpected challenges of life.

The TCs and I read the book together at the beginning of the semester before discussing the concept of harboring as a framework for the courses. We discussed the text's title, the ways the characters harbored each other, the teacher's role in harboring, and what harboring looks like in a virtual context. As a group, we defined harboring as a context-specific, relationship-based, embodied experience of both offering and nurturing connected support for one another. We then generated ideas for how we could, individually and collectively, harbor one another throughout the semester.

In the capstone courses, I made an intentional decision to embody harboring in virtual spaces through my instructional design and pedagogical decisions. For example, I chose to address the TCs as a "CoHeart" rather than a "cohort" to stress the importance of sharing a collective group identity as an enactment of care. I also included the following supports in order to nurture harboring as an enactment of care throughout the semester:

- A Room to Talk (ARTT): an instructor-free space for the CoHeart to talk about personal and professional challenges, modeled after ARTT in the novel. This allotted time provided the CoHeart an opportunity to harbor one another on a weekly basis.
- Harboring Stories: TC narratives shared with the CoHeart during class about ways they were harbored—or not—during the week and how that impacted their mental health, spirit, and general wellbeing. Harboring story-telling time functioned as a critical nexus of theory and practice as the CoHeart further theorized, concretized and operationalized the concept of harboring and explored new possibilities for the implementation of harboring and being harbored.
- Digital Group Chat: a private, instructor-free, digital group chat in which TCs were encouraged to engage in authentic "unfiltered" conversations.

TABLE 19.1 Participant Information

Participant	Gender identification	Credential	Placement Grade Level	Placement School Type
Jane	female	English	11	Urban Charter
Levi	male	English	6	Suburban Public
Fergie	female	elementary	1	Suburban Charter
Robin	female	English	7	Suburban Public
Sasha	female	social science	11	Urban Charter
Dolly	female	elementary	3	Suburban Public
Miley	female	elementary	1	Urban Public
Sarah	female	elementary	K	Suburban Public
Jackie	female	math	7 & 8	Suburban Public
Hermione	female	elementary	4	Suburban Public

Note. Each participant in the study self-selected a pseudonym.

Methodology

This chapter is situated in arts-based research (Barone & Eisner, 2012; Leavy, 2015, 2019; Mulvihill & Rwaminathan, 2020), which aims to re-present data as a research puzzle (Clandinin & Caine, 2012) with an emphasis on making space for participants' voices to unlock possibilities for the future of teacher education.

O'Donoghue (2014) states that arts-based educational research "operates for the betterment of society, [and] how it can or ought to address societal needs and problems prompts us to consider more carefully the relationship between doing, representing, disseminating and creating conditions for understanding and action" (p. 14). In this chapter, the arts-based re-presentation of the data invites teacher educators to consider these stories for the possibilities they offer for care in teacher education.

The ten participant TCs in this study ranged in age from 22–24 years old and were enrolled in EDUC 530 and EDUC 531 during the fall 2020 semester. Each participant voluntarily chose to participate in the study and signed an informed consent form. The university's Internal Review Board granted approval for this study. This chapter features found poems from five of the ten participants. Table 19.1 is included in order to provide information about the participants' genders, credential types, placement grade levels, and placement school types.

Data collection took place during the penultimate week of the semester and was triangulated from three sources to increase reliability and trustworthiness: (1) a Google Form questionnaire inquiring about participants' stressors, as well as modes and examples of harboring throughout the semester; (2) a one-hour focus group Zoom session on similar topics; and (3) an end-of-the-semester video clip that captured what participants learned over the semester. Each video clip recording was transcribed. Following collection, data were compiled and organized for data analysis.

In order to re-present the findings in a way that authentically shares participant narratives, I utilized the concept of found poetry. A found poem can be described as "the process of taking words, phrases, or whole passages found in data, usually narrative-style interview data, and reframing them as poetry by changing the spacing, line breaks, and by adding and deleting certain words" (Butler-Kisber, 2005, as cited in Sjollema et al., 2012, p. 208).

Under the umbrella of arts-based research (Leavy, 2015, 2019), found poetry can be used in the data analysis process to sense-make (Eisner, 1997), evoke emotions (Richardson, 1994), and bring the researcher "closer to the data in different and sometimes unusual ways that can yield new and important insights" (Prendergast, 2006, p. 235). Arts-based researchers use a variety of different mediums to maintain trustworthiness with the participants, ensure the credibility of their data, and triangulate the findings while keeping the data authentic and humanized (Wiggins, 2011). Found poetry is one methodological approach within arts-based research that can allow researchers to arrive at new understandings by summarizing data in original, compelling ways.

I created a found poem (Patrick, 2016) from each of the ten participant's data as part of the data analysis process. Creating these found poems allowed me to engage with data in a way that humanized the concept of harboring for each participant. As Leggo (2018) noted, poetry has the capacity to "invite conversations about what it means to be human on the earth in the twenty-first century" (p. 20). To generate the found poems, I read through all of the raw data several times. As I read, I annotated to identify repeated phrases, highlight key ideas, and note powerful phrases for each participant. I then wrote a one-page memo for each participant to understand what was essential to their definition and understanding of harboring in connection to care. After writing each memo, I went back to the data and constructed the poems to maintain as many of the participant's original words but oftentimes in a different order to highlight the central ideas and concepts from the data.

Creating found poems allowed me to stay "faithful to the data" (Szto et al., 2005, p. 150) and honor participant voices by retaining as many of their original words, unique syntax, diction, and key ideas as possible. In the following section, I present some of the poems; however, generalizability is not a goal or objective of arts-based research (Barone & Eisner, 2012). Rather, arts-based research offers the individual story that others might find resonance with:

> Arts based research emphasizes the generation of forms of feeling that have something to do with understanding some person, place, or situation. It is not simply a quantitative disclosure or array of variables. It is the conscious pursuit of expressive form in the service of understanding. (Barone & Eisner, 2012, p. 7)

After reading the completed poems in three rounds, each poem was coded using qualitative methods as outlined by Saldaña (2016). The three major themes that emerged from the found poems were a sense of belonging, connection to others, and purpose. These themes suggest that harboring can be an important framework for understanding, navigating, and engaging in care in teacher education.

Teacher Candidate Narratives of Harboring

The found poems revealed that harboring happened across a wide variety of contexts throughout the semester and took place between the (1) professor and TCs; (2) members of the CoHeart; (3) TCs and their mentor teacher; and (4) TCs and their students. Of the ten participant poems that were constructed, five poems were selected for inclusion in this chapter based on the poem's ability to highlight two of the three themes and different relational contexts for harboring facilitation in order to showcase the variety of ways harboring took place. Each of the following found poems represents one of the ways in which harboring manifested during this research study and highlights two of the themes that emerged from the data analysis. Table 19.2 provides the title of each poem, the major themes exemplified in the poem, and who facilitated the harboring, as described by each participant.

The data is intentionally presented in the found poetry format in order to provide an opportunity to engage closely with the lived experiences and voices of each participant. Brief comments are offered following each poem to connect to the larger context of care through harboring in teacher education. However, as previously mentioned, the poems and discussion of the poems are not intended to generalize experiences for all TCs. Rather, they highlight ways programs can facilitate harboring to support TCs' success throughout teacher education.

TABLE 19.2 Overview of Found Poems

	Poem Title	Themes Exemplified	Facilitation of Harboring
Found Poem 1	Jane's Story: Harboring to Combat Anxiety	Sense of Belonging Connection to Others	Professor to Teacher Candidate
Found Poem 2	Sarah's Story: Support when Support Lacked	Sense of Belonging Connection to Others	Teacher Candidate to Teacher Candidate
Found Poem 3	Hermione's Story: Dock and Land	Purpose Sense of Belonging	Teacher Candidate to Mentor Teacher
Found Poem 4	Fergie's Story: The Unapologetic Hug	Sense of Belonging Connection to Others	Mentor Teacher to Teacher Candidate
Found Poem 5	Levi's Story: Leave the Light On	Purpose Connection to Others	Teacher Candidate to K-12 student

Note. Each poem highlights two of the three themes.

Jane's Story: Harboring to Combat Anxiety

Our professor harbored every single one of us
more than we would ever deserve.
We message her at any day of the week,
and she'd *always* answer us.
She'd always respond to help us on the edTPA
and help us navigate student teaching.
It didn't matter what time of day.
I don't think we could have gotten through this
without her.
She's so dedicated to helping us – it's more than just "a class" to her.
She knows we need help in real life situations as we student teach.

For me, EdTPA was a very anxiety provoking experience.
I lost sleep over the assessment a lot –
not because I was working on it –
but because I had anxiety about it.
I had anxiety about the lessons,
anxiety about recording,
anxiety about making everything *perfect*.
Anxiety.

My professor was there for me during all of it.
I told her about my anxiety from edTPA and
she walked me through all the things that I could control.
We talked about all the things I could do
and all the ways I could ensure I would pass.

My professor gave me encouragement
in order to ease my nerves,
but she also gave me specific strategies and ideas
of how I could prepare and write in a more logical way.
That eased my nerves.
She grounded me.

Anyone can encourage you –
your family,
your friends,
but someone who is an expert in the field knows
exactly what you need to do.
And so her encouragement weighted a lot.
She grounded me.

Jane's story highlights how teacher educators can support TCs with high-stakes assessments. As Jane explained, teacher educators have an important lens into the requirements and expectations of these exams. Therefore, they have a unique opportunity to offer TCs care in this context. For Jane, care looked like responding to messages promptly, offering encouragement based on professional experience, and offering strategies and ideas for success. For Jane, the edTPA assessment was daunting but the professor's enactment of care allowed her to be successful in her efforts. Teacher educators can harbor TCs through these assessments—not just the mechanics of the assessment but care for the whole person who is completing the assessment. The support Jane received reveals a sense of belonging and connection to others through her relationship with the professor.

Sarah's Story: Support when Support Lacked

Harboring means a judgement free zone
to share emotions
and feel supported.
Harboring asks,
"How can I be here for you right now?"

My CoHeart asks these questions,
but my mentor teacher
never asked that question.

She treated me as a babysitter for her class
or someone to push work onto.

I was teaching the entirety of the online Zoom meetings,
and she would keep her camera off
and walk away from the computer.
I know this because I would sometimes say her name
to ask a question and she would not answer.

She could have harbored me
by giving me feedback on my lessons,
turning on her camera while I was teaching,
and coming prepared and actually planning.
She could have harbored me by treating me like a mentee,
rather than a co-teacher.
She could have asked,
"How can I be here for you right now?"

In class one day,
I shared this with my CoHeart.
The tears fell as I stumbled through my words.
After I shared,
I looked at my phone.
All of my classmates had each sent me a text
to check in on me
and offer words of support.
I could feel their love.
They asked,
"How can I be here for you right now?"
That is what it means to be harbored.

Sarah's story highlights how teacher educators can provide space for TCs to enact care for one another. Because the TCs felt comfortable with one another, they were able to offer Sarah encouragement directly. They were relationally connected and able to offer her what she needed. As this poem shows, care was facilitated by the instructor who created a caring environment, but it was enacted between the TCs. Teacher educators can create environments where TCs are brave enough to be vulnerable and loving enough to respond to that vulnerability. Sarah's story reveals both a sense of belonging and connection to others through the harboring she received from her peers.

Hermione's Story: Dock and Land

Harboring is
somewhere where you can dock and land –
don't have to think about anything.

You can throw your anchor down,
and someone is there to pick you up;
you can let go.
you can forget.
you can just be.

My mentor teacher texted me Sunday night
and said my wife has an emergency appendicitis.

He said,
"I won't be there tomorrow."
I said
"Don't worry.
Please don't worry about anything.
I've got it under control.
He said,
"Thank you so much."

He didn't have to do anything for school.
In that moment, he had to worry about
his kids,
his wife,
all these things – so
worrying about his class and the sub
shouldn't be one of his worries.

He can throw his anchor down
and I can pick him up;
he can let go.
he can forget.
he can just be.

Hermione's story highlights the harboring that can take place between a TC and their mentor teacher. As teacher educators, we might incorrectly assume that the mentor teacher is always the one who mentors, guides, and supports the TC. However, Hermione's story reveals that TCs have the power to harbor their mentor teachers. This found poem reveals harboring as a multi-dimensional complex concept that blurs the boundaries between mentor and mentee. Hermione's sense of belonging with her mentor teacher also led to feelings of great purpose as she was able to effectively care for her mentor teacher and consequently her students by taking on responsibilities.

Fergie's Story: The Unapologetic Hug

Harboring is a big hug –
one of those hugs that holds you up
when you feel like your legs are about to give out.
Or
like one of those hugs where you can feel your worries wash away
and you're reassured that you're going to be okay.
Harboring is the hug.

Before I got there, the first grade team
was already a family.
So I was nervous about how I would fit into the picture.

When I got there, the first grade team
welcomed me in with such open arms.
They cared about what I had to say,
cheered me on as my biggest fans,
made me feel safe,
and calmed my fears about teaching
and life in itself.

When I was there, the first grade team
included me in everything.
They always let me be my authentic self
unapologetically.
I let them be who they are,
unapologetically with me.

When I was with them, the first grade team
gave me a big hug -
like one of those hugs where you can feel your worries wash away
and you're reassured that you're going to be okay.

This found poem highlights how mentor teachers can harbor TCs. Fergie extends the concept of harboring to explain that entire grade level teams can nurture harboring for TCs. This poem highlights a sense of belonging and connection to others that Fergie experienced in her clinical experience.

Levi's Story: Leave the Light On

Harboring is a dock
with open with welcoming arms

ready
to take in any weary travelers.
Sometimes you need a lighthouse to reel in people
who need a rest from their journey.
It's
always leaving a light on for anyone
that needs some love.

My student has been struggling.
Her mom had COVID
and her dad isn't in the picture.
She's got a lot going on,
And she's falling behind.

I met with her and she was telling me
that she had surgery last week.
And she hasn't been able to get her work in.

I shared my story –
I had a major surgery just last spring
and I fell behind in my work, too.

I told her "I understand your experience,
and I want you to know that I care about
you as a person.
I want to make sure you're doing okay."

Right then –
her entire tone,
flipped completely.

She turned in a rough draft all in one day.
And now she's telling me about
how much she loves writing
and that she's going to email me
for more comments and suggestions on her work.

All it took was
always leaving a light on for her
because she needed some love.

Levi's found poem showcases how TCs can facilitate harboring for the students in
their class. In making space to share his own story with a student, he is able to

facilitate care that the student needed in the moment. This poem highlights Levi's ability to connect with others, and through that connection, he experiences purpose in his clinical experience.

New Possibilities for Harboring in Post-COVID Teacher Education

After creating the found poems and reviewing the raw data again, it became clear that there was minimal commentary that the semester and its consequent harboring took place in virtual spaces. This suggests that harboring is not limited to digital teaching and learning but focused on reclaiming humanity and connecting in new ways; therefore, the findings have implications for the enactment of care in teacher education in any post-COVID classroom.

Harboring Requires Customization and Imagination

The found poems suggest that the efforts the TCs felt harbored across the various dimensions of the program throughout the semester. When reflecting upon why these efforts were successful, it became apparent that harboring was strategically and intentionally designed with specific TCs in mind, based on relational knowledge and previous experiences with the candidates. Therefore, the pedagogy and curriculum of harboring was constructed based on specific TCs in a specific program with a specific instructor. The facilitation of harboring in this specific context does not yield one-size-fits-all suggestions or recommendations for harboring pedagogy or curriculum; rather, the findings of this study suggest that harboring is essential for holistic care in teacher education, and the construction of harboring should be highly localized and specific based on different cultural contexts (Boucher, 2020). Teacher educators are encouraged to ask new questions and imagine new possibilities about ways to meet the needs of TCs in their specific contexts. Harboring is a concept that is meant to continually evolve as our TCs continue to grow and change. Teacher educators are encouraged to consider this concept on highly personal levels that bring forth innovative customization and awaken imagination to consider care in new ways.

Harboring Invites Engaged Pedagogy

Employing the concept of harboring into the teacher education coursework can be an embodied experience of bell hooks' (1994) concept of engaged pedagogy:

> Engaged pedagogy not only compels me to be constantly creative in the classroom, it also sanctions involvement with students beyond the setting. I journey with students as they progress in their lives beyond our classroom experience. In many ways, I continue to teach them, as they become more capable of teaching me. The important lesson is that we can learn together,

the lesson that allows us to move together with and beyond the classroom, is one of mutual engagement. (p. 205)

Harboring can function as an embodiment of engaged pedagogy because it requires the instructor to continually revisit the concept of care. Care is not a fixed-item on a check list; rather, with each TC and the unique challenges of each semester, care in the form of harboring must be continually pursued. Furthermore, as the instructor of these courses and researcher of this project, I learned more about what it means to harbor one another from the TCs throughout the semester and beyond. I am not the harboring expert; rather, we journey together in co-learning what it means to truly harbor one another. Harboring was an act of mutual engagement and informs my future work as a harboring instructor and human being.

Harboring is Essential in Post-COVID Teacher Education Programs

As anxiety, depression, and suicidal ideation continue to rise (Mental Health America, 2021), there is a continued need to build harboring into teacher education programs. While COVID-19 served as the catalyst that ignited a passion to intentionally embed harboring into the curriculum, it is an area that needs sustained attention and focus. The found poems suggest that as programs return to in-person learning experiences, embedding harboring is essential. As new post-COVID issues arise, helping TCs remain relationally connected and experience care in the context of harboring will be foundational in learning skills to survive and thrive as successful classroom teachers in our everchanging world. Harboring should not only be facilitated between the course instructor and the TCs; rather, structures should be put in place for harboring to be extended into the K-12 clinical experience between TCs and mentor teachers as well as TCs and their students. Teacher educators can work alongside K-12 school partners to explicitly build this concept into program partnerships in order to best support TCs.

Harboring Can Extend into K-12 Classrooms

The found poems also highlight that harboring can take place across multiple planes of a teacher education program. As the instructor of the course, my intention was to facilitate harboring in two primary ways: (1) between myself as the course professor and TCs; and (2) between members of the CoHeart. However, harboring extended far beyond these spaces, suggesting that teacher educators who embed harboring as a part of the learning experience can open new possibilities for harboring across multiple spaces of teacher education. Hermione's story about harboring her mentor teacher suggests that harboring can benefit the TCs as well as mentor teachers. By intentionally embedding this concept throughout the semester, the candidates expanded it into their specific contexts, suggesting that by inviting harboring into the explicit curriculum, programs can extend harboring—and care—into K-12 schools and classrooms.

By facilitating, observing, and learning from the TCs' stories of harboring, I arrived at new understandings of teaching and learning. Through engaging in harboring alongside the TCs, we, together, moved beyond the limitations of the classroom and into new possibilities. Teacher educators willing to embark on this journey of harboring alongside TCs can open new pathways and possibilities for teacher education.

References

Barone, T., & Eisner, E. W. (2012). *Arts based research.* Sage Publications.
Boucher, M. L. (2020). *More than an ally: A caring solidarity framework for white teachers of African American students.* Rowman & Littlefield.
Clandinin, D. J., & Caine, V. (2012). Narrative inquiry. In A. A. Trainor & E. Graue (Eds.), *Reviewing qualitative research in the social sciences* (pp. 166–179). Routledge.
Eisner, E. W. (1997). The promise and perils of alternative forms of data representation. *Educational Researcher, 26*(6), 4–10.
hooks, b. (1994). *Teaching to transgress: Education as the practice of freedom.* Routledge.
Leavy, P. (2015). *Method meets art: Arts-based research practice.* Guilford Press.
Leavy, P. (2019). *Handbook of arts-based research.* Guilford Press.
Leggo, C. (2018). Holding fast to h: Ruminations on the arts preconference. *Artizein: Arts and Teaching Journal, 3*(1), 15–25.
Mulvihill, T. M., & Rwaminathan, R. (2020). *Arts-based educational research and qualitative inquiry: Walking the path.* Routledge.
Noddings, N. (1984). *Caring: A feminine approach to ethics & moral education.* University of California Press.
Noddings, N. (1988). An ethic of caring and its implications for instructional arrangements. *American Journal of Education, 96*(2), 215–230.
Mental Health America. (2021). The state of mental health in America. *Mental Health America.* https://mhanational.org/issues/state-mental-health-america.
O'Donoghue, D. (2014). Doing arts-based educational research for the public good: An impossible possibility? *International Journal of Education & the Arts, 15*(1), 1–15.
Patrick, L. (2016). Found poetry: Creating space for imaginative arts-based literacy research writing. *Literacy Research: Theory, Method, and Practice, 65*(1), 384–403.
Prendergast, M. (2006). Found poetry as literature review: Research poems on audience and performance. *Qualitative Inquiry, 12*(2), 369–388.
Richardson, L. (1994). Nine poems: Marriage and the family. *Journal of Contemporary Ethnography, 23*, 3–14.
Saldaña, J. (2016). *The coding manual for qualitative researchers* (3rd ed.). Sage Publications.
Sjollema, S., Hordyk, S., Walsh, C., Hanley, J., & Ives, N. (2012) Finding home: A qualitative study of homeless immigrant women. *Journal of Poetry Therapy, 25*(4), 205–217.
Szto, P., Furman, R., & Langer, C. (2005). Poetry and photography: An exploration into expressive/creative qualitative research. *Qualitative Social Work, 135*(4), 135–156.
Wiggins, J. (2011). Feeling it is how I understand it: Found poetry as analysis, *International. Journal of Education & the Arts, 12*(3), 1–12.
Woodson, J. (2018). *Harbor me.* Puffin Books.

20

NAVIGATING NEW LANDSCAPES AFTER COVID

Cultural Geography as Care for Prospective English Teachers

Jessica Gallo and Abigail Navarro Muñoz

In the year after COVID-19 gripped the United States, prospective teachers preparing to enter classrooms for the first time in January 2021 faced complex challenges on their teaching journeys. The pandemic changed the cultural geography of schools—both the physical environment of schooling and the culture of classrooms that prospective teachers had envisioned from their own education experiences and teacher education programs. Not only would prospective teachers begin their teaching in unfamiliar classroom landscapes (i.e., digital, hybrid, socially distant), they would also have to re-envision how to interact with students, create classroom communities, and support students through a time of intense uncertainty in our schools.

In this chapter, we invite readers to inhabit our shared thinking space as we negotiate the cultural geography of our teaching during the pandemic. In this qualitative research study, we asked: How do teachers and middle school students make sense of rapidly changing school environments during COVID-19? Through our narratives and our students' narratives, we share approaches for prospective teachers and teacher educators to explore the cultural geographies of learning environments during and after the pandemic.

Cultural Geography in Education

Cultural geography describes the ways in which people interact with their environments. In cultural geography, "culture" refers to an array of ideas, behaviors, and identities that shape and are shaped by individuals' surroundings, including "how cultures are distributed over space, how places and identities are produced, how people make sense of places and build senses of place, and how people produce and communicate knowledge and meaning" (Rogers et al., 2013,

DOI: 10.4324/9781003244875-25

p. 87). Furthermore, Rose (2021) argues that "culture is both a question of habits (of ingrained manners of doing, practising and living) and a question of meaning (of investment, care and representation)" (p. 952) within a physical place.

Classroom cultural geography has long been part of teacher education as prospective teachers consider how to design their learning environments. Much has been written about the role of space and place in educational environments (e.g., Diamond et al., 2021; Gruenewald, 2003). While these approaches are not always characterized as cultural geography, they have common elements that examine the connections among place (physical, digital, and virtual environments), space (emotional and affective responses to environments), and identity (concepts of self, peers, and groups).

The connections among and distinctions between place and space in cultural geography can be difficult to tease out. Generally, *place* refers to the tangible environment, including digital and virtual places, while *space* is considered a more abstract concept that incorporates the affective, emotional environment. This distinction is not meant to fully separate the two concepts. Rather, place and space are intertwined.

Additionally, our identities as teachers and learners are intricately linked with our learning environments. Tani (2017) explains that "the meaning the environment has cannot be detached from its experiencer; it is not something that can be analysed by its physical characteristics, but it is constructed by an individual through living and experiencing it" (p. 1505). Thus, "through these contexts, places can be open, supportive sites where individuals as actors have agency to direct their future communities, identities, and cultures" (Cole, 2009, p. 22).

Context and Study Design

As a white teacher educator at the University of Nevada, Reno, an emerging Hispanic-Serving Institution, Jess knew the group of prospective English teachers in her Fall 2020 Methods of Teaching English class—which included Abi—were about to launch into their student teaching at a time of great turmoil in education. She wondered how best to prepare the prospective teachers in her classes, not only for their earliest teaching experiences during the pandemic, but for a long career in education beyond COVID-19.

As a daughter to Mexican immigrants and a prospective teacher, Abi wondered if she was ready for her student teaching that spring semester. Abi had many volunteer and tutoring experiences but student teaching would be her first full-time English teaching experience. After many of her university practicum experiences were eliminated or cut short in 2020, owing to the pandemic, she was set to begin her internship at Mountain View Middle School (MVMS) for a combination of in-person and online teaching (all names of schools and K-12 students are pseudonyms). MVMS has some of the wealthier students in the city, relative to other middle schools in the district, and is racially diverse, with 61% of students identifying as white, 24% identifying as Hispanic, and 15% identifying as two or more races, Asian or Pacific Islander, Black, or Native American (Nevada Department of Education, 2020).

Jess and Abi spoke regularly throughout Abi's student teaching experience. From these conversations, we developed a qualitative study to examine how students and teachers adapted to the changes caused by the pandemic. The data for this study consists of middle school students' daily reflections from Abi's writing prompts in her student teaching classroom, 13 individual interviews with Abi's middle school students, and Jess and Abi's weekly fieldnotes of teaching observations and challenges. Abi selected student interview participants using purposeful sampling to represent a cross-section of her students' experiences.

To analyze our data, we read student journal entries and interview transcripts multiple times to look for cultural geographic themes using a priori codes of identity, place, and space from our review of cultural geography literature. Sample codes include *feeling disconnected* (space), *aha moments* (identity), and *unfamiliar setting* (place). With the student data grouped into narratives of identity, place, and space, we compared these themes to our own teaching and research reflections. Analyzing students' reflective writings and interviews alongside our fieldnote data revealed how attention to cultural geography helps us to care for our students and ourselves during and after the pandemic.

Navigating Our Landscapes

In this section, we describe the three themes that arose from our data analysis: identity, place, and space. These aspects of cultural geography capture the impact of the changing learning environments on our students' experiences and our own teaching practices.

Identity: Discovering Ourselves

In cultural geography, there is a reciprocal connection between individuals' identities and their surroundings. We shape our identities to suit our perceptions of norms and cultures within a place; by extension, the ways that we enact our identities also shape the culture of the place. As an English educator, Jess recognizes that a major purpose of teacher education is to help prospective teachers shift their identities away from *university student* and toward *teacher*. In this regard, teacher education is inherently attuned to the cultural geographies of teachers and schools, and beginning teachers are frequently very focused on how their students will perceive them.

Abi was subject to this feeling in her internship. At the start of the pandemic, Abi adapted easily to online teaching and enjoyed the convenience of being able to help students from the comfort of her room behind a computer screen. If she was unsure of a definition, a response, or an example to give her students, all she had to do was find the answers with a quick Google search on a separate screen without anyone knowing. As her internship moved from primarily online to primarily face-to-face, Abi feared that students would tear her apart, once she did not have internet support:

> When tutoring at my old high school, I was comfortable speaking to the students, at times reverting to Spanglish and catching myself using Spanish grammar in English. But teaching in person at MVMS will be different. I am unsure whether I will be able to see myself in the students, and nervous that they will realize I am not a great English teacher. This school intimidates me. I have yet to find my identity as a classroom teacher. How will I respond to a question I do not know in front of all my students?

Abi feared that her teaching abilities would be greatly impacted by her insecurities about the changes in the classroom setting. She worried that her students would perceive her as a less skillful teacher if she was not able to respond to students' questions quickly and smoothly.

Many conversations in Jess's Fall 2020 methods class revolved around adapting practices for online, face-to-face, or hybrid teaching environments because the prospective teachers expressed concern that the change in classroom environment would impact their teaching identities. One of the ways that Jess supported teacher identity development was by frequently reminding students that they are professionals with specialized expertise about how best to educate middle and high school students. For example, when the prospective teachers asked Jess if their unit plan topic or essential question was "okay" for the assignment, she always responded by asking what they were trying to accomplish as teachers, what they valued about the topic, or what adolescents might find interesting about their unit plans. Often that meant that the prospective teachers' questions were met with additional questions about their goals, concerns, and knowledge of their students.

There is no doubt this can feel frustrating for beginning teachers who are looking for the keys to being a good teacher (and a good grade on an important assignment), but this type of collegial conversation builds autonomy and habits of mind that will carry them through unique teaching situations in the future. It requires prospective teachers to discover, analyze, and explore their epistemologies of teaching and learning with the guidance of an experienced teacher. Through this practice, Jess supported their identity development from student to autonomous classroom practitioner.

As Abi continued to work through planning and teaching processes in her internship, her thinking shifted away from worries about how students would see her toward how students themselves connected and grew:

> Over the course of my internship, I realized that the identity of an individual is more impactful in the environment of the classroom than the place itself.

I worked closely with the students that fell behind, oftentimes reteaching full lessons for students while others worked independently. I did not think too much about students that did very well in all classes.

Angela was one of these students, always diligent and insightful in her work. During her interview, she expanded her thoughts on learning during COVID-19:

> I think I'm doing pretty well. It also depends because I don't learn much on my hybrid days. It's more like a day for independent work. It's more homework and all that, like catching up and stuff, so I think I'm probably learning less but for what I'm given, I'm doing pretty well. I have straight As. I think it's been harder for other people to adapt, but I feel like for the most part it's not necessarily learning; it's about doing your schoolwork.

Even though Angela continued to see herself as an A student, the learning she was doing in this new environment was not as meaningful as it had been before the pandemic. She felt disengaged and began to see schoolwork as tasks to complete rather than relevant learning.

In order to challenge students like Angela at all levels, Abi adapted her daily writing prompts to connect with her lessons, shifting from creative writing to questions that prompted critical discourse and encouraged students to connect concepts from the class as they navigated spaces outside of the classroom. This shift allowed her to assess each student's interests and learn more about and from them. Like Jess, Abi wanted students to have autonomy in their education. Teachers at all levels want to guide students in their own discoveries and learning experiences, allowing them to take initiative and have a say in their education. We want to create an identity-rich environment in which our students are not just completing tasks; they are also shaping who they are as learners and individuals within that environment.

Place: Constructing the Classroom Environment

COVID-19 precautions in Abi's internship and Jess's university courses caused drastic changes to the physical classroom that required us to re-envision how to construct our classroom environments. Both Abi and Jess consider relationship-building an important aspect of learning but the shift in the landscape made it difficult to envision how relationship-building happens when teachers and students are unable to be in the same place at the same time. Virtual learning, even when it included synchronous meetings, fostered detachment from relationships, accountability, and genuine interactions.

In the synchronous online methods class, Jess wanted to create the feeling of being in a classroom together and building authentic relationships, even if students were separated by miles and time zones. To do this, Jess adapted the traditional literature circle format to the Zoom classroom. Randy Ribay's (2020) novel *Patron Saints of Nothing* was the common book for the semester; each prospective English teacher read the novel with a different reader response role in mind. During the in-class novel discussion, Jess popped into each breakout room to join the conversation and build a sense of sharing a virtual classroom. She was careful to participate authentically in students' conversations; the pop-ins were meant to show interest in the discussion, not just monitor time on task or adherence to an assignment.

After the initial book discussion, Jess and the prospective English teachers spent time discussing how the literature circle approach might work in a physical classroom space as compared to their virtual version. While the prospective teachers raised questions connected to the physical environment of a classroom (e.g., noise level, physical groupings, paper and book management), the conversations also included concerns about digital environments. They wondered how to encourage student accountability when they could not see or hear all students, the impact of students who would not turn on their cameras or did not have access to a microphone, and how to manage the hurdle of unstable internet access in a learning environment that relied so heavily on technology. We brainstormed solutions, like using the chat feature, pairing small group breakout rooms with shared Google docs, and using texting backchannels for students with unstable connections to participate with the help of peers. These conversations inspired important thinking about the role that place can play in teaching.

Abi's internship experience also gave insight into the difficulties of virtual engagement and learning. Among Abi's first observations as a prospective teacher in a fully online, synchronous teaching format was the idea that the structural change of learning environments led to student detachment from the accountability of work and class participation. During synchronized meetings, students simply did not attend; of the students that joined, few had their cameras on, which made it difficult to know students and differentiate them from one another. During class discussion, fewer students were inclined to share or talk. Once meetings ended, some blank screens remained, leading Abi to believe that some students simply joined the online meeting and fell asleep or physically left their devices. Access to online synchronous meetings from any place allowed students to join from wherever they wanted. Abi's students occasionally waved hello from the comfort of their bed, joined the call from a vehicle, or shared their views of the snowy landscape they would be snowboarding while they listened to class lessons. Suddenly, schools were no longer about being in a particular place for the purpose of learning. Instead, students could "consume" class lessons in the same way they consumed YouTube videos. Abi asked herself, "How can teachers hold students accountable for learning through a device screen?"

When returning to face-to-face, socially distanced learning in the classroom, Abi noticed that students were awkward with social interaction. She expected difficulties with classroom management in the face-to-face setting but was surprised when students mirrored behaviors similar to those she had seen in remote settings: "I was able to see students, but they seemed distracted by something in the distance." When Abi asked questions or attempted to lead class discussion, students stared blankly onward, as if they needed to reorient their behaviors to account for sharing a physical place again. As a result, Abi rearranged her classroom to encourage more eye contact among students and to help them readjust to in-person interactions.

For many teachers, the pandemic brought into sharp focus the impact that place has on teaching and learning, and many of us struggled to adapt our approaches to the changing environments. However, by taking a cultural geographic approach and acknowledging that changes in the place of learning deeply affect our relationships with that learning, we can help our students and ourselves navigate those changes more thoughtfully. One way to do this is to prioritize students' meaning-making within their current learning environment rather than trying to control the environment to maintain previous relationships with and understandings of classrooms.

Space: Creating Meaningful Connections

During the pandemic, we noticed that our students formed and reformed their relationships with schooling as a result of the changes to their surroundings; in other words, the affective, emotional space of the learning environment changed as the physical place changed.

For Jess, creating a supportive affective space in the methods class posed a different kind of challenge beyond the logistical concerns of organizing the new virtual place. Jess requires her future English teachers to design a three-week conceptual unit plan for a hypothetical classroom, an assignment that feels enormous, overwhelming, and extremely high-stakes to prospective teachers. To lessen the anxiety, Jess wanted to create a space where students could talk to her and each other to work through the unit planning process together, so she devoted at least an hour of each three-hour evening class to workshop. During this time, the prospective teachers could turn off their cameras to work independently, meet in breakout rooms with peers, or conference with Jess to address any questions. Sometimes in the conferences, the prospective teachers would share their fears about the unit plan; Jess would listen, reassure, and support them in making pedagogical choices that made sense to them.

Using class time this way gave the prospective English teachers the time they needed to do the hard thinking of unit planning but it also helped them to feel like professionals developing their teaching rather than students completing class assignments. In reflecting on the unit-planning workshops, Abi explained that she became attached to her instructional unit because it was an expression of her work as a teacher, not just a big assignment to complete. The community of the methods class provided a supportive learning space for the prospective teachers to envision their own classrooms beyond their work as university students.

When Abi's internship shifted to in-person instruction, she was intentional about designing unit plans that promoted student autonomy while sparking their interest. The daily personal writing time she experienced in Jess's class inspired creativity and personal reflection for her and her peers because they had time and space to process their feelings and share their personal writing with one another. Abi wanted to create that kind of thinking space for her middle school students too. She began choosing writing prompts that asked students to reflect on their feelings about learning during the pandemic, which fostered strong personal interactions with and among students. She gave them the space to work through their feelings and was able to create a stronger class community as a result.

One interaction with Niall confirmed for Abi the importance of supporting students' emotional responses to classroom environments. As she was welcoming students in the hallway, Abi noticed that Niall was hesitant to respond. Later, while students were working independently on the day's lesson, Abi offered to help Niall with his assignment in the quiet hallway:

> I expressed my concern and interest in how he felt. Niall spoke about the amount of stress he was under and touched on the home changes he was going through. Although Niall repeatedly apologized for not going into much detail, I was grateful that he trusted me as much as he did. I under- stood the lack of concentration and motivation one could have while griev- ing. Rather than returning to class, I suggested walking around the school's hallways, since walking often helped me when I felt restless. Niall and I walked, sometimes in silence, other times recognizing the overwhelming feelings one can have with so many other things going on. That day I received the first personal email from a student to my district email—Niall thanked me and expressed his appreciation for my interest in his well-being.

In Niall's final interview, he reinforced his emotional connections with classroom spaces:

> At the end of 7th grade, it was a lot more fun because you had all your friends. You had most of them in your class and it felt more lively. The school did. I like the social aspect of it. And I feel like you learned a lot more from your teachers, not that they don't care now, but they, like, cared a little bit more. Back then, I mean. They care now; they do a good job, but the school just felt, like, alive with kids everywhere.

Abi assisted Niall in navigating an emotional space that affected his learning while using the physical landscape of the school. As Abi and Niall walked the physical environment, together they transformed the place by attaching new meaning to the emotional space. This helped Niall work through the challenges he was experiencing at home and at school.

Like Niall, other students expressed a loss of social interaction and worried about strained friendships that once formed part of their shared space and support system in school. In her interview, Gabrielle shared how the pandemic had changed her social relationships since, because of social distancing guidelines, students attended in-person classes every other day:

> It has given me the chance to see new people. It's almost given me this feeling like I'm a little more outgoing than I would have been if it was last year because I would have been comfortable and I would have had a certain place that I associate myself with. Like, "this is my group, these are my friends." But now a lot of people probably don't have the same friends on the same day, and it pushes you to talk to new people.

Gabrielle's expression of the importance of a shared social space shows the connections between place and space. When the school environment changed, so did her interactions with people in the school environment. While Gabrielle focused on the positive impacts here, many of her peers expressed sadness at the new distance they felt among their friends. Adapting to this new space pushed students out of their comfort zones, allowing them to create new interactions and reflect on the liveliness of school before the pandemic.

Cultural Geography as Care for Teachers

Approaching teaching and learning through a cultural geographic lens allows us to consider how the environment of a classroom affects the physical and digital places, the affective and emotional spaces, and the identity development of our students. For prospective teachers and teacher educators interested in using a cultural geographic lens, we suggest several ways to consider identity, place, and space in concert with teaching commitments and values. By considering these aspects of cultural geography, we can adapt to new learning environments to suit the needs of students in unstable or unpredictable environments. These recommendations stem from our research and teaching during COVID-19 but they are flexible enough to contribute to teachers' ongoing classroom cultural geographies well beyond the pandemic.

The first step in considering cultural geography in teaching is acknowledging that crafting a physical and emotional environment means we are also shaping how students see themselves as learners within that environment. We wanted our students to see themselves as autonomous, intelligent, capable writers who could accomplish hard things even when everything in the world seemed upside down. When we faced the need to adapt our teaching, we knew that we also needed to support students in adapting, too. We did so by providing time for interactions in which students could talk about their feelings, reactions, and understandings of their learning environments. Additionally, we sought ways to encourage a multidirectional transfer of knowledge—in other words, we found opportunities to learn from students and share thinking space with them. Supporting students in their expressions of knowledge makes curriculum more meaningful and relevant as they engage in authentic conversations. Through identity-building adaptations like these, we can develop the affective elements of a classroom community and help students feel supported, even in the midst of drastic change.

During COVID-19, we understandably felt lost without access to the physical classrooms that define our teaching. In virtual classrooms, we cannot control the physical place where students are learning and, often, students cannot fully control their physical environments either. However, we can structure virtual classrooms that support students in building new relationships with their new learning environments. This includes using small group conversations, activities that encourage student reflection, and specific conversations about students' interactions with their changing school landscapes. When we can inhabit a shared physical place, we can continue to consider our students' cultural geographies by mindfully arranging the physical classroom to foster increased student social interactions, support students' emotional and affective responses, and foster positive connections to the physical place.

The ambiance and "feel" of the classroom environment are important in creating meaningful and long-lasting memories with students. We can develop meaningful connections with students by expressing interest in their well-being through small acts, like welcoming students into the class, allotting time for social interaction and communication between friends, and creating shared emotional experiences within a physical landscape. This attention to the emotional space of a classroom supports students' engagement with content, as well. When we engage authentically with student conversations, we minimize students' feelings of being monitored and build stronger relationships that allow us to push them in their thinking and move beyond task completion. Helping students navigate their emotions can encourage positive connections, autonomous growth, and a productive learning space.

Finally, a cultural geographic approach requires an understanding that changes to the learning environment can impact student norms, etiquette, and classroom interactions. Being thoughtful about these behavior shifts can help us to be gentle with our students, especially when they react unpredictably to changes in their classroom environments. Moreover, we can be gentle with ourselves as we negotiate how to adjust and adapt our teaching while still maintaining our commitments to our pedagogical values. Seeing our classrooms through the lens of cultural geography allows us to care for our students and ourselves by thinking explicitly about the culture we create through our relationships with one another and our learning environments.

References

Cole, A. G. (2009). Mapping students' lives: Children's geographies, teaching and learning. *The Educational Forum, 73*(1), 20–32.

Diamond, J. B., Posey-Maddox, L., & Velázquez, M. D. (2021). Reframing suburbs: Race, place, and opportunity in suburban educational spaces. *Educational Researcher, 50*(4), 249–255.

Gruenewald, D. A. (2003). Foundations of place: A multidisciplinary framework for place-conscious education. *American Educational Research Journal, 40*(3), 619–654.

Nevada Department of Education. (2020). [*Mountain View Middle School*] Nevada Accountability Portal. http://nevadareportcard.nv.gov/di.

Ribay, R. (2020). *Patron saints of nothing*. Penguin.

Rogers, A., Castree, N., & Kitchin, R. (2013). Cultural geography. In A. Rogers, N. Castree and R. Kitchin (Eds.), *A dictionary of human geography* (1st ed.). Oxford University Press.

Rose, M. (2021). The question of culture in cultural geography: Latent legacies and potential futures. *Progress in Human Geography, 45*(5), 951–971.

Tani, S. (2017). Reflected places of childhood: Applying the ideas of humanistic and cultural geographies to environmental education research. *Environmental Education Research, 23*(10), 1501–1509.

21

LEARNING COMMUNITIES AS CARING COMMUNITIES DURING COVID

Caring as Relation that Empowers Teacher Education

Ceridwen Owen and Anne Whitney

The COVID-19 pandemic highlighted teachers' need to practice self-care, as stress and its effects hit teachers particularly hard (Evans et al., 2020; Kim & Asbury, 2020). Even before the pandemic, calls for teachers to engage in self-care were common. These calls, however, were rarely backed by any concrete support (Owen, 2020; Whitney, 2020). The dominant discourse of self-care too often centres whiteness, physical care, and individualism (Squire & Nicolazzo, 2019), excluding many groups and restricting collective caring. In this chapter, we illustrate how teacher learning communities that are focused on dialogic discussion and writing can be places of care that move beyond these exclusions and restrictions. Drawing on Owen's (2020) work on the needs and development of early career English teachers, Whitney's work on writing groups (Fallon & Whitney, 2016; Whitney, 2009, 2020; Whitney & Badiali, 2010), and our experiences as teacher educators working with learning communities during the COVID-19 pandemic, we outline how learning communities are already places of self-care via caring as relation and argue for what this expanded vision of self-care offers to teachers, preservice teachers and teacher educators.

The Place of Care in the Work of Teaching

As teacher educators in Australia (Ceridwen) and the United States (Anne), we work amidst neoliberal education performativity measures where teachers' worth and progress is linked to "outcomes, effectiveness, performance standards, service delivery to 'clients', customer satisfaction and accountability" (Kostogriz, 2012, p. 398). These measures ignore the "deeply relational, affective, and ethical" (p. 399) work that teachers engage in daily with students, colleagues, families, and the community. Further, performance measures position self-care as "irresponsible" insofar as it

DOI: 10.4324/9781003244875-26

diverts energy from production; caring, therefore, is a form of resistance (Ball & Olmeda, 2013).

From the perspective of many teachers in both the Australian and US contexts, teaching is about determining, considering, and meeting the needs of students and of teachers (Noddings, 2012). These needs include both affective and cognitive, as teaching and learning occur between people rather than in isolation (Kostogriz, 2012). Noddings' (2012) care ethic thus positions care as relational rather than individual, integrating intellectual needs with emotional and well-being needs. Care, and by extension self-care, then becomes a collective responsibility rather than an individualist pursuit.

Focusing on the needs of teachers, self-care can promote healing from stress and/or trauma and move the individual toward liberation from the conditions causing the stress and/or trauma (Boehr et al., 2020; El-Osta et al., 2019; Molinier, 2021). Yet advice and resources for teachers' self-care usually have been, at best, only superficially beneficial and, at worst, supportive of systems of disempowerment or inequity. "Wellness" initiatives in corporate settings, for example, can be read as "'responsibilising' [sic] the subject to absorb and internalise [sic] structural faults in the material conditions of employment" (Murphy, 2021, p. 112). Self-care often is framed by individualism and Western, colonized understandings of time (Ahmed, 2012; Squire & Niccolozzo, 2019), thus decontextualized from the problems causing the injury and from the intersecting identities of the selves needing the care. We instead embrace a vision of self-care as intersectional and political, always.

Learning Communities

Teacher learning communities, whether framed as professional learning communities, communities of practice, or teacher networks support professional development (Doecke et al., 2008; Hayes, 2007; Netolicky, 2020; Parr et al., 2020) as well as teacher agency and advocacy (Biesta et al., 2015). Yet pre-pandemic, the increasing commodification of education reduced space for the relational and ethical dimensions of teaching and teacher education (Kostogriz, 2012). Teacher-led learning communities were increasingly either replaced or their agendas co-opted by administration-sponsored purposes and structures (Anderson, 2017). Noddings (2012) argues that these metrics and standardizations result in a competitive environment of learning where the results of students and teachers being better than others is valued over cooperation and a focus on the forming of "full, moral and happy lives" (p. 778).

Yet, even as teachers and their learning communities are increasingly influenced by institutional prerogatives and directions, policies and initiatives, there are ways that teachers, pre-pandemic, were managing to withstand the pressure from these forces to maintain their ideologies and the "social practice" (Kostogriz, 2012, p. 402) of teaching (see also Allard & Doecke, 2014; Ball & Bowe, 1992; Biesta et al., 2015; Connell, 2009; Gillborn, 1994; Troman, 1996). In the following section, we provide examples of teacher-led writing/learning communities to show how these communities enabled participating teachers to engage with the ethics of care through dialogic discourse about experience. We see these practices of experienced teachers as core elements of being a teacher; consequently, preservice teachers must be empowered to form and engage in such learning communities as well.

The English Education Praxis Group

Ceridwen, a teacher and teacher educator, has co-facilitated the English Education Praxis Group in Victoria (Australia) since 2018. Based at Monash University, the group met on average four times a year. The learning community included an average of 30 English teachers and educators from various contexts (e.g., public-funded and independent schools, regional and metropolitan schools, secondary schools and universities) and from various professional experiences (e.g., preservice teachers to retired teachers, academics and PhD candidates), though on average no more than 15 attended any single meeting.

Before each meeting, the group would read a selected article about English education: for example, writing that considers teachers as writers, the changing experience of English teachers, teaching in high stakes environments, and the ethical work of English teaching. On arrival, the first 30 minutes were spent writing, followed by 90 minutes of discussion. Participants would reflect on their teaching experiences and understandings in response to the reading, their writing, and others' views, values, and beliefs.

Participant views shared in a wider study of this professional learning community (Owen, 2020) provide an understanding of the value of this group to its participants. Tiffany commented that the learning community made her feel "sane," like she was "not alone," that there were "other people out there that think like [she does]" (p. 155). She saw the teachers in the community as willing to critically consider ill effects of various government-endorsed approaches, such as standards-based reforms. Charlotte also appreciated dialogically engaging with "like-minded teachers" (p. 155), though she also valued the explicit theoretical dimension of the community's practice. By basing discussion on research articles and by drawing together academics' and practicing teachers' knowledge and experience, the group moved beyond the "immediacy of day-to-day teaching" (p. 156) and provided Charlotte with a variety of perspectives in which to consider her experiences and her views, values, and understandings. Ally and Hunter, both in their first year of teaching and very good friends, noted that one of the reasons they enjoyed the community and continued to participate was the range of ages and experiences in the community and the lack of hierarchy; they did not feel like "newbies" (p. 155).

The group was a place of listening, dialogue, critical thinking, dialogic discussion and writing, and a place where like-minded educators could make thoughtful connections between English and life that were not bound by a particular school, agenda, perspective, or oversight measures. The participants did not explicitly focus on Noddings' (2012) ethic of care yet their reasons show that the English Education Praxis learning community was a place of care: There was a focus on the intellectual, emotional, social, and moral dimensions of teaching and the development of trust and empathy amongst the members of the group. Participants' presence and ideas were valued outside of their status as employees or as the producers of preferred metrics; instead, they were treated as peers with ideas to contribute and friends with feelings to share.

Centre Teacher-Writers

Since 2008, Anne has worked with the Centre Teacher-Writers (CTW) in Pennsylvania (USA), a group of teachers that has met periodically for shared writing experiences (Whitney & Badiali, 2010). Teachers who attend span from kindergarten to high school level, with experience ranging from one year to more than 30, and with a range of past writing experience. Meetings are small, with an average attendance of five and a range of one to 20. Meetings typically involve some writing time, some time for sharing, and talk about whether and, if so, where the writing might ultimately be shared.

CTW supports teachers writing for a range of purposes that the teacher-writers have found and shared. Some have produced articles for publication in peer-reviewed journals aimed at practitioners; others, wanting to push back against neoliberal testing policy initiatives they deemed harmful, secured an opinion column in the local newspaper. Still others chose less public writing, reflecting and learning from classroom experiences or processing personal experiences. While the writing itself does matter, the teacher-writers also reported that sharing and receiving feedback were important on their own, in "a contextual relationship of reciprocity" (Fallon & Whitney, 2016, p. 61). Karen's comments show how group relationships prioritize and enact emotional connections:

> When you're reading about somebody else's feelings and experiences; it's amazing how [they] can remind you of similar experiences or invoke certain feelings that I may have, but haven't thought about in years. Sometimes those invoked things are feelings and memories [that] may have been buried. So, by having somebody else open up over their experiences, [it] can actually open a little reservoir of thought in [your] own mind. (Fallon & Whitney, 2016, p. 69)

While CTW was initially convened as a professional learning community with a writing focus, through this kind of reciprocity it quickly became a caring community in which professional learning was a benefit (but not the core motivation for meeting) and writing was a way of working (but usually not an end in itself). In other words, repeated cycles of writing, sharing writing, and trading feedback in ways that integrate intellectual and emotional experience, and in a space outside of mandated professional activity, created space for caring in the context of professional learning. This echoes Dawson et al.'s (2013) notion of teacher writing groups creating "breathing space" for teachers "to make sense, heal, escape, laugh, and play" (p. 97).

Over the years, CTW members have written and talked about death, divorce, depression, parenting, and medical issues, as well as curriculum and teaching, educational policy, and broader systems of power and inequity. Members of Ceridwen's English Education Praxis Group have written and talked about their personal and professional identities, the changing nature of their work, and resisting commodification of their work (or not resisting and considering leaving the teaching profession) while sharing food, feelings, and friendships. While a managerial view of professional development might frame this activity as inefficient, since it is not tied to any specific classroom action or stated learning objective, we see it as supporting deeper, more contextualized, professional learning, framing learning communities as caring communities. We, like Cohen (2010), see professional identities as negotiated through practices of interaction with colleagues. Further, we see professional learning, like any other human endeavor, as intersectional (Crenshaw, 1994), always engaged in the context of multiple and themselves intersecting identities, positionalities, and arcs of experience. Professional learning, like any learning, occurs within the context of the broader lived experience of being human and being human(s) together.

Learning Communities as Sites of Care in Pandemic Times

A refined understanding of learning-communities-as-caring-communities transforms notions of self-care from personally and individually nurturing to more collectively (and more politically) healing and liberatory. Here, we describe activities of care experienced in these Australian and American learning communities during the pandemic. We offer these anecdotally, being composites drawn from real texts and comments rather than quotations from any member's actual statements. One interesting feature of caring in these learning communities in the midst of a pandemic (but not one we are able to address within the scope of this chapter) was strong reluctance to ask teachers to participate in anything formalized as "research" during this time, even though ongoing research activities had been a constant feature of both groups pre-pandemic. To present teachers with IRB consent forms or ask for permission to make recordings felt wrong in the context of the traumatic experiences so many were having. Further, we ourselves as researchers were beyond the capacity to do so.

In March 2020, as teachers were taxed with inventing remote schooling with few resources and even less time, Anne began to receive texts from teacher-writers, sharing sentiments like "I wish I had some space to step back and write for a moment," "It's so fast and unrelenting. I need to write, soon" and "I wish I had

CTW to help me through this." These sentiments intensified as conditions for teaching developed across a summer break and then a return to the physical classroom (which carried many unanswered questions about the safety of such) in hybrid form, with some students in school and others simultaneously remote (which was imposed locally without warning and after assurances to the contrary, just a week before classes began in late August). And, of course, all members were also experiencing personal challenges; for example, Anne, who might normally have convened meetings, also contended with a shift to all-remote teaching, a divorce, and facilitating her own children's learning from home just as health problems were also occurring. None of the group were in good condition to lead, and it seemed impossible that anyone might be able to make time to show up—but we decided to try.

In a series of Zoom sessions held on weekday evenings, teachers met using a roughly consistent format: First, a bit of writing to a prompt; second, a bit of sharing (usually one-on-one partner sharing followed by whole-group sharing); and third, a prompt for writing into the coming weeks. Prompts included "What is drowning you/What is keeping you afloat?" and "What do you need/What do you have to offer?" These sessions were publicized explicitly as self-caring sessions rather than as professional learning times, with titles like "Write/Restore/Reflect/ Renew." While all teachers internationally were welcomed and invited via social media, only two teachers joined us who had not been active pre-pandemic. We suspect this reflects the importance of vulnerability and trust in these communities; *during* crisis is a terrible time to start new in community-building.

As in the USA, Australian teachers were significantly stressed by the conditions of the pandemic; in one study, 50 percent of Australian teachers reported that they were undertaking up to an extra six hours of work each week (Ziebell et al., 2021) with the "emergence of significant wellbeing and mental health problems" (p. 10). As Melbourne undertook the longest lockdown in the country of over three months, Ceridwen's experience with the English Education Praxis group illustrates the difficulties that occur when communities are based on goodwill and a sense of joint purpose but are not essential in terms of "getting the job done."

As a leader of the group, Ceridwen found herself unable to find a way to facilitate meetings. Undertaking the final stages of her PhD study, teaching at university, and homeschooling two primary-aged children left little mental space or physical time for organizing. In the absence of Ceridwen's organizing force and the members' unwillingness for another Zoom meeting at the end of a day of staring at screens, the group did not meet. Yet, smaller groups continued to have contact and find ways to care for one another.

For example, Ceridwen and one member, Joe, began to have late night chats as dogs were walked and time was found away from children, families, and work. These chats became an important contrasting experience to day-to-day difficulties and monotony. At times hilarious, other times despairing, these conversations offered companionship and a way to engage in dialogic storying together. Central to these discussions was the uniqueness of the moment, where unlike any other time in their careers, the pandemic brought teaching into their living rooms and families into their classrooms. Through their discussions, they began to make sense of this: the blurring of boundaries and identities; the connection between work, values, beliefs and home; and the English teaching community. Under traumatizing conditions, these conversations enabled them to embrace the difficulty rather than ignore it, while messages from institutions (such as Joe's school and Ceridwen's university) were to just "carry on." In a time when they were constantly receiving the message to put on a brave face and continue to show up for others, these conversations enabled them to be vulnerable, to support each other, and to practice self-care.

While small groups of people found a way to engage in these discussions during the pandemic, it is worth reflecting on why the English Education Praxis Group formally did not continue past March 2020 and the CTW did not continue past December 2020. This speaks, we suggest, to the difficulties of professional learning communities that sit next to or outside of official structures. The pressures of the pandemic meant that teachers could not find the time, or justify it, to meet and dialogically talk and write. While in this chapter we advocate for the ability of learning communities to operate at the individual and group level, the impacts on these learning communities during the pandemic do suggest challenges to their ongoing stability.

Self-Care as Shared and Liberatory

While of course each learning community is unique, ours offer context for needed discussion of care and self-care in teacher professional development and, by extension, to teacher education. Common across all the learning communities discussed in this chapter is their potential to be spaces of recovery and liberation from the conditions of *both* the pandemic that resulted in stress and trauma for teachers, preservice teachers and teacher educators *and*, more broadly, the neoliberal educational discourse that frames educational labor.

Learning communities based on care ethics endorse cooperation, passion, and the exploration of teachers' voices and experiences. The focus shifts from teachers competing to teachers cooperating, from teachers meeting skill and knowledge metrics to teachers dialogically and collectively developing their practice and their understandings of teaching and learning. Such learning communities enable teachers to undertake the technical work of schooling as dictated by various institutions, such as governments, statutory bodies, and school authorities while also engaging in a creative, social, and dialogic experience (Kostogriz & Doecke, 2013).

Two key commonalities characterize the activities of our teacher learning communities during the pandemic. First, they were driven by explicit needs not met in the school setting. Anne's teacher-writer friends texted, "I need to write;"

Ceridwen and Joe agreed they needed contrast from the unrelenting sameness of quarantined days. This resonates with Noddings' (2012) view of caring as centering needs both intellectual and affective. In response to these needs, spoken and written reflection of the types we have described in the pandemic context are known to be supportive in both cognitive and affective areas (Bolton, 2010; Farrell, 2013; Niederhoffer & Pennebaker 2009; Robbins et al., 2006).

Second, both had developed community practices of care pre-pandemic. These practices included dialogic discourse and writing, theoretically informed or inspired discussion, and making connections between worlds (not necessarily isolated to the world of the classroom: personal-professional boundaries blurred as learning communities engaged members' multiple roles, relationships, and identities). They also included the establishment of vulnerability and trust. These practices were not mandated by some pre-existing format for the community, as might be issued by an employer, and they were not automatic; instead, they had been developed over time as teachers co-learned and cultivated ways of dialogic writing, reading, and conversation (Noddings, 2012). This is in keeping with findings that teacher learning communities support sharing, trust, growth, and the development of reflexive practices (Doecke et al., 2008; Kostogriz & Doecke, 2013; Netolicky, 2020; Owen, 2020).

All of this might seem less than urgent in the pandemic context, were it not for the ways it also points to a rethinking of care in teacher education and teacher self-care, more generally, as collective and liberatory. Literature on activism, especially but not limited to Black and Womanist activism, has emphasized how the kind of self-care Audre Lorde (1988) characterizes as "self-preservation" and "an act of political warfare" necessitates the development of "collective-self" care strategies, which reach beyond the individual to the group in ways that sustain political resistance (Ortega-Williams, 2021).

Teaching has been seen as a caring profession in a way that undermines its claims to status (Hargreaves & Goodson, 1996), and this notion has supported the systematic discrediting of teachers' expertise. At the same time, caring has been left out of managerial educational discourse, even while it is used to continually devalue and control teachers. In the face of this, teachers in shared learning communities can enact a "care amongst ourselves" (Molinier, 2021, p. 103–104) that in turn makes space for "the kind of politics that recognizes care [and] requires an intersectional analysis (of class, race, and gender) of its social conditions as well as of the ways of thinking and subjectivities that are mobilized by survival" (103–104). As Ball and Olmedo (2013) have explained,

> Resistance to dominant discourse(s) and the technologies in which they are shaped implies that we must change our understanding of what being a teacher is all about. All of this involves constant and organised work on the self, that is, the "establishment of a certain objectivity, the development of a politics and a government of the self, and an elaboration of an ethics and practice in regard to oneself" (Foucault, 1997a, p. 117). (p. 93)

The practices of caring together that teacher learning communities have engaged in, pre-pandemic and through the pandemic, have opened space to do just that. It is not only personal "breathing space" (Dawson et al., 2013) that forms in caring teacher learning communities; it is also collective space for the processing and reflection on social and political conditions in which teachers live and work.

To conclude: The use of learning communities framed as sites of self-care, shaped by/with teacher-leaders themselves, can support pre- and inservice teachers and teacher educators in the affective, relational, and ethical work of teaching. More significantly, this kind of self-care can not only assist individual teachers in surviving a time of crisis, it can also assist teachers at any stage in collectively pushing back against the educational-industrial complex. We see neoliberal, managerial framing of the teaching profession as an ongoing, structured crisis for educators; this baseline crisis is then punctuated by pandemics, disasters, and other shorter-term problems that the wider public might recognize as crises. Just as teacher educators support preservice teachers and early career teachers in developing inquiry stances, we must also foster stances of care, along with the skills and motivation to engage in forming and leading teacher learning communities. Both the caring and the learning communities are means of resistance, equipping teachers to persist in caring for themselves and each other in ways that not only get them through the crisis of a pandemic or lockdown but also strengthen them for the battle over education as a whole.

References

Allard, A., & Doecke, B. (2014). Professional knowledge and standards-based reforms: Learning from the experience of early career teachers. *English Teaching: Practice & Critique, 13*(1), 39–54.

Ahmed, S. (2012). *On being included: Racism and diversity in institutional life.* Duke University Press.

Anderson, G. (2017). Participatory action research (PAR) as democratic disruption: New public management and educational research in schools and universities. *International Journal of Qualitative Studies in Education, 30*(5), 432–449.

Ball, S. J., & Bowe, R. (1992). Subject departments and the 'implementation' of National Curriculum policy: An overview of the issues. *Journal of Curriculum Studies, 24,* 97–115.

Ball, S. J., & Olmedo, A. (2013). Care of the self, resistance and subjectivity under neoliberal governmentalities. *Critical Studies in Education, 54*(1), 85–96.

Biesta, G., Priestley, M., & Robinson, S. (2015). The role of beliefs in teacher agency. *Teachers and Teaching, 21,* 624–640.

Boehr, C., Carlson, S., Deters, A., Dickman-Burnett, V. L., Lester, A. J., Raider-Roth, M., Mellon, B. A., Theurer, P., & Tyler, S. (2020). Relational mentoring and the centrality of self-care. In C. Woolhouse & L. Nicholson (Eds.), *Mentoring in higher education: Case studies of peer learning and pedagogical development* (pp. 195–214). Springer International Publishing.

Bolton, G. (2010). *Reflective practice: Writing and professional development.* Sage Publications.

Cohen, J. L. (2010). Getting recognised: Teachers negotiating professional identities as learners through talk. *Teaching and Teacher Education, 26*(3), 473–481.

Connell, R. (2009). The work of teaching. *History of Education Review, 38*(2), 9–16.

Crenshaw, K. (1994). Demarginalizing the intersection of race and sex: A Black feminist critique of antidiscrimination doctrine, feminist theory and antiracist politics. In A. M. Jaggar (Ed.), *Living with contradictions: Controversies in feminist social ethics* (pp. 139–152). Routledge.

Dawson, C. M., Robinson, E. L., Hanson, K., VanRiper, J., & Ponzio, C. (2013). Creating a breathing space: An online teachers' writing group. *English Journal, 102*(3), 93–99.

Doecke, B., Parr, G., North, S., Gale, T., & Australia Department of Education, Employment, Workplace Relations. (2008). *National mapping of teacher professional learning project: Final report.* Department of Education, Employment and Workplace Relations.

Evans, C., O'Connor, C. J., Graves, T., Kemp, F., Kennedy, A., Allen, P., Bonner, G., Reza, A., & Aya, U. (2020). Teaching under lockdown: The experiences of London English teachers. *Changing English, 27*(3), 244–254.

El-Osta, A., Webber, D., Gnani, S., Banarsee, R., Mummery, D., Majeed, A., & Smith, P. (2019). The self-care matrix: A unifying framework for self-care. *SelfCare Journal 10*(3), 38–56.

Fallon, L., & Whitney, A. E. (2016). "It's a two-way street": Giving feedback in teacher writing groups. *Teaching/Writing: The Journal of Writing Teacher Education, 5*(1), Article 4.

Farrell, T. S. C. (2013). Teacher self-awareness through journal writing. *Reflective Practice, 14*(4), 465–471.

Gillborn, D. (1994). The micro-politics of macro reform. *British Journal of Sociology of Education, 15*, 147–164.

Hargreaves, A., & Goodson, I. (1996). *Teachers' professional lives: Aspirations and actualities.* Routledge.

Hayes, T. (2007). 'A part of the continent': Professional identity, professional learning communities. *English in Australia, 42*(2), 59–63.

Kostogriz, A. (2012). Accountability and the affective labour of teachers: A Marxist–Vygotskian perspective. *The Australian Educational Researcher, 39*, 397–412.

Kostogriz, A., & Doecke, B. (2013). The ethical practice of teaching literacy: Accountability or responsibility? *Australian Journal of Language and Literacy, 36*, 90–98.

Kim, L. E., & Asbury, K. (2020). "Like a rug had been pulled from under you": The impact of COVID-19 on teachers in England during the first six weeks of the UK lockdown. *The British Journal of Educational Psychology, 90*(4), 1062–1083.

Lorde, A. (1988). *A burst of light: Essays.* Firebrand Books.

Molinier, P. (2021). Care amongst ourselves: Self-care as a therapeutic and political experience. In N. Araujo Guimarães & H. Hirata (Eds.), *Care and care workers* (pp. 93–105). Springer International Publishing.

Murphy, B. (2021). Against wellbeing: The problem of resources, metrics and care of the self. *Alternative Law Journal*, 1037969X211007580.

Netolicky, D. M. (2020). *Transformational professional learning: Making a difference in schools.* Routledge.

Niederhoffer, K. G., & Pennebaker, J. W. (2009). Sharing one's story: On the benefits of writing or talking about emotional experience. In S. J. Lopez & C. R. Snyder (Eds.), *The Oxford handbook of positive psychology* (pp. 621–632). Oxford University Press.

Noddings, N. (2012). The caring relation in teaching. *Oxford Review of Education, 38*(6), 771–781.

Ortega-Williams, A. (2021). Organizing as "collective-self" care among African American youth in precarious times. *Journal of African American Studies, 25*, 3–21.

Owen, C. C. (2020). *Becoming an English teacher: The shaping of everyday professional experiences in early career teaching* [Thesis, Monash University].

Parr, G., Bulfin, S., Diamond, F., Wood, N., & Owen, C. (2020). The becoming of English teacher educators in Australia: A cross-generational reflexive inquiry. *Oxford Review of Education, 46*, 238–256.

Robbins, S., Seaman, G., Yancey, K. B., & Yow, D. (2006). *Teachers' writing groups: Collaborative inquiry and reflection for professional growth.* Kennesaw State University Press.

Squire, D. D., & Nicolazzo, Z. (2019). Love my naps, but stay woke: The case against self-care. *About Campus, 24*(2), 4–11.

Troman, G. (1996). The rise of the new professionals? The restructuring of primary teachers' work and professionalism. *British Journal of Sociology of Education, 17*, 473–487.

Whitney, A. E. (2009). Writer, teacher, person: Tensions between personal and professional writing in a National Writing Project Summer Institute. *English Education, 41*(3), 235–258.

Whitney, A. E. (2020). Teachers writing, healing, and resisting. *Teaching/Writing: The Journal of Writing Teacher Education, 9*(2), 11.

Whitney, A. E., & Badiali, B. (2010). Writing as teacher leadership. *English Leadership Quarterly, October*, 2–3.

Ziebell, N., Acquaro, D., & Pearn, C. (2021). Examining the impact of COVID-19 Report Summary. *Australian Education Survey.* Melbourne Graduate School of Education.

22

PROMOTING A CRITICAL-STRUCTURAL APPROACH TO TEACHER CANDIDATE CARE AFTER COVID

Meghan A. Kessler

Early in the fall of 2020, I was engaged in a Zoom seminar with that semester's cohort of elementary teacher candidates. These candidates were approximately two weeks into their student teaching experience, and all were teaching in fully virtual or hybrid modalities. These early weeks of the semester are usually an on-ramping period, characterized by a lighter teaching load as they acclimate to their school, curriculum, colleagues, and students. By this time, they are also usually experiencing a range of rich emotions: nervousness, excitement, budding love for their students, and great anticipation for the professional-personal adventure beginning to unfold.

As part of our welcoming ritual at the beginning of class, I asked each teacher candidate to share one word that summed up their week, with a brief story to illustrate. As they shared, I jotted notes on a notepad, writing each name with their summative word alongside. By the end of the conversation, my heart sank as I scanned the list: *overwhelmed, exhausted, isolated, disappointed, uncertain, over it.* While many of these emotions would certainly come up during even the smoothest of traditional student teaching semesters, Fall 2020 brought numerous new challenges as candidates were flying relatively blind into a new horizon.

While my initial response was to offer a gesture of emotional support—warm reassurance, congratulations on their self-awareness, strategies for self-care—I realized that there were broader forces at play that contributed to the stress of the moment. Adding to my teacher candidates' experiences were the myriad structural, cultural, and political discourses that came to characterize the launch of the 2020–21 school year. These manifested in heated arguments about school reopening, brutal politicization of COVID-19 precautions, and frustrated or fearful comments by seasoned mentors. These candidates were engaged in their capstone experience of learning to teach, yet their—and their colleagues'—professional efficacy, job satisfaction,

DOI: 10.4324/9781003244875-27

emotional well-being, and even physical health and safety were potentially on the line (Kessler, 2020). Further, our society's deep structural inequities, racial injustices, and economic disparities were being laid bare, stoking deep concerns about the lives of their students and communities. As one researcher put it early on, "What has happened is like a giant tidal wave that came and sucked the water off the ocean floor, revealing all these uncomfortable realities that had been beneath the water from time immemorial" (Rodriguez, 2020).

As the world moves forward through each new chapter of the COVID-19 pandemic, I have come to realize that these candidates needed much more than words of encouragement and self-care strategies, no matter how important these can be. Specifically, I now realize that I had not sufficiently equipped them to identify and interrogate the structural, cultural, and political discourses connected to the profession and the positionalities of teachers. It is my hope that this chapter will serve as one step in that process for teacher educators. In so doing, I argue for a new, critical-structural approach to teacher candidate care.

Introducing the Framework

In my research on the pandemic's impact on inservice teachers (Jones & Kessler, 2020; Kessler, 2020) and preservice teachers' (Kessler & Gray, 2022) pandemic-era teaching, I have found that the emotional toll on teachers at all levels of experience is extremely concerning. Care, in all its definitions and manifestations, is more important than ever. Of relevance to this chapter is care as it has been theorized by Noddings (1984, 1986, 2013). Noddings' ethic of care (1984, 2013) theorizes this kind of care as reciprocal and contextualized, in which the one-caring and the cared-for negotiate the act of caring. The ways in which teachers realize responsive relationships with students is complex and informed by context, often realized as layered interactions (Jones, 2017).

However attentive to the contextual realities of teachers' work, this conceptualization of care is still concerned with the relationship between teacher and student. Noddings (2012) stated that teachers are dependent on students' responses to realize this sense of caring. In effect, teachers' (caring) work is defined by interactions with students—and this emotional engagement while teaching can become exhausting (O'Connor, 2008). Further, when coupled with cultural values of educational productivity and accountability, the imperative to care can become challenging and perhaps even problematic. As evidence of this, discussions of self-care for teachers have become a popular way to support teachers' emotional well-being and satisfaction in the profession (e.g., Gonzalez, 2017; Harper, 2020; Sweet, 2019; Venet, 2014).

Although many schools and administrators are doing their best to support teacher self-care and well-being, there are professional and structural barriers (e.g., teacher workload, external accountability) that make this more than an individual responsibility for teachers. This tendency to assign individual responsibility for larger social or structural problems is rooted in neoliberal ideologies (Ward, 2015). While definitions of neoliberalism can vary slightly, here I use it io refer to epistemic and economic values that stress individual responsibility, efficiency, and productivity of educators (Tuck, 2013).

Care is frequently discussed in terms of an individual imperative yet, as Endres (2007) notes, scholars often ignore how paradoxically teachers are situated at the "crucial, if uneasy points of intersection between formal, systematic institutions and more personal relations" (p. 172). Further, Ball (2015) argues that it is important for scholars—and I would add, teacher educators and teachers—to consider "the ways in which policies both change what we do (with implications for equity and social justice) and what we are (with implications for subjectivity)" (p. 306). Therefore, it might be worth redefining care to include a critical-structural perspective.

Identify, Interrogate, Advocate Framework

To redefine care in terms of a critical-structural approach means to support teacher candidates' overall contextualization of their teacher-selves and their work. Here, I take critical-structural perspective to mean that which addresses the workplace/professional and policy contexts in which teachers work. To equip candidates in this contextualization, I have developed the following framework as a kind of conceptual organizer and step-by-step process. I refer to this as the Identify, Interrogate, Advocate (IIA) Framework (see Figure 22.1).

This framework borrows lightly from a tool for practicing mindful self-reflection and compassion popularized by psychologist and mindfulness meditation teacher, Dr. Tara Brach. Brach's (2020) framework, RAIN, calls on individuals to pause in a moment of distress or emotional difficulty to R-Recognize or identify the realities of one's current experience; A-Allow by accepting the experience as it is or seeing it clearly without judgement; I-Investigate without overanalyzing; and N-Nurture oneself with patience and self-compassion. Research has found that consistent practice of mindfulness strategies like Brach's RAIN can support teachers' social-emotional wellness and resilience (Roeser et al., 2012). Further, professional development opportunities that build teachers' capacities to engage in mindfulness practices can support the *whole* teacher and protect against burnout (Abenavoli et al., 2013).

FIGURE 22.1 Identify, Interrogate, Advocate Framework

However, I would argue that these kinds of interventions are just a starting point, albeit a lovely place to start. Many of the stressors that necessitate individual practices like mindfulness are caused by external factors. Ravitch (2011) once referred to these stressors, specifically increasing high-stakes accountability and standardization, as resulting in the "simmering rage" (para. 5) that eventually spilled out into the numerous teacher rallies and union activism of the last decade. Further, the assignment of individual responsibility to structural problems is a key component of a neoliberal ideology that positions teachers as enactors of efficient and technical services or workers in education assembly lines (Au, 2011), a perspective that can serve to erode collectivism, further marginalize already disenfranchised communities, alienate teachers and learners, and threaten empathic citizenship and democratic engagement (Apple, 2006; Vassallo, 2013). Therefore, I argue that individual interventions or enactments of care should be accompanied by additional efforts to grow teachers' and teacher candidates' broader, structural awareness of their work and positionality.

Operationalizing the IIA Framework

While teachers' work during the COVID-19 pandemic certainly presented a unique set of challenges, it took place upon a well-established foundation of discourses about what it means to be a "good" teacher and who or how schools—and, by extension, teachers—are intended to serve. While a full accounting of these discourses would be beyond a single book chapter, I will focus on a few that I believe might help teacher educators reconceptualize and enact a new kind of care. This includes the identification and interrogation of policies that assign individual (teacher) responsibility to larger structural or social challenges and the imperative to advocate for policies or institutional changes that redistribute responsibility in a more sustainable, humane way.

How to Identify?

Mindfulness practices can help individuals pause and notice their experience in new ways. I apply this to the experiences of teachers and teacher candidates for the first step in the IIA Framework: *Identify*. As it relates to a critical-structural approach to new teacher care, I encourage teacher educators to equip teacher candidates to identify moments of tension between their professional values or identities and the demands of teaching. As noted above, often teachers are encouraged to practice self-care as a means of coping with the stressors of their work. However, this might ignore or diminish the fact that many policies contradict teachers' own professional knowledge or desires in the classroom.

Santoro's (2018) work reframes the dissonance between policy, cultural expectations, and teachers' values as relating to the moral and ethical commitments of teachers. She found that the structural, cultural, and political proliferation of standardization and high-stakes accountability, deprofessionalization, and overall distrust are to blame for teachers' wide-ranging dissatisfaction. This demoralization occurred "when pedagogical policies and school practices threaten the ideals and values, the moral center, teachers bring to their work—things that cannot be remedied by resilience" (p. 5). With the influence of the federal initiatives No Child Left Behind and Race to the Top, testing, standardization, and increased technical managerialism in teachers' work have become the norm. These trends in accountability have continued to gain prominence during the pandemic as we worry about "pandemic learning loss" for our most vulnerable students (Mervosh, 2021). It is important, then, that teacher educators share with their teacher candidates some of this literature and the specific, informed criticisms to contextualize policies within the larger arc of history.

Research has also found that teachers eventually experience fatigue and burnout when constantly evolving expectations reach a tipping point (Dilkes et al., 2014; Dworkin, 2008; Orlando, 2014). The particular toll of accountability, surveillance, high-stakes testing, and standardization is well-documented. Scholars have found that the high-stakes testing and intense accountability of the last few decades threaten teachers' sense of professional autonomy (Anagnostopoulos, 2003; Grissom et al., 2014; Wright et al., 2018) and lead to increased turnover (Wronowski & Urick, 2019). The overall effects of low morale and motivation among teachers (Byrd-Blake et al., 2010; Finnigan & Gross, 2007), might eventually lead to challenges recruiting and retaining high quality teachers in schools that are under-resourced and serving historically marginalized populations (Clotfelter et al., 2004). These are important issues for teacher educators to address with their teacher candidates.

How to Interrogate?

One of the key benefits of mindfulness practice is the ability to de-identify or pull oneself back, so to speak, from a moment or stimulus to see things more clearly. However, if I encourage an externalized, critically oriented version of this practice, it is more appropriate to equip teacher candidates to *interrogate* their profession as situated within a complex web of social, cultural, and political forces. This moves beyond simply appreciating the complexity and contextualization of teachers' care-work, as discussed above. Many of these forces are manifested in the language and policies of schools. While I might not advocate that every teacher candidate develop a graduate-level appreciation of any number of theoretical frameworks, a general critical-sociocultural approach can be of service here to help candidates understand that our collective actions constitute sociopolitical structures that determine the conditions under which the work of teachers is done.

For example, introducing candidates to the ways in which knowledge, language, and power are interconnected (Foucault, 1972, 1977) can provide a deeper appreciation for teachers' embodied frustrations in the current era. Ball

(2003) has argued that neoliberal reforms, in particular, cause teachers to perform inauthentically, or at least act in cynical compliance, if not outright resistance, owing to inner conflicts: the "ground of such struggles is often highly personal" (p. 216). When considering how these forces are at work in care for teachers during the pandemic, these discourses are evident in the assignment of individual responsibility (i.e., self-care) for structural and social challenges (i.e., overwork and overwhelm; Ward, 2015).

Further, a basic understanding of the influence of neoliberalism in education reform might help teacher candidates interrogate the aforementioned tensions that they identified in the previous step of the IIA Framework. Neoliberalism is something of a catchall term that can be understood as "epistemology, economic strategy, and moral code rolled into one" (Tuck, 2013, p. 325). However, for the purposes of this chapter and to support explication of the IIA Framework, I will focus on two manifestations of neoliberalism in the making of teachers: individualization and measurement.

When considered through a Foucauldian (1977) lens, the tenets of neoliberalism can be seen in any number of school policies, and teachers are often held individually responsible for structural inequities and even myths about the successes of schools (Berliner, 2013; Berliner & Biddle, 1995). From this perspective, policies mandating accountability or standardization act as disciplinary powers, holding teachers in a "mechanism of objectification" (Foucault, 1977, p. 187) that scrutinizes their individual teaching accomplishments via high-stakes testing or teacher evaluation, even positing them as scapegoats when metrics are not met. Therefore, it is important to help teacher candidates cultivate an understanding of the power constructs that inform the possible enactments of the teacher's role. This is not to encourage cynicism or deny individual responsibility. However, individual tensions or frustrations are not necessarily the fault of a single individual; rather, they are the result of larger discourses of power to which we are all subject.

How to Advocate?

The final step in Brach's (2020) RAIN practice is to nurture and offer care to oneself. From a critical-structural perspective, this can be translated to advocating for the profession and fellow teachers. Recently, a former teacher candidate of mine who had just finished his fourth year of teaching was discussing the many ups and downs of his teaching experience during the last few years. Not only was he working in a large urban district with layered administrative and state mandates, but he and his colleagues had also traversed a long teachers' union strike and the outbreak of COVID-19. He had been through more than the average teacher in his first few years of teaching. However, the enduring lessons that he took from this unusually tumultuous experience were how deeply he cared for his students and just how vital it is to develop collective, collegial support among teachers. With this in mind, I close my discussion of the IIA Framework with the final step, *advocate*. Advocacy will certainly vary among different teaching contexts, political climates, and support structures but it is necessary to move teacher educators forward in enacting a critical-structural approach to care with their teacher candidates.

First, as teacher educators, we must use the privileges associated with our positions to build platforms and amplify the voices of teachers, including the voices of our own teacher candidates. Our scholarship, service commitments, and community engagement are all opportunities to share the stories and concerns of the teacher workforce. Teacher educators can consider hosting events at our institutions that bring teachers across the career spectrum together to build community and share knowledge, resources, and support. Teacher educators should also encourage and model sustainable professional boundaries. A caring, dedicated teacher does not need to be available to students, their families, a principal, or colleagues at all hours. Grading, planning, and preparation for teaching is like a gas: it will fill whatever container we provide for it, yet might explode under all that pressure. Therefore, teacher educators must help their candidates build a container that it is less likely rupture.

Second, it is vital that we support the work of teachers' organizations, unions, and advocacy groups. Therefore, I encourage teacher educators to help candidates learn about professional organizations that advocate on behalf of teachers. While this suggestion might come with a bit of political baggage in certain communities, teachers' unions remain one of the most powerful resources available to teachers. Even in small school districts, the collective can be stronger than the sum of its parts. Teachers' unions and professional organizations are great educational resources for teachers looking for opportunities to become engaged, as well. If formal professional organizations are not available in local school districts, teacher educators can encourage candidates to seek out like-minded colleagues who may serve as advocates for those less experienced or with whom they feel safe sharing their needs and concerns.

My final suggestion is to support teacher candidates in the development of their advocate voice. Too often we bemoan the public's misunderstanding of teachers' work, knowing that many do not have a full view of the complexity of what we do (Labaree, 2008) and view teachers as little more than babysitters (Nelson & Lewis, 2016). However, if teacher educators support teacher candidates in exercising a voice that advocates on behalf of the profession—a voice that is unafraid to speak the truth about their complex and layered work—candidates might be better equipped and more comfortable speaking out earlier and louder in their careers. As a former social studies teacher and now social studies teacher educator, I encourage my candidates to exercise their advocate voice with friends, family, and even local and state legislators. Often, national political races and policies receive the most attention, but it is the decisions of our more immediate policymakers that matter most in shaping the rules, mandates, and working conditions of teachers. In my own experience, local and state legislators are often interested to hear from teachers and university students in their constituency. School board members, municipal leaders, and statehouse representatives care about the health and stability of the communities they serve and should take care to listen to the voices of those with whom we entrust some of our most precious resources.

Conclusion

In the introduction of the second edition of *The Challenge to Care in Schools* (2014), Noddings updated the concept of responsive systems to be contextualized within the trends of standardization and accountability accelerated by the No Child Left Behind and Race to the Top reforms. Certainly, these trends have mattered a great deal in the lives and work of teachers during the past two decades, leading to increased stress and decreased retention (Grissom et al., 2014; Wright et al., 2018; Wronowski & Urick, 2019). Yet, the churn of education policy and reform is a well-established reality for teachers, one that has been found to leave them feeling burned out, demoralized, or fatigued.

Furthermore, as concern over pandemic learning loss increases, we have seen public and policymaker scrutiny of teachers. While many families appreciated the difficulty of teachers' work in the early days of the pandemic, we now see threats and violence at school board meetings for mask mandates (Kamenetz, 2021), demonstrating that individual battles are where structural problems are realized. Knowing that policy and power discourses (Foucault, 1972) are intertwined with teachers' understandings of self and agency, teacher educators can play an empowering role in mitigating the pressures that threaten the emotional resilience and professional longevity of their teacher candidates, thereby enacting care via critical policy awareness.

It is my hope that the framework of *Identify, Interrogate, Advocate* can help spur reflection and conversation among teacher educators and their candidates. Without a roadmap for identification and investigation, can they be ready to advocate for themselves, their colleagues, and their students once they enter full-time teaching placements? As we transition from the years of pandemic teaching, the swiftly shifting demands of education policy and reform—and their manifestation in the lives/work of teachers—necessitates closer consideration of why and how we should care for teachers, especially those preparing to teach. We do want emotionally resilient teachers but we should also want teachers who are prepared to criticize and call out the influences beyond individuals that are to blame for the problems they face. In short, individual interventions should be bolstered by systemic change. Otherwise, we are preparing teacher candidates who are simply resilient, but not resistant against systems that are marginalizing them, their students, and their students' communities.

References

Abenavoli, R. M., Jennings, P. A., Greenberg, M. T., Harris, A. R., & Katz, D. A. (2013). The protective effects of mindfulness against burnout among educators. *Psychology of Education Review, 37*(2), 57–69.

Anagnostopoulos, D. (2003). The new accountability, student failure, and teachers' work in urban high schools. *Educational Policy, 17*(3), 291–316.

Apple, M. W. (2006). Understanding and interrupting neoliberalism and neoconservatism in education. *Pedagogies, 1,* 21–26.

Au, W. (2011). Teaching under the new Taylorism: High-stakes testing and the standardization of the 21st century curriculum. *Journal of Curriculum Studies, 43*(1), 25–45.

Ball, S. J. (2003). The teacher's soul and the terrors of performativity. *Journal of Education Policy, 18*(2), 215–228.

Ball, S. J. (2015). What is policy? 21 years later: Reflections on the possibilities of policy research. *Discourse: Studies in the Cultural Politics of Education, 36*(3), 306–313.

Berliner, D. (2013). Effects of inequality and poverty vs. teachers and schooling on America's youth. *Teachers College Record, 115*(12), 1–26.

Berliner, D. C., & Biddle, B. J. (1995). *The manufactured crisis: Myths, fraud, and the attack on America's public schools.* Addison-Wesley.

Brach, T. (2020). *Radical compassion: Learning to love yourself and your world with the practice of RAIN.* Penguin Life.

Byrd-Blake, M., Afolayan, M. O., Hunt, J. W., Fabunmi, M., Pryor, B. W., & Leander, R. (2010). Morale of teachers in high poverty schools: A post-NCLB mixed methods analysis. *Education and Urban Society, 42*(4), 450–472.

Clotfelter, C. T., Ladd, H. F., Vigdor, J. L., & Diaz, R. A. (2004). Do school accountability systems make it more difficult for low-performing schools to attract and retain high-quality teachers? *Journal of Policy Analysis and Management, 23*(2), 251–271.

Dilkes, J., Cunningham, C., & Gray, J. (2014). The new Australian curriculum, teachers and change fatigue. *Australian Journal of Teacher Education, 39*(11), 4.

Dworkin, A. G. (2008). School reform and teacher burnout. In J. H. Ballantine & J. Z. Spade (Eds.), *Schools and society: A sociological approach to education* (pp. 119–126). Pine Forge Press.

Endres, B. (2007). The conflict between interpersonal relations and abstract systems in education. *Educational Theory, 57*(2), 171–186.

Finnigan, K. S., & Gross, B. (2007). Do accountability policy sanctions influence teacher motivation? Lessons from Chicago's low-performing schools. *American Educational Research Journal, 44*(3), 594–629.

Foucault, M. (1972). *The archaeology of knowledge.* Vintage.

Foucault, M. (1977). *Discipline and punish.* Vintage.

Gonzalez, J. (2017, June 19). Why it's so hard for teachers to take care of themselves. *Cult of Pedagogy.* www.cultofpedagogy.com/teacher-self-care.

Grissom, J. A., Nicholson-Crotty, S., & Harrington, J. R. (2014). Estimating the effects of No Child Left Behind on teachers' work environments and job attitudes. *Educational Evaluation and Policy Analysis, 36*(4), 417–436.

Harper, J. (2020, March 12). *5 strategies for teacher self-care.* ASCD. www.ascd.org/el/articles/5-strategies-for-teacher-self-care.

Jones, A. (2017). *Relational knowing and responsive instruction* (Unpublished Doctoral Dissertation). University of Illinois at Urbana-Champaign.

Jones, A. L., & Kessler, M. A. (2020). Teachers' emotion and identity work during a pandemic. *Frontiers in Education, 5,* 1–9.

Kamenetz, A. (2021, September 30). School boards are asking for federal help as they face threats and violence. *NPR.* www.npr.org/sections/back-to-school-live-updates/2021/09/30/1041870027/school-boards-federal-help-threats-violence.

Kessler, M. A. (2020). *An unfolding crisis in the satisfaction and supply of teachers in Illinois: Insights and recommendations for policymakers in light of COVID-19.* [Peer Reviewed Policy Spotlight]. University of Illinois System Institute of Government and Public Affairs.

Kessler, M. A., & Gray, P. L. (2022). First-year teaching during the pandemic: Isolation and resilience. *Critical Issues in Teacher Education, 29,* 10–22.

Labaree, D. F. (2008). *The trouble with ed schools.* Yale University Press.

Mervosh, S. (2021, July 28). The pandemic hurt these students the most. *The New York Times.* www.nytimes.com/2021/07/28/us/covid-schools-at-home-learning-study.html.

Nelson, J. L., & Lewis, A. E. (2016). "I'm a teacher, not a babysitter": Workers' strategies for managing identity-related denials of dignity in the early childhood workplace. In S. Vallas (Ed.), *Research in the Sociology of Work* (pp. 37–71). Emerald Group Publishing.

Noddings, N. (1984). *Caring: A feminine approach to ethics and moral education.* University of California Press.

Noddings, N. (1986). Fidelity in teaching, teacher education, and research for teaching. *Harvard Educational Review, 56,* 496–507.

Noddings, N. (2012). The caring relation in teaching. *Oxford Review of Education.* 38, 771–781.

Noddings, N. (2013). *Caring: A relational approach to ethics & moral education* (2nd ed.). University of California Press.

Noddings, N. (2014). *The challenge to care in schools* (2nd ed.). Teachers College Press.

O'Connor, K. E. (2008). 'You choose to care': Teachers, emotions and professional identity. *Teaching and Teacher Education, 24,* 117–126.

Orlando, J. (2014). Veteran teachers and technology: Change fatigue and knowledge insecurity influence practice. *Teachers and Teaching, 20*(4), 427–439.

Ravitch, D. (2011, February 21). Why America's teachers are enraged. *CNN.* http://edition.cnn.com/2011/OPINION/02/20/ravitch.teachers.blamed/index.html.

Rodriguez, R. (2020, April 10). Time to fix American education with race-for-space resolve. *Harvard Gazette.* https://news.harvard.edu/gazette/story/2020/04/the-pandemics-impact-on-education.

Roeser, R. W., Skinner, E., Beers, J., & Jennings, P. A. (2012). Mindfulness training and teachers' professional development: An emerging area of research and practice. *Child Development Perspectives, 6*(2), 167–173.

Santoro, D. A. (2018). *Demoralized: Why teachers leave the profession they love and how they can stay.* Harvard Education Press.

Sweet, M. (2019, February 28). *Educators: You have permission to take care of yourself, right now.* Mindful Schools. www.mindfulschools.org/personal-practice/educators-you-have-permission-to-take-care-of-yourself-right-now.

Tuck, E. (2013). Neoliberalism as nihilism? A commentary on educational accountability, teacher education, and school reform. *The Journal for Critical Education Policy Studies, 11*(2), 324–347.

Vassallo, S. (2013). Resistance to self-regulated learning pedagogy in an urban classroom: A critique of neoliberalism. *Journal for Critical Education Policy Studies, 11*(1), 239–281.

Venet, A. S. (2014, December 22). 7 self-care strategies for teachers. Edutopia. www.edutopia.org/discussion/7-self-care-strategies-teachers.

Ward, L. (2015). Caring for ourselves?: Self-care and neoliberalism. In M. Barnes, T. Brannelly, L. Ward, & N. Ward (Eds.), *Ethics of care: Critical advances in international perspective* (pp. 45–56). Policy Press.

Wright, K. B., Shields, S. M., Black, K., Banerjee, M., & Waxman, H. C. (2018). Teacher perceptions of influence, autonomy, and satisfaction in the early race to the top era. *Education Policy Analysis Archives, 26*, 62.

Wronowski, M. L., & Urick, A. (2019). Examining the relationship of teacher perception of accountability and assessment policies on teacher turnover during NCLB. *Education Policy Analysis Archives, 27*, 86.

INDEX